THE ANCIENT PATH

Rediscovering Manhood

Michael F. Elmore, MD

Thus says the Lord, "Stand by the ways and see and ask for the ancient paths,* where the good way is, and walk in it; and you will find rest for your souls." But they said, "We will not walk in it."
Jeremiah 6:16

*viz. the tried and true ways of Judah's godly ancestors.

For My people have forgotten Me. They have burned incense to worthless gods and they have stumbled from their ways, from the ancient paths to walk in by paths, not on a highway.
Jeremiah 18:15

Cover Photograph

I took the photograph on the front cover while hiking with my son in Antelope Canyon in Northern Arizona. The top of the canyon is very narrow and sun light enters only for a short time in mid day. The arid terrain results in fine dust that constantly floats down into the canyon and silhouettes the light that enters. As I watched the beam of light slowly move across the canyon, the tumbleweed on the ground was suddenly ignited when the light struck it. I wondered if this was how the burning bush appeared to Moses on Mount Sinai. As Moses received God's direction – a path to follow – so too, beyond the flaming tumbleweed is a path leading deeper into the canyon. It is a metaphor for all men and the path God desires we take to maximize our manhood.

Library of Congress Control Number: 2007900800
ISBN 10 0-9660594-9-2
ISBN 13 978-0-9660594-9-6

Printed in the United States of America
May 2007

Unless otherwise noted, Scripture taken from the NEW AMERICAN STANDARD BIBLE © 1960, 1962, 1963, 1968, 1971, 1972, 1973, 1975, 1977, 1995 by the Lockman Foundation. Used by permission.

Scripture quotations marked (AMP) are taken from the Amplified® Bible, Copyright © 1954, 1958, 1962, 1964, 1965, 1987 by The Lockman Foundation. Used by permission.

Scripture marked (GNB) is from the Good News Bible © 1994 published by the Bible Societies/HarperCollins Publishers Ltd., UK Good News Bible © American Bible Society 1966, 1971, 1976, 1992. Used with permission.

Published by:
MCK, Inc.
8051 South Emerson Avenue, Suite 200
Indianapolis, IN 46237

Cover Design & Illustrations by Kristofer Designs, Austin, TX

Dedicated to my wife, Christine, who taught me what the real meaning of life is all about.

ACKNOWLEDGEMENTS

First, and foremost, I wish to thank my wife, Christine, for allowing me the time to write this book. On many of our vacations, she was gracious enough to not only permit me the time to write, but she also acted as a valuable critic. For the thirty-two years of our marriage, she has been my foremost encourager. Without her support this work would never have been completed.

I wish to thank my pastor, Gary Johnson, for his spiritual guidance and friendship over the years which have had a great impact on me. My deep appreciation goes to Pastor Jim Bricker, Jeff Cardwell, Eric and Diana Faulkner, Doug Harty, Larry Lane, David Michel, Pastor Charles Lake, Lyndon Rivera, Tim Rogers, Harold Schubert, Jason Barlow Smith, Russ Spicer, Win Tuner and Scott Veerkamp who all reviewed the manuscript and gave me invaluable advice. Some contributed personal stories that are contained in this book.

The cover design and art work throughout the book are the work of my incredibly talented and creative son, Christopher, who has always been my "Boy of Destiny." Kelly, my oldest daughter, did an outstanding job critically reviewing the final manuscript. If you purchased this book or any of my other publications through Amazon. com, it is due to my youngest daughter Kimberly's marketing and computer skills. It was a joy to have the opportunity to work with them.

The quality of the book is in large part due to my editor, Julie Yamamoto, who lives in Olympia, Washington. She pored over the various drafts and wielded her red pen like a skilled swordswoman. Her help was truly indispensable.

As is true in many professions, what one learns in school is simply a foundation for the real learning that comes in its application. This book is fashioned by the countless encounters I have had with my patients since I started practice in 1977. They have shaped my approach to the way I practice medicine and the way I live my life.

TABLE OF CONTENTS

INTRODUCTION

Every time I hear of another marriage going bust, it makes me sad, and I must admit, I get angry. It seems so unnecessary. I always wonder why husbands and wives can't just get along with each other? However, with the divorce rates at 50% or greater around the country, it appears difficult for couples to stay together.

I remember in 1974 walking down the aisle getting ready to commit to my wife-to-be *for life*! I was nervous, and as I walked down the aisle, I remember asking myself, "Am I making the right decision?" Mind you, I wasn't afraid I was marrying the wrong woman. No, I was afraid I wouldn't be able to honor my commitment. Fortunately, our marriage was like a glove that fit perfectly. I find it difficult to understand when people say how hard it is to make their marriage work. Was my success due to the fact that I just picked the right woman? I don't think so. No, my observation is that no matter how fantastic a wife is, a man can screw up his marriage without even trying! This book is about how this happens and how you can avoid it.

Some people have incredible lawns. You drive by their homes and you are in danger of having a wreck because you can't take your eyes off their lawn. It's immaculate! We all realize a lawn like that does not just happen. It takes hours, even days, of work and know-how. The sad point is that many men take better care of their yard than their marriage. They spend more time fussing over their car than their wife. The key to a great marriage is the same as for a great lawn – time and know how. This is not rocket science!

Most men are clueless when it comes to women. Why shouldn't we be? After all, no one gave us a book about women and how we should behave around them, or more importantly, how we should act around them to get what we want! Most of us just act macho like we always do around the guys, and that only makes matters worse.

I believe that men have lost their way. They are struggling, and their lives provide evidence of this. Many men have been unsuccessful in their relationships with women. It is disconcerting that so often they have abandoned their children to be raised by other men while they themselves are rearing another man's children. Men have become poor role models for their sons who are destined to repeat their father's path. Some men have been tripped up by mid-life crises, others are addicted to pornography and many are dishonest in their dealings with others, both personally and at work.

It seems that men are trying to find their way through life without a compass or at best with one that is defective. I believe this is unnecessary and avoidable.

The questions are these, how did all this come about and why do so many men find themselves in this situation?" There are, of course, many reasons. I believe we have been programmed by the American dream, and it is destroying us. In my book, *Stress & Spirituality, How to Conquer the Stress in Your Life and Achieve Your Spiritual Potential*, I point out that achieving the American dream requires you and your spouse to work very hard to finance the lifestyle we seem compelled to attain. [1] The end result is that we get all the "stuff" associated with the American dream only to see our marriages and relationships ruined.

Most people fail to understand the difference between success and significance. Many people are very successful by the world's standards, but their lives lack significance. Hence, they are discontent and dissatisfied. They may have everything, yet have nothing. I see this over and over again in my office as one patient after another files in and out.

Even more disturbing is that we find the same situation in our churches. Often, there is no apparent difference between the behavior of men in the church and those outside the church. This is a most serious indictment against the effectiveness of the church. What good is our religion if it doesn't work? This question may sound like heresy, but I couldn't be more serious. If patients repeatedly come to me but none of my treatments were effective, what kind of doctor would I be? Would you keep coming back? I don't think so!

I believe the ineffectiveness of the church is due to the disparity between the façade the church creates and what Jesus is really all about. Jesus is real. He is all about relationships. He is all about real love. But in the church, our love is often conditional, not real. It is judgmental. If you meet the conditions, you are loved. If you don't, you are judged, and you receive the *left foot of fellowship* (viz. you get the boot). We have to be real like Jesus. We must understand what Jesus is really all about. He is our example. We must allow the Holy Spirit to make us like Him. We must be conformed to His image. But we must also realize that this is not something we can do by ourselves.

The Holy Spirit does it as we yield to Him.

We have often substituted a relationship with the church for a personal relationship with God. Our relationship with others or to an organization can never substitute for our personal relationship with Jesus. This is putting the cart before the horse.

Several of my closest friends were kind enough to review the first draft of this book. The most frequently asked question was, "Why? Why did you name your book *The Ancient Path*?" The answer is in essence quite simple, "Because it fits." The book of Jeremiah is not the most uplifting book in the Bible. If someone is desirous of learning more about God and Christianity, the Book of Jeremiah is definitely not the first book of the Bible I would direct them to read. Rather, I would encourage them to read something like the Gospel of John.

Several years ago, as I was reading my Bible, I read these verses:

*Thus says the Lord, "Stand by the ways and see and ask for **the ancient paths**, where the good way is, and walk in it; and you will find rest for your souls." But they said, "We will not walk in it."*

Jeremiah 6:16

*For My people have forgotten Me. They have burned incense to worthless gods and they have stumbled from their ways, from **the ancient paths** to walk in by paths, not on a highway.*

Jeremiah 18:15

When I read these verses, I was struck by the words *the ancient path*. For days that phrase stuck in my mind. Finally I realized that those words were applicable for men today. *The ancient path* was the tried and true way of Judah's godly ancestors. They strayed from it and got themselves in serious trouble. So too, today, men have strayed from the path that God intended. As a result, they are finding themselves in serious trouble, too.

As I talk to men in my office, many feel hopeless. They think that too much water has gone over the dam. *It's too late*, they tell me. But, it is NEVER too late to turn to God! It is never too late to yield yourself to Him and watch Him change your life and the lives of those around you.

I find the phrase *the ancient path* to be particularly relevant for

9

men today. Many have gotten off the ancient path, the path that God intended for them to be successful in their home and life. I have never met a man who marries who does not want to be a good husband and father. But, I have met many men who don't seem to know how. This book is about how to rediscover and maximize your manhood. The message for you today is that even if you have blown it, God offers you the promise of restoration and a better future. No matter how bad your present situation may be, God has a guarantee for you that if you get on His ancient path, your life will get better. If you then stay on His path, your life can be incredible, even better than you could ever imagine. You can become the man of character and integrity God wants you to be and your family so desperately needs you to be.

I have divided this book into three parts. The first, Recognizing How Life Works, is the getting started section and deals with first things first. Without a proper foundation, you can't go forward. Part two, Understanding Women, is essential for success in life and marriage. Finally, in part three, I speak about Establishing Your Spiritual Foundation. This is where you will find the strength for all you do in life.

FOCUS

TRUTH (What is the focus – the essential truth of this chapter?)

There is an Ancient Path available to me – a road I can get on and follow to maximize my manhood.

APPLICATION (What does this truth mean to me? How is it relevant in my life?)

Whether my relationship with my wife is good, blah or terrible, it can be terrific! There is hope.

ACTION (What should I do about it? How can this truth benefit my life?)

I need to learn exactly what this Ancient Path is and get on it! Pray: Dear God, teach me about this Ancient Path and help me get on it.

PART I

RECOGNIZING HOW LIFE WORKS

CHAPTER 1

FINDING SIGNIFICANCE AND PURPOSE IN LIFE

Having been a doctor for more than thirty years, not many things shock me. In my residency, I was required to run a busy metropolitan hospital emergency room from 11 PM to 7 AM - you know, the time during which the local "knife and gun club" always meets! What people do to one another is disgusting. I learned a lot about people and human dynamics. In my practice, the stories I'd heard about what went on in my patients' lives often brought me to tears.

Several years ago, I learned that one of my friends, also a physician, was having an affair. That really shocked me. I suppose this was so for a couple of reasons. What's the big deal about an affair? They go on all the time. Well, to me this was different. In many ways this friend was like me, and that scared me. It upset me that he cheated on his wife, lied to her about it and then subsequently divorced her to marry his mistress. It is difficult when you know both parties, and they are your friends. Suddenly you feel like you are put in the middle and have to choose sides. But the real problem for me was that I thought he had the perfect life. He had it all – a big house with all the amenities, all the "toys," a wife who was devoted to him, good kids and a great medical practice, and he was very active in his church. For me it was like looking in a mirror. I thought, "If it can happen to him, it can happen to me!!!" That frightened me – a lot.

For weeks the whole situation haunted me. I read several books on mid-life crises trying to figure out what happened. You need to understand. I love my wife and my family, and I didn't want anything like that to happen to me. I even asked my wife, "Honey, do you think I have ever gone through a mid-life crisis?" She replied, "Yes, dear." I couldn't believe it. "When?" I asked. "It started when you were eighteen and hasn't ended yet!" she answered. "You didn't even know me when I was eighteen!" I responded. "No. But, I can guess what you were like," was her response. You can never win these discussions with your wife. Anyway, that didn't particularly help me one way or another.

It took several months to finally figure it out to my satisfaction. There is a local African-American pastor in Indianapolis who has a very large church. Although I have never met him, I like him a lot. I read an interview he gave in the newspaper. One comment he made has always stuck with me, "Once you get your spiritual foundation in order, everything else falls into place." That was it. I knew that my friend had always talked a lot about church and was very active, but much of it was superficial. He lacked the spiritual foundation to protect him from the temptation. But, that was only part of it. He also let his guard down. He didn't do what it takes to protect his marriage. In essence, that is what knowing how to rediscover your manhood is all about. It involves those two things: 1. Developing your spiritual foundation and 2. Protecting your marriage by keeping your guard up.

THE PHASES OF LIFE

There are several phases in life that we all pass through. I have diagramed these in the diagram that follows. Many men seem to progress through life never appreciating these phases. They never recognize how life works. While they are in one phase, they are always anticipating and dreaming about how good the next phase will be. As a result, they don't seem to enjoy the phases, but merely pass from one to the next. Let me describe these phases.

During the early phase of life, we receive our **education**. Initially, we learn everything from our parents and older siblings. Then off to school we go, and the learning process expands to our teachers and fellow students. Usually, the focus of our education ultimately leads to our **career.** At some point, we get **married** and go on to have a **family**. Coincident with marriage and family comes the accumulation of **things**. We buy a house, purchase furniture, get one or more cars, etc. This part of life involves a lot of *doing* to achieve success. It usually requires both spouses to work to earn enough money to have everything they both want and feel they need to make the American dream a reality. Unfortunately, all this *doing* comes with a price. It creates a lifestyle that can be very destructive to the marriage and the family structure.

I first became interested in the phases of life when I looked around and saw several of my friends and colleagues going through nasty midlife crises. Many ended up divorced or addicted to a substance such as alcohol. I wondered what happened to their apparently perfect lives. What happened to cause this? Although many factors were unique to each situation, the bottom line seemed to be that success was not enough. Although they had everything in one sense, they had very little in another.

Many years ago, I was doing medical mission work in Guatemala with my friend Dr. Gary Pitts. Gary was a medical student at the time. Toward the end of our week together, he pulled me aside and said something that struck me as very profound, "When we arrived here, I immediately sensed that something was different compared to the United States, and I couldn't quite put my finger on it. Finally, it came to me. Back home people have everything but they are discontent and unhappy. But these people have almost nothing, and they are happy and seem to enjoy life." Gary was challenged by this, and he hasn't been the only one. Many who have gone with me on a short-term mission trip to a developing country have also observed and been impacted by this observation.

The problem is that our society places an undue emphasis on success. One way to look at this is to realize that there are two "S's" in life. The first is the S of Success and the second is the S of Significance. We need a proper balance of these two. What do I mean by the S of significance? It is not uncommon for a man to reach a point in life where he looks around and asks, "What does all this really mean?" Men inherently want their lives to count for something. They want to know that somehow their life has made some sort of difference. Rising to a position of respect in a company or accumulating all of life's materialistic toys is not enough. The resulting emptiness men experience often leaves them disillusioned, perplexed and not knowing where to turn. Unfortunately, they often go in the wrong direction, along a destructive path. This is why a man may have an affair, shirk his responsibilities at home, leave his job to seek some sort of adventure or, out of general depression, end up with substance abuse. All of these acts occur because he no longer knows where he is going and has lost hope. People desperately need hope. Hope is defined by Webster as "desire accompanied by anticipation or expectation." Hope energizes us. Once we have direction and know where we are going, we have the hope that provides the drive we need to go on. Without it we are stuck not knowing what to do.

THE PHASES OF LIFE

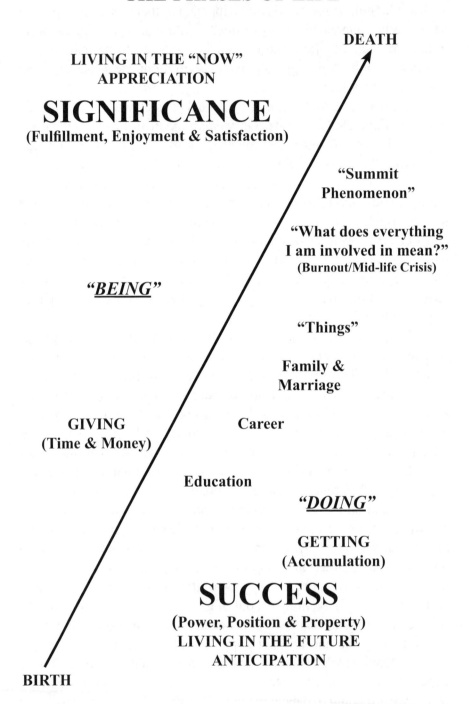

DEATH

LIVING IN THE "NOW"
APPRECIATION

SIGNIFICANCE
(Fulfillment, Enjoyment & Satisfaction)

"Summit
Phenomenon"

"What does everything
I am involved in mean?"
(Burnout/Mid-life Crisis)

"BEING"

"Things"

Family &
Marriage

GIVING
(Time & Money)

Career

Education

"DOING"

GETTING
(Accumulation)

SUCCESS
(Power, Position & Property)
LIVING IN THE FUTURE
ANTICIPATION

BIRTH

The key to preventing this type of problem is to understand that the second S in life, significance, is something that should be part of all the phases of life. If you incorporate significance into each phase of life, a midlife crisis can often be prevented.

Scott Veerkamp is a very successful realtor in Indianapolis. At the start of his career, he was confronted with his growing success and the lack of significance in his life.

I was raised on the Southside of Indianapolis in a family that I wouldn't trade for anything. My parents gave me all the love and nurturing that anyone could ask for. I am especially grateful to my dad who showed me how to be a good father and husband by the way he loved me and treated my mom. My mom helped me through some pretty tough times as a teenager. I made some bad decisions with regards to drug use that could have, without her intervention, been my demise.

By age 26, my life was going well. I was married, we had a son and had purchased a nice house. My income was well into six figures, and I was experiencing "The American dream."

Then I started a company called Eastern Express which was a trading house for commodities from the US to the former Soviet Union. I was getting bids for panty hose, blue jeans, shampoo, computers, etc. Many companies were asking for products. Then I got "the big one!" I received an order from a very powerful, wealthy company called Infolux Ltd. The dream I had been chasing, now seemed a reality. I sold this company 12 late model used cars. They were a "probationary batch," as they called them, which would be delivered according to our agreement. If all went well, they would buy 300 to 500 cars per year. The transaction required that I accompany the cars as a sign of good faith. I was to meet with the principals of the company to make sure we could work together.

I arrived in Moscow three weeks before the cars arrived, in early November 1992. I was given a warm welcome from the principals of Infolux, and they provided me with a driver while I was there. I had several appointments a day with other companies who wanted to do business with me. I was given a special tour of the Kremlin and Lenin's tomb, a viewing of the largest diamond vault in the world, and I met with the principals of the Bolshoi Ballet to discuss the possibility of a US tour.

It was all very glamorous, but it quickly turned into a nightmare when the cars arrived. The men who had put so much stock in me suddenly became very disenchanted when they inspected the cars. I understood the gist of what they were saying by their body language and the octave levels in their voices. At first I did not realize how much trouble I was in. They took me to an old run down building and then the "thugs" came in. They started screaming that the cars were not what I said they were going to be. I had no doubt in my mind that these guys, who I later came to understand were part of the Russian Mafia, intended to take my life. I negotiated to pay for the estimated damages in exchange for my life.

I made it back home, put together the money that I had agreed and sent it to their affiliates in New York City. I was off the hook but was left with horrible memories, a mountain of debt, no job and no desire to EVER do business in a foreign country as long as I lived.

It was March of 1993, and I slumped into serious depression. I tried to make ends meet by selling cars wholesale, cleaning carpets and doing other jobs. When I couldn't make ends meet, I borrowed money from my parents. Of course, that really helped with the whole self esteem issue.

I decided to get back into Real Estate sales which I had done previously. I reasoned that if I could make a bunch of money all this would go away. I started interviewing with new home builders that I had known before. One Tuesday I had two interviews. During my first interview I was offered a sales job that was sure to pay six figures, which brought me incredible relief as I needed a six figure income just to service the debt that I had incurred. I accepted the job and was to start the following week. I decided to go to the second job interview and not mention that I had already taken another job. Maybe the second interview would be more lucrative than the first? The interview went very well, and at the end, the owner asked, "Scott, what are your priorities in life?" I knew he was a very "religious" man, so I responded, "GOD, FAMILY and WORK." He said, "That sounds great; let's have another interview on Friday." We agreed to meet at 11:00 AM.

Over the next couple days, I couldn't seem to shake what I had said, "GOD, FAMILY and WORK." It was the GOD part that bothered me because I didn't know God and didn't know that it was possible to "know" Him.

When Friday came, I was at home getting ready for my interview, and I remember feeling really down. I had been thinking about what had happened in Russia and the financial mess that I had gotten my family into. I started pondering the age old questions, "Who am I, and what purpose, if any, do I have in this life?"

On the way to the interview, I was overwhelmed with despair and started crying uncontrollably. I pulled the car over and cried out to God for help. I remember my words like it was yesterday, "God, if you are listening, I need help. I am so tired of who I am and the messes I seem to get into. I want to be a good husband and father. God, teach me to be the Christian young man that You want me to be." I dried my eyes, blew my nose and tried to put on my "business hat" to be prepared for the interview. I arrived at my destination and was sitting in the lobby waiting for my appointment. When the owner came out, we went back into his office. He went behind his desk like he did on our first interview. But this time he didn't invite me to sit down, nor did he sit. Rather he said, "Scott, I tried to call you this morning because I wanted to save you a trip. I talked to the builder that you used to work for, and he told me that you sure did sell a lot of homes, but that he found out that you were running some Russian escapade out of his model home before you left him high and dry one week end. Scott, I am not interested in having a loose cannon in my company no matter how many homes you can sell."

I quietly said, "Ok," and as I reached down to pick up my brief case, he reached over his desk and grabbed my arm. As I looked up, he said, "In our first interview you said that God was number 1 in your life. What's the real story?" Immediately I was reminded of my prayer, and I was overwhelmed with emotion. Feeling like a total fool, I started crying. This man who didn't know me from Adam walked around his desk and held me in his arms until I calmed down. Then he sat me down and asked me this question, "Scott, if you were to die today would you go to heaven, hell or do you know?" I went down the road of, "Well, I have done things wrong in my life, but I have done some good things too." He then looked at me and said; "Do you want the good news or the bad?" I said, "I am not sure if I can take too much more bad news in my life right now." He then said, "We really don't need to talk about the bad news anyway, do we?" I said, "Probably not." He said, "The good news is that you can KNOW that your eternal destination is heaven before you leave this office today." It was the greatest news I had ever heard. He opened up his Bible and pointed out that God loved me and wanted to save me if I would simply ask Him. That day, March 8, 1993, I prayed and asked Jesus Christ to forgive me of my sins and to be my personal Lord and Savior. My whole life changed forever.

I am very grateful to Bob Buford for his books *Halftime,* [1] *Game Plan,* [2] and *Stuck In Halftime,* [3] which helped me develop a second-half strategy for the second half of my life. In addition, these books taught me how to articulate and see the application of success and significance in my own life and in the lives of others.

The characteristics of the second half of life often become a reality only after we reach the point when we ask, "What does all this really mean?" This is what I call the Summit Phenomenon. At this summit, we may experience a period of burnout which can be very helpful because it forces us to slow down long enough to evaluate our lives. A healthy second half of life is characterized not so much by getting as it is by giving. Significance comes from extending ourselves to others. The secret to enjoying each of the phases of life is to focus not just on the doing so necessary to achieve success, but also on being. This allows us to derive pleasure and enjoyment from and to experience significance during each phase.

At this point, you may be wondering, "What does he mean by doing and being?" I spoke on this topic to a group of medical and surgical nurses. I asked them to tell me all the things that occupied their time each day. We composed a list that included the usual things: the need to just get up (rather than sleep in), help the kids prepare for school, get breakfast for everyone, prepare lunches, transport the kids to school, go to work, etc. Next, I asked them how they felt at the end of the day. Did they feel incredibly satisfied with all they had accomplished? Their answer was an emphatic, "No!" They went to bed exhausted, frustrated and emotionally drained.

So I posed this question: "Is there a solution to this dilemma?" They weren't sure. Then, I gave them an example of how their daily lives could be different. I explained that I used to teach a class at my church entitled *Achieving Your Spiritual Potential.* One night, a young woman in the class shared an insightful experience. She had struggled with the concepts of *doing* and *being* over the preceding weeks. When it started to make sense to her, she went home determined to put these concepts into proper order. The next morning after getting up, packing a couple of her children off to school and caring for her son with mental retardation who needed to be tube fed, she looked around at all that still needed to be done. There were dirty dishes in the sink, a huge pile of laundry by the washer and the house was a mess. Her youngest son was still at home and wanted to play. It was at this point that she made a conscious decision. The *doing* (dishes, laundry and house) would have to wait. She chose *being* instead. She got down on the floor and for the next half hour played with her son. After that she went to work on the dirty dishes, the laundry and cleaning up the house.

Everyone was anxious to hear the result. She went on, "This has been the most incredible week of my life!" After playing with her son, she noticed that his whole disposition changed and not just for a few minutes but for the entire day! Somehow he was more obedient and her relationship with him had become closer. She continued each day during that week to focus on some aspect of *being*. Commensurate with this was her recognition that as a mother and housewife all the things she had to *do* all day long were no longer just drudgery but her ministry. She had been given a most important job that was highly significant – the raising of her family. Everyone looked to her. She had established balance in her life. As she chose to *be* each day, everything she had to *do* took on significance.

One of the most important fundamental concepts we need to understand is the difference between doing and being. *Doing* is easier to comprehend since it seems to come more naturally to us. *Doing* is important because it is essential for a productive life and involves the many necessary activities that we carry out daily. There is nothing wrong with *doing* or any of the many activities associated with it. If that is all we focus on, however, our life will be very unbalanced. Although there can be tremendous fulfillment in *doing* because of all we achieve, the satisfaction associated with these accomplishments is oftentimes short-lived.

So what then is *being*? How does *being* differ from *doing*? I think the best way to understand the difference is to look not only at what we accomplish through our *doing,* but also look at whether we enjoyed the experience of the accomplishments.

Have you ever looked forward to completing a particular task, only to find that you were disappointed and experienced a let down after the job was done? This feeling occurs with an overemphasis on *doing.* On the other hand, *being* makes you focus on taking time to slow down a bit to realize why you are doing something. *Being* reminds us to "smell the roses" along the way. A good example is your job. We often work hard and come home so exhausted that we are not able to truly enjoy and appreciate what we have accomplished. *Being* emphasizes taking the time to simply enjoy what we are doing. In my class, I have been amazed to see how difficult it can be for people to comprehend where *doing* ends and begins. I try to direct them to look at specific activities and help them discover, as honestly as possible the *doing* and *being* with each. Let me share a few examples that might help clarify this difference.

As a physician, I need to see many patients each day. It is easy to become overwhelmed by all that I have to *do*. If I am not careful, I get trapped into the *doing* of my daily activities. If this happens, I come home worn out and frustrated by what I have left undone. But, if I take a moment to think about why I went into medicine and how much I enjoy helping people, then my focus on what I am *doing* changes. My work necessitates a certain amount of *doing*. But it also has the potential to provide deep significance and satisfaction if I focus on building relationships with my patients and trying to help them solve their problems. I find that, as I do this, I am more likely to be attuned to my patient's spiritual needs, which allows me to be more receptive to the prompting of the Holy Spirit.

Sometimes, being attuned to patients involves counseling or asking if they would like me to pray with them. These moments deepen my relationship with them, and they allow me to be much more effective as a physician since I am not just treating their physical problems. I always teach my medical students and residents that the *doing* of medicine is the *care* we provide which is what we bill for. But the reason patients return is from the *caring* (the *being*) we give. Despite a hard day, I usually return home elated and exuberant. Do you find that your work is drudgery or fulfilling? Can you think of ways to focus on the *being* in order to enrich the experience of your work?

Another example of *doing* versus *being* that most of us can relate to is in our role as parents. Parenting can be the most difficult job in the world, and I see many parents who go through all of the right motions, but never really seem to enjoy the experience. Again, the solution is to see the tremendous significance there is in *being* a parent. I remember when my daughter, Kelly, was very young. She loved to play the game "Chutes and Ladders." I must admit, I hated that game. The object is to move your piece up the game board so many squares at a time. If you land on a square with a ladder, you move up, but if you land on a square with a chute, down you go! I seldom got a ladder and routinely got a chute, much to my daughter's enjoyment. Just when I thought I was getting somewhere, she would squeal with delight as, once again, I entered a chute and found myself plunging back down the board. It was at times like these, that I purposely had to force myself to engage in activities that I disliked. In so doing I began to realize the tremendous power of *being*. During these games I felt most fulfilled as a father and inwardly recognized that I had met a need of my child. We need to see ourselves as God's instruments even in the day-to-day performance of routine activities. When we recognize that our duties are our sacred responsibility as parents in training and nurturing our children, then each of the activities takes on special significance.

Many professional people seem to find it difficult to just have fun. I can recall many physicians, lawyers, businessmen and other professionals who decided to take up a sport such as golf or tennis as a hobby. They told me it was "just to have fun and relax." The next thing I knew they started taking a few lessons to try to improve their game. Before long they were playing in competitive tournaments and traveling on the circuit. Somehow their competitive natures had taken over, and all of the fun was gone. Their hobby became another form of work. Some of this attitude derives from the tremendous focus that is required of professionals to achieve a level of competence needed to practice the profession. Their training "brain washes" them. They are unable to detach themselves from the way they were trained and act differently in other areas of life.

While I was in medical school, residency and fellowship training, I was so focused, it was impossible for me to go out and simply enjoy a football game or other event. I felt guilty because I was not accomplishing something! I was in practice for ten years before I ever went on a vacation without taking a medical journal to read. Fortunately, God has helped me overcome this oversight.

Consider for a moment an activity as simple as eating. How many times have you raced through a meal just to satisfy your hunger? Did you enjoy the meal? Eating the meal becomes almost like work - something you had to complete or *do*. The next time you eat, practice enjoying every bite and savoring the taste.

Even an activity like attending church can be just *doing*. Do you go to church because it is the right thing to do, out of a sense of obligation or fear of God? Or do you go with a sense of appreciation to worship your Divine Creator who loves you and sent His Son to die for you? Do you go to help others and minister to them? Many people are trapped in the legalism imposed by the Do's and Don'ts of religion. They are working their way into heaven, or at least trying to. But, this is not how salvation works. You can't work your way into heaven. That is the whole point. God wants a personal relationship with you. He has already done all of the work. You are saved by His grace, not by your own doing. Your doing should be driven by your love for Him and your relationship with Him. It is done in appreciation for all Jesus did for you.

I encourage you to make a list of those things that occupy most of your time. All of us wear many hats for the roles we play. For each of the items on your list, consider how you are involved in *doing* and *being*. Then ask yourself why you do each of these activities and what God's purpose is for you in doing them? Since God gives meaning and purpose in our lives, there should be some significance associated with each activity. Just performing the activity belongs to the realm of *doing*. This is what we call success. The significance in each of the activities belongs to the realm of *being*. When you find yourself feeling trapped and not enjoying the activity, see if you can begin to focus more on God's purpose for the activity in your life and begin to see yourself accomplishing the activity for His glory rather than your own. You will see that your outlook regarding these activities can change dramatically. If you force yourself to change your focus on these activities on a daily basis for several weeks, you can create a new habit, accompanied by more enjoyment in each of the activities.

My good friend, Margie Hart, started an organization named Esperanza de Jesus Cristo, to help Hispanics on the south side of Indianapolis. She gave me some additional thoughts on *being* and *doing*. She said, "*Being* is practicing the present moment with all that God gives. Children are always *being* rather than *doing*. That is what Scripture means in this passage, 'You must be like a child to enter the kingdom of God.'" She encouraged me, "Eat like a small child – feeling, smelling, swishing – do all like a child. To be in the presence of God, we float into each moment, aware of the smallest details, delighting in them with thanksgiving. Then you let the moment just ripple over you like a wave. All experience begins with wonder. This is eternity." Do you get the impression that Margie has learned to live her life a little differently than most of us?

Do you realize that God has a specific purpose for your existence? This realization is the key to achieving true enjoyment while on earth. God has given you certain talents and strengths. You can choose to use them for your own good, to fulfill your own personal agenda, or you can use them for His Kingdom. Do you see yourself called to a purpose? What is your passion in life? What are your talents and strengths? How are you using them? How do you want to use your life to make a difference?

I met Jeff Cardwell in the 1980s when we attended the same church. It was through a mission trip to El Salvador that God showed him the difference between success and significance in life. That trip changed his life forever. Here is his story.

My goal as a kid was to be a millionaire by the time I was 30. I achieved that goal in 1988 at the age of 28. My daughter was born that year and my life was moving fast.

However, I ran into a snag the following year when my wife developed a severe infection of her hand. The doctor told us that if the infection went into the bone, he was afraid that she would lose her hand. While she was in the hospital in isolation, I asked the doctor if we should go to the Mayo Clinic or somewhere else. "Money is not the issue. Whatever it costs to get her well is no problem," I said. What the doctor said next devastated me, "It is not a matter of money." I had been raised in a poor home, and when I looked around as a child it appeared to me that money could solve any problem. Now I realized that was not true. I went to church on Easter Sunday 1989 and rededicated my life to God. All the other solutions had failed me. I was what I call a "Crash Christian." I had crashed and landed in God's lap. After that, I lived in faith and turned the control of my life over to God. At first, the realization that much of my life was out of my control was hard to take. But my life began to turn around. My wife got better. That summer, I got involved with Habitat for Humanity and started helping others, not just focusing on myself.

In May of 1990, Dr. Mike Elmore spoke at our church one evening about his recent mission trip to Guatemala. I leaned over and told my wife that one day I wanted to do something like that.

The idea of adventure travel appealed to me, but I was not a medical person. Although the seed was planted that night, there was no opportunity for me to go.

Throughout the next 10 years, I worked with my partner building designer homes costing a million dollars or more. We also did land development for subdivisions. In the late 90's, I hosted my own radio show for home improvement. God blessed us, and we were very fortunate.

My daughter went on a mission trip to El Salvador in June of 2000, and my wife said I had to go to protect her. But God had other plans for me. My daughter became fast friends with a young El Salvadoran woman named Maria who facilitated our mission work. They became like sisters. One night, we were in the Prayer Tower at King's Castle, and Maria prayed for me, saying, "You need to make time for God in your life." That was a defining moment for me. I knew that God had spoken through Maria. I decided to simplify my life and make time for God.

When we returned home, I told my partner that I was going to sell him my half of the home-building business. He said he could not afford to buy me out. "Yes, you can," I said, "I am going to sell it to you for $1!" "I don't want anything but to refocus and simplify my life. I never want to miss another opportunity to go on a mission trip."

Now, 6 years later, everything I am doing in my life is in some way connected to that trip.

REGAINING YOUR SENSE OF PURPOSE

What is your life all about? What do you want it to mean? People instinctively want their lives to count, and many are searching for purpose. The Latin root for the word purpose means "for + place." Webster defines purpose as "something one intends to get or do, intention, aim; resolution, determination; the object for which something exists or is done." But how do you find out what your purpose is? People search in a variety of ways. Some say you have to "look within" to find your true purpose. But I believe that you must first begin by looking up to God, your Creator, to find the reasons He created you. The bottom line is that you were made by God for

God. Once you understand this, there are a number of benefits. You can focus your energy and simplify your decisions. You are given meaning to your life and help to prepare for eternity with God. All this will reduce your stress. Jesus said that the Holy Spirit would "teach us all things." He will lead you along the path and teach you the very essence of life.

A couple of years ago, I read an article in the morning paper stating that 80 to 85% of Americans disliked or frankly hated their jobs. I was astounded. How sad that so many people dislike going to work. Many times in life we may not be able to change our circumstances, but we can change our attitude toward those circumstances. Let me share an example.

I am often overbooked with appointments, which is not unusual for most people. We all have too much to do. The temptation for me is to work as hard and as fast as possible to see every patient. But when I do this, I am often providing *care* but am not *caring*. Care is *what I do for my patient* and caring is *who I am to my patient*. As you might expect, caring is what gives me the most satisfaction and significance in my practice. When I realize that I am not enjoying what I am doing, I know I have slipped back into the mode of only *doing*. So, I determine not only to provide care but also caring. By reestablishing the balance of *doing* and *being*, I once again begin to enjoy what I am doing. Not only am I providing care, but in the process of caring for others, I am connecting with them.

Despite all the changes in medicine over the past twenty-five years, there is one thing that has not changed. When I enter an exam or hospital room, my patient is there and I am there. The same is true for other health care professionals, whether they be nurses, physical therapists, speech therapists, occupational therapists, dietitians, etc. After all, most health care professionals chose their profession not just because they wanted to "fix people," but to practice their altruism, compassion and empathy. These words express the concept of service and the profound connection to others that occurs when we not only provide care but choose to care. Caring sends a message to our patients, "Your life matters to me. It is unique, important and sacred." Caring seeks to understand and see life through the patient's eyes. It seeks to understand how the patient feels.

This attitude is particularly important because many people seem to live in denial of death. They don't do well when confronted by their own mortality and have never spent time considering their immortality (what happens after they die). This is a paradox in the United States because we deny death and view it as the ultimate human weakness. This seems to be an adaptive response in our culture which emphasizes power, achievement and control. Yet these qualities seem futile and their importance evaporates when death is knocking at the door. We need transcendence to give meaning and purpose to life. At these moments health care workers have one of the greatest privileges of life. They have the opportunity to function as healers acting as facilitators and communicators as they help their patients express their concerns.

It is at times of crisis that our spirituality is challenged and sometimes shattered. It is an incredible privilege to come alongside another to help them in these times and in the aftermath as they seek to put everything back together again. Sometimes we may have very little to say, but there is tremendous value in our presence. This silent presence is referred to as *receptive silence*, and it sends the message, "Yes, this is a very difficult situation, but I am here with you to help in anyway I can." I have found that at times like these, the less I do, the more I accomplish and the less I say, the more I communicate. It is in these actions that we are *caring*, not just providing care.

The problem of job dissatisfaction centers around whether you see your work as just a job or as a calling. Whatever you do, if you give it to God and ask for His direction, your job then becomes a calling. All of us come into contact with other people in the course of doing our jobs. Our attitude toward our work becomes critical as others watch us. I will have more to say about work in Chapter 8.

There is an old story about three medieval stonecutters who were constructing a large medieval cathedral. An observer approached the first and asked if he liked his job. He replied, "All day long all I do is cut stones, day in and day out. It is so boring and monotonous. I hate it!" Next, the observer asked the same question of the second stonecutter. He answered, "I really appreciate this job because it pays me well enough to provide for the needs of my family. Even though the job is somewhat tedious, nonetheless, I have the satisfaction of knowing I am working for them." Lastly, the observer inquired of the third worker. His reply was very different from the other two. "Everyday I am given the opportunity to cut stones which will be used to construct this magnificent cathedral. When it is finished, everyone

28

who enters will sense the greatness and awesomeness of God. God has given me this opportunity to be used to ultimately demonstrate His greatness to others. It is such a wonderful privilege!" What was the difference? Each of these men did exactly the same thing all day long. But how they saw their job and their attitude were what made the difference.

We are instructed to do everything "as unto the Lord." Are you doing this? If you are not, what kind of difference do you think it would make if you adopted this attitude?

LIVING IN THE "NOW"

So many people live so far into the future that they find it difficult to enjoy the present. I would advise you to refuse to be lured by anticipation. I'll explain.

For many years, I was always looking ahead. I spent so much time anticipating what was going to happen that I lost my joy for what was going on in the present. When I was in grade school, I couldn't wait to move on to high school. Then I couldn't wait to go to college in order to prepare for medical school. But by my Junior year in college, I couldn't wait to get to medical school so I could study "what was really important." During my first 1 ½ years of medical school, although I was finally studying what was really important, I couldn't wait to start seeing patients. In my Senior year in medical school, I longed to be an intern. When I was an intern, I longed to be a resident. As a fellow in gastroenterology, I couldn't wait to get into practice. When I got into practice, I talked to other doctors who had been in practice for a few years and they said, "I can't wait until I retire!" That hit me. I thought, "They still have 30 years to practice!" So, I realized I had to change; I was always frustrated by living in the future.

Now I choose to focus on the present. It is very important for me to live each moment as if it is the most important moment of my life. Some people call this "living in the now." As I disciplined myself to do so, I noticed an intense satisfaction for the many things that I do and experience each day. It's not that I don't anticipate what will happen or don't plan for the future. I do. But, it doesn't consume and rob me of what is going on now.

When someone asks me what the best part of my day was, I

have difficulty answering the question. I so thoroughly enjoy every encounter with people all day, that each one was the highlight of the day. I know that sounds like something from a Hallmark card, but it's true, and it can be true for you, too.

I have come to realize that any sense of control I have is really an illusion. Think about it. You don't even have control over whether your car will start in the morning. Even if you have it checked and serviced regularly, the time will come when it just won't run. On the way to work, how much control do you have over the drunk who is driving toward you in the opposite lane? None of us can control the weather or what the stock market does. I am no longer discouraged by any of these uncertainties because I commit my life to God and put every aspect of it in His hands. He is now in charge - not me. I know that He is definitely in control of all things. I ran my life for twenty-six years on my own. Then one night I slipped out of bed onto my knees, and I turned it over to Him. My life runs a lot better with Him driving than me. There is a bumper sticker that says, "God is my Co-pilot." Recently I saw another bumper sticker that said, "If God is your Co-pilot, you better move over!"

Two of my favorite Scripture verses are found in the Book of Proverbs. I quote these to God as I am praying everyday on the way to work.

"Commit your works to the Lord and your plans will be established."   **Proverbs 16:3**

"The mind of man plans his way, but the Lord directs his steps.   **Proverbs 16:9**

As I quote these, I ask God to establish my ways and the ways of my family because I have committed them to Him. I ask Him also to direct my steps and those of my family. You can try doing this every day, as well. You will be amazed at the difference it makes.

VISION

"Where there is not vision, the people perish."
                                                    Proverbs 29:18

Albert Schweitzer phrased the essence of this verse differently when he said, "The tragedy of life is what dies inside a man while he lives."

When I was growing up in Buffalo, New York, our family attended a Lutheran Church. Whenever a missionary came to speak to our Sunday school class, I was always terrified. I would sit in the back of the room and slump down in my seat. For some reason, I had this fear that God would call me to be a missionary and send me to Africa. I thought that if the missionary couldn't see me, maybe I could escape this fate. This fear followed me into my adult life. As a physician, I saw other doctors going off to foreign lands to be a missionaries, even if for only a week or two. I had within me a critical spirit, and when I looked at them I thought, "You have got to be kidding! Those guys don't live very exemplary Christian lives, but somehow when they land on foreign soil, WHAM-OH they are missionaries!!!" Later I had to ask God to forgive me for a judgmental attitude. I actually remember praying, "Dear God, I have no desire to go outside the USA. My neighbors and patients need my help. The mission field is ripe here, I don't need to go to some foreign land, and in fact, I am NOT going unless you change my heart." I have come to realize that God loves it when we pray honestly from our hearts, and He loves a challenge.

Not long after my prayer, I received a call from Dr. William Standish Reed, the Founder and President of the Christian Medical Foundation (CMF) International. He wanted to do a Midwest regional conference for CMF in Indianapolis. He asked if I would be willing to help his people in choosing a location and assisting in the logistics. The conference was set for June, 1989. Two weeks prior to the conference, he called again to tell me that Dr. Julio Fuentes, a surgeon from San Marcos, Guatemala, would be attending the conference. He told me that he had had the opportunity to operate with Julio in San Marcos once and that he was a very fine surgeon. Julio wanted to watch some endoscopy procedures, and Bill asked if he could spend a couple days observing me at the hospital. I said, "Sure."

When Julio and his wife arrived in Indianapolis, I quickly realized that Julio spoke no English, and I spoke no Spanish. Fortunately, his wife was bilingual. Over the next two days, Julio was with me continually. Sometimes his wife was around, and at other times she wasn't. But, somehow it didn't seem to matter. I could tell that Julio was very bright and knew what was going on. I learned that in all of Guatemala, endoscopy was offered in only two cities. His town of

San Marcos had a population of 60,000, but also served as the referral center for some 300,000 indigenous Mayan Indians who lived in the many small villages scattered in the mountains that surrounded San Marcos.

After spending the two days together at the hospital, Julio and I along with our wives attended the two day conference. One afternoon they came to our home to visit. Five days after we met, I took Julio and his wife to the Indianapolis Airport. Julio's wife said to me, "Michael, Julio would like to invite you to come to Guatemala," and I heard myself reply, "I would love to come!" Later, as I drove home, tears were running down my cheeks. I said, "God, you tricked me! You changed my heart!"

In April of 1990, I went to Guatemala for the first time. One of my daughters, our pastor's daughter who wanted to become a nurse, and a pharmaceutical representative accompanied me. Julio had arranged for us to do gastroenterology clinics at the National Hospital in San Marcos. We evaluated over 100 patients in four days and performed endoscopy on over forty of them. Since none of us spoke Spanish, we depended heavily on Julio's wife. In the evenings, we ate dinner together and told jokes. I found out that Julio and I had the same sense of humor. All four of us felt that week was one of the best times of our life. I promised Julio I would return, and I kept my promise. I have been back every year since then. In our eighteen trips, more than 300 people have accompanied me to Guatemala, and we have cared for thousands of patients. I desperately wanted to communicate with the people and have learned enough Spanish to get myself into trouble. As a result of my experiences in Guatemala, God also led me to Peru, Columbia, Costa Rica, El Salvador and Nicaragua.

If someone would have told me in 1989 before Julio came to Indianapolis that I would have ever made any of these trips, I would never have believed them. But now my whole life revolves around all the friends I have in Central and South America. My Latino friends say that my problem now is that I have "a Latino heart trapped in a Gringo's body." That is a transformation that only God can do. Thank goodness that God is still in the business of changing hearts.

As a result of these mission trips, God has shown and taught me many things. I have come to realize that short-term mission trips are a way to benefit mankind by allowing people to use their knowledge, skills, talents and energy to help others less fortunate. People who have gone on these trips with us often speak about how their lives are changed forever. I always tell people that if they choose to go on one of our trips, it may be the most dangerous thing they ever do. At first they think I am speaking of physical danger, but soon they come to realize what I mean. Think about it. When was the last time you gave up a week of your vacation, paid $1000 or more, traveled to a developing country where you didn't speak the language and committed to help the people there, expecting nothing in return. Most Americans have never experienced this. When you give of yourself like this, God always blesses your efforts and your life.

I have frequently said, "Everything in life seems to take off when you start focusing on doing good for others." I have advised my children not to waste their time in life trying to associate with those who are wealthy, famous or politically powerful, rather to search for people who are helping others and bond to them. You will have the most exciting and fulfilling life you could ever imagine.

What is your vision for life? Many people don't seem to have one. They just live year after year plodding along. In one of my journals, I came across something I had written several years ago:

I have a deep sense of purpose, spiritual calling, destiny and understanding of why God put me on earth. It is my relationship with Him and this calling that propels me through life.

Do you feel the same way? If you don't, it is my sincere hope that, by the time you finish reading this book, you will.

William W. George said, "Visionaries can dream of a future unthinkable to others and then lead people to enable the dream to become a reality."

I have come to recognize that one person empowered by God can not only make a difference, he can make a huge difference. The Bible says:

For the eyes of the Lord move to and fro throughout the earth that He may strongly support those whose heart is completely His.

II Chronicles 19:9

If you are committed to God, He wants to use you to make a huge difference. He will guide and direct you through His Holy Spirit, and give you meaning and purpose in life.

33

FOCUS

TRUTH (What is the focus – the essential truth of this chapter?)

There is a big difference between success in life, which focuses on doing, and significance, which emphasizes being in life.

APPLICATION (What does this truth mean to me? How is it relevant in my life?)

By understanding these differences, I can choose to live a life of balance and truly enjoy each moment of every day.

ACTION (What should I do about it? How can this truth benefit my life?)

Pray: *Dear Jesus, help me to recognize the difference between the doing and the being in my life so that I can achieve the balance of success and significance You desire.*

CHAPTER 2

MADE IN HIS IMAGE

*Then God said, 'Let Us make man in Our image (likeness),
according to Our likeness; and let them rule over the fish of the sea
and over the birds of the sky and over the cattle and over all that
creeps on the earth.' God created man in His own image, in the
image of God He created him; male and female He created them.*
Genesis 1:26-27

Imagine for a moment that you owned your own business. It could be any kind of business. You have a large building which houses all the wares you sell, several offices for your administrative staff, a reception and waiting area, etc. You see yourself as a very good business man who is very attentive to every aspect of your business. However, there is just one problem. There is a room in your building that you don't know about. In that room is "Command Central." You know somehow that it exists, but you really don't understand it or know much about it. You take it for granted because everything is getting done, orders are being processed, items are being sold and money is coming in just fine.

Then one day, things start going wrong, and you can't figure out what the problem is. There is a serious issue in Command Central which you don't understand because of your ignorance of the room and what goes on in there. Hence, everything starts falling apart. Next thing you know, your bankers show up and cancel your line of credit because of your failing balance sheet. Subsequently, your business goes under, and you are left wondering what went wrong. Everything seemed fine for so long.

This scenario may seem a little bizarre, but I am here to tell you that this is exactly how most men live their lives. There is, in fact, a part of them that they are unaware of that is their "Command Central." They may live their lives for many years doing "just fine." But eventually, problems start to appear, and they don't know what went wrong or how to fix the problems. The problems often show up in several areas. It may be failing health, a broken marriage, trouble at work, etc. None of these are really the problem; rather they are symptoms of the problem.

Let's explore what's going on hoping to gain some insights into how to prevent these problems.

SPIRITUAL HUNGER IN AMERICA

Our society has changed so much since I was raised in the 1950's. In those times, people often considered what was good for the community. But now they ask, "What is good for me?" We used to think what was best for the company. Now we think, "What is best for me?" Society's thinking has radically changed, focusing more on individualism. People no longer want a job just to support their families. They also seek work that is stimulating and will help them in their personal growth. Loyalty to companies has been eroded by large company scandals. In addition, many companies hire the fewest fulltime workers possible, seeking instead to employ part-time workers or to work with specific project teams only for a specified period. When the project is done, everyone moves on.

It is estimated that the average employee will have as many as seven major job changes during his or her lifetime. These factors have led to changes in the attitudes of employers to employees and vice versa. The feeling of loyalty companies have to their employees, and employees to their companies, has almost disappeared. My father and grandfather might have worked their whole lifetime for one company from which they retired; this is seldom the case today.

The spirit of individualism has led to changes in how people see the church and how it affects their religious commitment. People are often less attached to a church and sometimes attend more than one church, in search of the right children's programs, the right preacher, the right small groups to meet their needs, etc. This shopping around approach has led to an overall decrease in people's involvement with and commitment to any one particular church where their efforts might make a difference.

The focus on self, combined with the spiritual vacuum that exists, has led to a spiritual hunger of huge proportion. People seem to be turning in every direction from standard forms of religion to the New Age, the occult and even to satanic practices. There is a fascination with "near death" and "out of body" experiences. For example, the best seller *Embraced by the Light,* written by Betty J. Eadie, focuses on these experiences. [1] The vast number of books sold is a testimony to the spiritual hunger within our society.

An excellent evaluation of these types of experiences is presented by Maurice S. Rawlings in his books *Beyond Death's Door* [2] and *To Hell and Back.* [3] As a cardiologist Dr. Rawlings has resuscitated literally hundreds of patients during cardiac arrest. This has given him a first hand opportunity to question patients in the midst of and immediately after resuscitation during their lucid moments. Many described the typical heaven-like experiences. However, many others described hell-like experiences that were so terrifying that they quickly repressed them into their subconscious to such a degree that they could not recall them even a few hours later! Dr. Rawlings noticed that many of those who experienced the hell-like encounters radically changed their lives, often turning to God.

So, "Are we a religious people or aren't we?" The Gallup Poll in 1990 indicated that in the United States, we are indeed a religious people with a strong fundamental religious heritage. The poll indicated that 95% of those surveyed said they believed in God and 72% stated that religion was the most important influence in their lives. [4] In addition, 77% stated they believed their physicians should address spiritual issues as part of their medical care and 48% even wanted their physician to pray with them.

The results of a more recent survey conducted by the MacArthur Foundation were summarized in the February 16, 1999 edition of *USA Today.* [5] The MacArthur team surveyed 3,032 Americans looking specifically at midlife development. The study looked at the religious lives of 1,800 people, ages 35-64, and noted that although religion was endorsed by most of the people, there was a tendency towards a very eclectic faith. This eclectic faith did not demand firm convictions or frequent attendance at religious services. Half of people surveyed said that they attended church at least 1-3 times a month or more. One quarter attended a service once a week. 50% attended less than once a month; of these 21 % never attended church at all. A majority of Americans (73%) stated that religion was either very or somewhat important to them and 71% considered themselves either very or somewhat religious.

What does this mean? David Kinnaman of the Barna research group in Ventura, California, market researchers specializing in faith in

American culture, stated "spirituality in the United States is a mile wide and an inch deep." He indicated that, although interest in spirituality is at an all time high in the United States, people have often developed a hybrid personal faith and that this faith integrates different perspectives from different religions, many of which seem to be contradictory.

Obviously, people are on a spiritual journey. While this can be a good thing, the resurgence of interest in spirituality also means that people are running off in many different directions in an attempt to be fed spiritually. What kind of spiritual food are they receiving, and what is it doing for their well being? Doctors need to recognize that these data indicate Americans see faith as playing a very important role in their lives. Dr. William Standish Reed, President and Founder of the Christian Medical Foundation, has written in his book *Surgery of the Soul: Healing the Whole Person-Spirit, Mind, and Body,* that society needs "a new medicine for the future which has as its central theme a greater orientation of both doctor and patient toward God through Jesus Christ and through the Holy Spirit … Christian physicians … should tell their patients that we may appear to be healers, but it is God who makes the sick whole." [6]

More than 15 years ago I wrote a booklet entitled *Understanding Your Digestive System,* to help patients learn about the various organs that make up the digestive system, see how each organ functions and gain insight into the diseases that affect each system. [7] Early in my practice of Gastroenterology I recognized that many of my patients' problems were profoundly affected by the stress they were experiencing in their lives. Because of this, I included a section on stress. This section explained the complicated relationship of a person's body, soul and spirit. So many people called to tell me how much they enjoyed and benefited from this information that I decided a second book dedicated to just this topic would be helpful to my patients. It took me awhile to formulate an outline, and I even drafted an initial manuscript. Then, as is frequently the case when I am writing something, I got tired of reading what I had written, and it got buried on my desk and forgotten. One day while I was making my rounds in the hospital, a delightful elderly woman who had just finished reading my first booklet looked up at me and said, "Young man, you must write another book. Only this time forget all the medical stuff, and just write about what you discussed in your last chapter on "Stress!" It was like my mother had spoken and I had better obey. So I dug out the initial draft and reworked it.

With the help of my family and friends, *A Christian Physician Looks At Stress & Healing,* [8] was published in May of 1996. My purpose in writing the book was to provide some answers to the difficult questions that some patients face in dealing with illness. Many have asked how I first got interested in stress. I always respond, "I firmly believe that the digestive system is the first line of defense against the stress we all encounter." After a patient has given me a litany of their symptoms, he or she often asks, "Do you believe that stress could do this?" My answer is, "Stress can do anything and everything!" I explain that since God created us with a body, soul and a spirit, it would be impossible for me to treat only the physical nature of an illness and ignore both the spiritual and psychological aspects that are so important in either causing and/or modulating a disease process.

CREATED: BODY, SOUL & SPIRIT

Many men suffer from a condition that I call *spiritual malnutrition.* Unfortunately, spiritual malnutrition often goes unnoticed, not only by the individual himself, but by those around him. "How do you feed your spirit?" To answer that question, we must have a clear understanding of the difference between the body, soul and spirit.

When the apostle Paul wrote to the church of Thessalonica, in his first letter he stated the following:

*Now may the God of peace Himself sanctify you entirely; and may your **spirit** and **soul** and **body** be preserved complete, without blame at the coming of our Lord Jesus Christ.*

I Thessalonians 5:23

From this verse we can see that we are created by God with a body, a soul and a spirit. Although the three are distinct, they are inseparable. We cannot divide ourselves up into body, soul and spirit. We are one. We are by nature spiritual beings created in God's image.

Defining these various aspects is difficult and very confusing. For example, it is difficult to adequately define the difference between the spirit and soul of man. In fact, Webster's dictionary defines the spirit as follows:

1 a) "the life principle, especially in man originally regarded as

an animating vapor infused by the breath, or as bestowed by a deity;
    b) the *soul*.

    2. the thinking motive, motivating, feeling part of man, often as distinguished from the body; mind; intelligence."

Similarly Webster defines the soul as:

    1. "an entity which is regarded as being the immortal or *spiritual* part of the person and, though having no physical or material reality, is credited with the functions of thinking and willing, and hence determining all behavior.

    2. the moral or emotional nature of man."

    I see a problem with both of these definitions. First, in defining the spirit, the word "soul" is used. Secondly, the definition of soul speaks of our "spiritual part." If you find this less than confusing, you certainly are more intelligent than I am.

    Patients come to me regularly wanting me to focus only on their bodily ailments. Perhaps they even allow me to engage in a discussion of a particular emotional turmoil they are going through. But, they may not even consider a discussion regarding their spiritual situation. If we cannot even define soul and spirit clearly, how can we begin to separate them and how can we expect to be healed if we focus our therapy on just one aspect alone?

    The writer of the book of Hebrews states:

For the word of God is living and active and sharper than any two-edged sword, and piercing as far as the division of soul and spirit, of both joints and marrow, and able to judge the thoughts and intentions of the heart.   **Hebrews 4: 12**

    Hence, it is only God who can divide the soul from the spirit. God never intended that we would be able to do so while we lived on earth.

    Although we cannot specifically separate our body, soul and spirit, I will attempt to give you a working definition of each. This will allow you to consider the essential aspects of each part and how they apply to your health.

BODY

    Most men have no problem understanding their body. The body is also known as our somatic component. When we are hungry, we eat to feed our bodies in order to prevent physical malnutrition. Wherever I travel in the US, there seems to be an obsession with exercise, conditioning and even cosmetic surgery. Proactive individuals seek regular medical check ups to maintain their health. Unfortunately, this is much more common in women than in men. Men tend to be macho and deny there could be anything wrong with them. If they paid as much attention to their personal health as they do their car or truck, they would be a lot better off. You can always buy a new vehicle. You only get one body.

SOUL

The soul is our emotional and mental dimension. It also involves our will and intellect. Many of us work hard to tend to our souls. We realize the importance of proper rest so that we don't become emotionally exhausted. We recognize how important it is to have time alone as well as time with our family and friends. We take vacations to "recharge our batteries." Cultivating proper relationships significantly helps and supports our mental health.

SPIRIT

Our spiritual dimension is our immortal, spiritual nature. Ways in which we tend to our spirit and prevent spiritual malnutrition are by spending time with God in solitude, meditating on His Word, and speaking and listening to God. I believe that this spiritual nature is our "Command Central." We can not see it, but yet it exists and is very real. When something goes wrong in our spirit, problems start to occur in all the other areas of our life.

A proper balance in life is essential to physical, emotional and spiritual well being. Yet balance is the most difficult issue we face. As we become more successful in our fast paced society, achieving balance becomes all the more difficult.

I encourage you to think about these working definitions for the body, soul and spirit. Examine your life in light of these three dimensions. Are you lacking in the necessary support in one or more? True health and well being involves the complex interconnectedness of these three dimensions. This is what I call "wholeness."

CREATED IN GOD'S IMAGE

God is Spirit (a spiritual Being), and those who worship Him must worship in spirit and truth (reality).   **John 4:24**

God often described Himself in the Bible as the "Living God." God is a spirit being. He is not the sun, moon or stars. He is the Creator of the sun, moon and stars. They are His creation. We should worship the Creator, not the creation. Also, God is not an image made of wood, stone or metal which are inanimate substances. God is not an animal or a man, which are also His creation. He is not the air or wind. He is not a "force," although He is very forceful; in fact, He is omnipotent (all powerful). God is a person with a personal Spirit body, a personal soul and a personal Spirit. His body is made of spiritual substance rather than of flesh and blood like that of man.

When the Bible says we are made in His image, it refers to our spiritual nature. The very nature of "spirit" defines who we are and how we are made. Often times we refer to a pet as having a particular type of "personality." By this, we are referring to his demeanor. But, animals are not persons, as we humans are. It is our personal spiritual nature by which we identify with God, by which we long to worship Him and by which we do worship Him. By definition this spiritual nature is and must be eternal, because we will exist eternally.

In our intimate relationship with Him, we are permitted to share in the Divine nature – a spiritual bonding, an indwelling of His Holy Spirit that "quickens" (gives life to) us. This bonding is the basis of our intimacy with Him. The idea of intimacy with someone you can't see is often difficult to comprehend. But I can assure you that your spirit desires intimacy with God, your Creator. Unless this occurs, you will suffer from spiritual malnutrition which will cause you problems in your "Command Central."

Spirituality should begin with our personal relationship with God. Jesus said that He is *the bread of life* and the *living water*. If we eat of this bread and drink of the living water, His promise to us is that we will never hunger or thirst again. One aspect of this book is about finding God - the true God. The other is about experiencing Him. My heart aches when I see so many people totally frustrated by life. Yes, life is hard, but nonetheless, it can be incredible, even joyous. Joy is not a word we seem to use much anymore, but it still has relevance for us today. Come! Meet the personal cosmic God of the universe, who formed you as a unique individual unlike anyone else in the entire world. It is He who inhabits and shouts to us in all nature, declaring His existence.

My desire is that you become spiritually fused, one with Him, and experience His overwhelming peace. See His power operate in your life. It is God who provides meaning and purpose to our existence. Life no longer has to be senseless and purposeless. This promise gives us hope to live now, and it supports us when our time comes to face death. Death ceases to be a threat to us. I can walk into the room of an individual who is dying and immediately sense, without even a word spoken, his spiritual condition. There is a stark contrast between those who have experienced and lived in the enduring sense of God's presence without fear and those who are terrified by the possibilities that await them.

MAN & ANIMALS

For a moment let us consider how humans differ from animals. Are we merely evolutionary descendants from one celled organisms? Are we nothing more than higher primates descended from apes and monkeys? I spent a significant amount of time over a four year period studying the theory of evolution and the theory of creation. What I was left with was a list of observable phenomena and their interpretation. I concluded that scientists are unable to prove evolution and Christians can't prove creation. In the end, I had to decide which theory was more believable.

Evolution is a theory. In my opinion, it is every bit as much a religion as the religion of creation. Both are philosophies that try to explain our existence. Since neither can be proved, one needs to decide which makes the most sense. After years of studying medicine and realizing the complexity of each individual cell of the body, I am literally overwhelmed that scientists can believe that something as incredible as just one human cell from any organ could have evolved by random mutation and chance. Literally, the whole of creation screams of design and incredible complexity.

In order for evolution to be true, there would have had to be a time during the evolutionary period when the Second Law of Thermodynamics was suspended. This law speaks of the entropy of a system increasing to maximum if left alone without intervention. Entropy is a measure of the amount of randomness or disorder in a system. It is the inherent process of degeneration leading to the disorganization of systems.

Let me give an example. If you move away from your home and do not return for 50 years, when you come back, in what state will you find it? Will the windows be clean, or will they be covered with dust and dirt? Will the inside of the house have improved or deteriorated? Will your lawn be overgrown with weeds, or will it be pristine and weed free? The Second Law of Thermodynamics demands that every aspect of your home and your property will have progressively become more disorganized and will have deteriorated, because you as the designer and organizer were not present and did not insert energy into the system to maintain it. So too, our human bodies if left unattended will not improve naturally. We see this in our day to day lives. That is why it is necessary to take care of our physical appearance and tend to the needs of our body. Yet, we are asked to believe by those who espouse evolution that we occurred as the result of random chance mutations and that these eventually evolved to the current complexity. The question is where did the incredible organization and complexity come from? Was it by chance, by accident, or through the direction of a designer?

Evolution is based upon the concept of evolving (going) from simple to complex. That means simple molecules gradually progressed to more complex molecules, complex molecules ultimately became simple living organisms and finally these evolved into more complex living creatures, eventually leading to man. However, this theory of evolving from simple to complex has been renounced by even Dr. Francis Crick. This is indeed ironic since Dr. Crick was responsible, along with James Watson, for discovering and elucidating the double helix structure of DNA (deoxyribonucleic acid) in 1953. How did this renunciation come about?

When scientists began to understand genetics and the information contained in genes, it opened up a whole new understanding and appreciation of life's complexity. For example, if one looks at a single Mycoplasma, a bacteria which is the simplest of all creatures in the animal kingdom, we find something quite amazing. The genes of a *single* Mycoplasma contain the information necessary to synthesize the 256 proteins necessary for its survival. If this information was typed out, single-spaced on paper, it would fill all the books in the world's seven largest libraries! Hence, when scientists realized this, they recognized that even the simplest of organisms were never "simple" but highly complex right from the start. As a result, the hypothesis that simple organisms evolved to more complex organisms no longer made sense.

Dr. Crick published an article in the Journal *Icarus,* entitled "Directed Panspermia" in 1973. [9] His thesis was that the incredible complexity of living systems and our knowledge regarding the early conditions on earth move the theory of spontaneous generation from the realm of plausible scientific theory to the miraculous. Since, as a scientific materialist, he could not accept the theory of intelligent design (viz. God), he resorted instead to the idea that life was brought to the earth by extraterrestrials billions of years ago. This does not solve the problem of how life began, it simply moves it to some other planet in some other galaxy.

Since evolution could no longer explain the complexity of human life and the use of supercomputers in the early 1970s showed spontaneous generation to be mathematically impossible, where were scientists left to turn? Like Crick, many turned to the theory of panspermia - the belief that the complex life currently existing on earth arrived here from some other planet in the universe. It was brought here by the "mother ship." Please excuse my sarcasm, but as a scientist myself, I am embarrassed by how scientists so readily accept this. I believe it is because they are desperate to explain man's existence on Earth through any means that do not require a designer, viz. God.

This discussion is important because it has implications regarding how we see ourselves as humans and how we relate to the other members of the animal kingdom. I believe that animals have instincts and emotions, but they do not have a spirit like humans. Only humans contemplate the meaning of their lives and the purpose of their existence. We alone pursue purpose for our lives. We alone focus on goals. We express our creativity in art. Since God created us in His image, we possess similarities to the characteristics of God. Since God is the Creator of all things, we too, desire to be creative. All the civilizations throughout history have possessed an innate belief in God thus demonstrating a religious focus.

Dr. Susan Blackmore in her book, *Dying To Live: Near Death*

Experiences, [10] stated that she believes our brains evolve in such a way as to desire meaning for our lives, and " … the idea that God created us for a special purpose is a lot more palatable than the idea that we just got here through the whims of 'chance and necessity.'"

Similarly, Dr. Herbert Benson, in his book *Timeless Healing, The Power Of Biology and Belief,* [11] stated that people have worshipped as long as they have existed and that somehow, instinctively, people have recognized that worshipping a higher power is necessary and good for them. He asked the question, "Are we wired for God?" He explains how we are "hard wired" with a lot of instincts such as the fear of heights, the fear of snakes, the fight or flight response and others. In contrast to animals, we ponder our mortality and wonder what will happen when we die.

Many times as I have stood by the bedside of a comatose patient speaking to him as if he understood me, I sensed that other physicians or nurses wondered about my sanity. On some occasions a nurse has come up to tell me, "Doctor, the patient does not hear you; he is comatose." I always point out to those health care providers that even though the body and soul may be asleep or in coma, I believe that the spirit is awake and is able to receive input. This is also true when patients are under general anesthesia during surgery. A number of studies have documented that the type of music played in the operating room and/or comments made by surgeons, anesthesiologists and others during the surgery, despite general anesthesia, have a direct impact on how quickly these patients recover.

Several years ago, I attended a conference in Santa Fe, New Mexico entitled "Creativity & Madness - Psychologic Studies Of Art and Artists." One of the presenters stated that what makes the difference between man and animals is man's creative mind. [12] Through art we sense fulfillment in knowing and expressing our gifts and talents. It is a means of self expression, a way to discover, explore, experience and heal ourselves. Creativity may be a transcendent path to the journey of life. Creativity is rooted in the unconscious mind and represents the interplay between our thoughts and our feelings.

Art is a way of experiencing the "self." Art helps us to organize our thoughts and converts them into a concrete form that can be touched and experienced. Art has been used as therapy for cancer patients, helping people to cope with what they are experiencing as a result of their disease. The more creative we are in life, the more enjoyment we experience. It is a way we continue to make our lives interesting every day. Our creativity seems to be fundamental to our concept of self worth and many of us seem to want to make a special contribution in some way to society. Creativity allows us to reach out to others, to share our beliefs, our values and literally ourselves.

GOD'S LOVE - HIS IMAGE

Recently, I was asked to read a book written by a fellow physician. I could tell he was struggling with many issues within Christianity. The more I read, the more I became convinced that his real problem was that he did not have a personal relationship with Jesus Christ. Yes, he knew about Jesus, but he had never come to really know Jesus. His mind was filled with intellectual facts about who Jesus was and what He had done, but his heart was empty. He had no connection with the Savior heart-wise. I agreed with many of his criticisms of Christianity as you will see in the following chapter. However, his intellectualization of Jesus and Jesus' message were, in my opinion, incorrect. He had been led down a path all too familiar to me. I had seen it many times. The Bible teaches that no one can come to God and believe the Gospel in and of himself. This only occurs by the action of the Holy Spirit who leads us to believe. Prior to this, we are described as spiritually dead, dead in our sin. God alone can *quicken the dead* which means to bring or give us new life.

It has been my observation that many who claim to be Christians always seem to over emphasize either the judgment of God or God's love. The former preach the Good News of the Gospel using it more like a hammer than the good news it was intended to be. Their message is, "Accept Jesus and be saved or spend eternity in hell." Where is love in that? You are encouraged to believe because of fear. That does not equate well with a God of love or the picture of Jesus as our loving Shepherd. When speaking to the elders of the Church at Ephesus, the Apostle Paul said:

*But I do not consider my life of any account as dear to myself, so that I may finish my course and the ministry which I received from the Lord Jesus, to testify solemnly of the **gospel of the grace of God**.*
— **Acts 20:24**

Paul emphasized the grace of God, not His wrath. Remember

47

that justice is receiving what you deserve, mercy is not receiving what you deserve and grace is receiving what you don't deserve. By focusing on God's wrath, many who call themselves Christians are actually turning people off to what Jesus was all about. They are approaching people who do not know God with a condemning spirit. Jesus never did that. Jesus' condemnation was for those who thought they knew everything about God but had it all wrong.

There is one aspect of Christianity that makes it unique and sets it apart from all other world religions. It is the only belief system where God came down to man to intercede for him. It is the only religion where the shedding of blood was by God Himself. Many pagan religions in contrast required human sacrifice to appease the gods. Can you imagine going to church to sacrifice your first born baby boy to appease the wrath of an angry god? This is at the crux of the difference. It can be summed up in one word – love.

Christianity is marked by a God of love. In fact, the Bible uses many words to describe God, but the one most used and most important is love. God is literally defined by the word love.

God is love ... **I John 4:16**

I have been fascinated by this and have frequently meditated on it. I do not believe it is even possible to read the Bible and understand it the way God intends unless you have first been touched by God's love. The very essence of who God is is pure love. Everything He does is determined by the properties of love. For example, the Bible says that God is perfect, holy, blameless. Not only has He never sinned, He is incapable of sin. Evil is completely inconsistent with who He is. The nature of evil is completely alien to Him. If you pour some oil into a glass of water and shake it up, the oil and water immediately begin to separate. Before long all the oil will be floating on the water with a very clear line of demarcation. Oil and water are totally alien. They are nothing alike chemically. They simply do not mix. Such it is with God's holiness and evil. They do not mix – ever! This is a difficult concept for us as humans to comprehend since sin comes so naturally to us.

Just imagine how you would act if love totally defined everything about you. You would never do another selfish thing. Your actions toward others would always be focused on their best interests and never your own. It has been said that in order to find yourself, you need to lose yourself in service to others. Maybe now we can begin to understand the Apostle John when he told us,

For God so loved the world that He gave His only begotten Son . . . **John 3:16**

This great truth explains how His great love for us motivated His plan of salvation.

By this the love of God was manifested in us, that God has sent His only begotten Son into the world so that we might live through Him. In this love, not that we loved God, but that He loved us and sent His Son to be the propitiation for our sins. **I John 4:9-10**

Propitiation is not a word we use today. It literally means to satisfy or appease. It was the turning away of God's wrath by Jesus' substitutionary atonement for our sin. No other religion on earth has ever existed where a god demonstrated his love like our God did. What amazes me most is not just that God did this but when He did it.

But God demonstrates His own love toward us, in that while we were yet sinners, Christ died for us. **Romans 5:8**

The next time you sin and feel like God can't forgive you, remember this verse. While you were in the midst of your sin, that is when God interceded for you. Our reaction when someone rejects and hurts us is to get angry, resent them and even lash out at them. God did just the opposite. Even before man rejected Him, God had already formulated a plan to solve the problem of man's separation from Him (due to His holiness) and to restore the relationship He wanted with us. That can only occur as the result of a supreme act of love.

Our love has its source in God's love, and His love reaches its full expression when we love others. When we love others, God Who is invisible becomes visible. The fullest and most dramatic expression of this is the sacrificial giving of one's life for another.

Greater love has no one than this, that one lay down his life for his friends. **John 15:13**

This is another way we have been created in God's image. God transforms us by the power of His Holy Spirit. The end result is that we become progressively less focused on ourselves and more on others. This capacity for us to love others is a manifestation of God's love at work within us. Through God's eternal purpose and grace, He not only reconciled us to Himself but He broke down the barriers that existed between us making it possible for us to love one another.

However, in contrast to God's love, our love is often inconsistent. His love is consistent, unchangeable and permanent. We can count on it!

Nothing ... will be able to separate us from the love of God, which is in Christ Jesus our Lord.   **Romans 8:38-39**

God delights in unchanging love.   **Micah 7:18**

I believe that love is the most powerful force that exists in the universe. God is only good, and everything He does is good. Was it wrong for God to create the potential for evil when He created the world? No! It was an absolute necessity. It was essential for us to have free will, in order that we would be like Him. I believe that our free will is another important way that we were created in His image.

One day I was doing procedures in our endoscopy area. Debby, the nurse working with me, and I were having one of our theological discussions. At one point she made this statement: "You are number one in God's eyes!" Wow! That hit me. Each of us is number one in God's eye. But how can this be? How can each one of us be number one in God's eye? The answer is God's amazing love. His immense love is great enough for each of us to be number one in His eye.

Three years after my son was born, my wife became pregnant with our first daughter. Prior to the birth I became concerned. I wondered if I would have enough love for her because I loved my son so much. Would there be enough love in me to go around? Well, when she was born, love just poured out of me. I didn't know where it came from, it was just there! I found out there was more than enough love for my son and her and my second daughter who came along a few years later. So it is with God. He has more than enough love for all of us.

I was at a wedding several years ago when the father of the groom stood up and announced he had three sons, and he loved them all equally, but differently, because God had made each of them unique and special. Similarly, God has made each of us unique. His love for each of us is very special and just as distinctively unique as He made each of us.

The uniqueness of God's special love for us is illustrated in twin parables that Jesus taught. The first is the Parable of the Lost Sheep found in Luke 15:1-7. It is clear from Jesus' frequent reference to shepherds that He regarded them with the utmost respect. They provided for their sheep a constant vigil, tender care and often times sacrificial heroism as they defended them against predators. Jesus' title of the "Good Shepherd" is further evidence of this admiration and identification. If you wish to know who God is and what He is like, all you need to do is examine Jesus' teachings on the activity and behavior of a shepherd. He drew word pictures that the people could easily understand and used depictions with which they were familiar. The whole relationship of a shepherd to his sheep literally screams of God's love for us.

The parable speaks of the one lost sheep out of the flock of one hundred that the shepherd goes off to find. When he finds the sheep, he puts it on his shoulders and rejoices as he returns to his flock. Although the lost sheep is a metaphor for a sinner who does not know God and is therefore lost, the parable speaks of God's intense concern for all of us.

The message is clear. Whenever we go astray, become lost, our Shepherd seeks us. He pursues us until He finds us, and when He does, He rejoices. He is thrilled. God's love is so great that He was not satisfied with the 99 sheep in the flock. No, His love compels Him to find the lost sheep. If you had ten children and lost one, would you say, "Well, so what, I still have nine." I don't think so! You would do everything you could to get your child back. Recognize this. If you go astray, God will use all of His power and resources to go after you and find you.

The second of the twin parables is the Parable of the Lost Coin in Luke 15:8-10. This parable paints the picture of a woman who lost a coin which was obviously of great value to her. She lights a candle and searches diligently until she finds it. When she finds it, she is filled with joy. This parable, too, is a metaphor. The lost coin represents the same thing the lost sheep represents. Just like a coin, people are sometimes lost. Both parables assert the value of just one life that is lost. As I will speak to in great depth later, God is all about personal relationships. He places incredible intrinsic value on each human life. Never underestimate this fact. The Bible tells us that God is impartial. To Him the value of the homeless alcoholic that lives on the streets is identical to the most prominent of our citizenry. The love of God, His love, drives Him in all He does. One lost soul, any soul that has gone astray garners His immediate attention and action. This is the essence of the Gospel message.

Did you know that God continually watches over you? His eyes are always on you! He is always listening to your voice!

For the eyes of the Lord are toward the righteous, and His ears attend to their prayer. **I Peter 3:12**

He is not watching and listening to see if you are going to do something wrong so He can punish you. No, He is watching you like a father watches his two-year-old child. That father knows that he has to watch his toddler or that toddler will get himself into trouble. Because of his love, he never takes his eyes off his child. He is not looking to punish him but to protect him. So it is with our heavenly Father. He constantly watches over us as a shepherd watches over his sheep. God's love for each of us is expressed in how He watches over us as our Shepherd. God is enthusiastic about each of us. He dedicates to each of us His time and energy.

Sheep are very timid animals that are afraid of just about everything. Our Shepherd comes and surrounds us not only to protect us from danger but to give us His peace. I love what Catherine Marshall said, "To know God as He really is – in His essential nature and character – is to arrive at a citadel of peace that circumstances may storm, but can never capture." When I read that, the phrase "citadel of peace" really spoke to me. Now when I am in the midst of trouble in my life, I remember that God has brought me to the Citadel of Peace and nothing can in any way harm me unless He permits it. And His promise to me is that if He does permit it, He will use it for good in my life.

The Apostle Paul prayed the following:

. . . that He would grant you . . . to be strengthened with power through His Spirit in the inner man so that Christ may dwell in your hearts through faith; and that you, being rooted and grounded in love, ***may be able to comprehend*** *with all the saints* ***what is the breadth and length and height and depth, and to know the love of Christ*** *which surpasses knowledge, that you may be filled up to all the fullness*

I suppose that most of us don't think that it is possible for us to *"be filled up to all the fullness of God."* But God never says anything He does not mean. The Apostle was under the inspiration of the Holy Spirit when he wrote those words. We read in Psalms:

Open your mouth wide and I will fill it.   **Psalm 81:10**

These are God's words as much today as of old since we know that God does not change. He is consistent throughout time. The Apostle Paul was speaking to Christians at Ephesus who had accepted and believed the Good News of Jesus Christ. Even though they had been saved and sealed by the Holy Spirit, Paul still prayed that:

... the eyes of their understanding may be enlightened.

Ephesians 1:18

There was even more for them – so much more than they could even comprehend. God wanted them to know that He intended to support them with His power.

... the surpassing greatness of His power toward us who believe.   **Ephesians 1:19**

He wants to do the same for you today. If we could only grasp that power Paul was speaking of, we would never doubt what God says. This is literally God's resurrection power working in us. God stands ready to do for us far beyond anything we could ever think or ever imagine!

Now to Him who is able to do far more abundantly beyond all that we ask or think, according to the power that works within us.

Ephesians 3:20

What is that power that is at work within us? It is none other than God's Holy Spirit that was given to us at our new birth. The message is very clear. God is not man, and we must never measure Him by human standards. He asks us to dream and to dream really big – to dream the impossible. God is not bound by human limitations. We must never limit Him with our mind.

Remember, God's eyes are constantly watching you, and His love and great power are always toward you.

How do we treat or, even better, prevent spiritual malnutrition? We have no difficulty seeing the need to eat when we are hungry to nourish our physical bodies. Likewise, when we are emotionally exhausted, we take a break or go on vacation. However, as natural as these are for us, we often neglect our spiritual needs. We become spiritually malnourished and are not even aware of it. If this neglect persists and we remain in a state of spiritual malnutrition, we are doomed to suffer the consequences. As a physician, I can state that improving your spiritual condition has many positive health benefits. Remember, "Once you get your spiritual foundation in order, everything else falls into place."

FOCUS

TRUTH (What is the focus – the essential truth of this chapter?)

God not only created me with a body and soul but with a spirit. In contrast to other animals, I am a spiritual being like God.

APPLICATION (What does this truth mean to me? How is it relevant in my life?)

Once I get my spiritual foundation in order, everything else in my life will fall into place.

ACTION (What should I do about it? How can this truth benefit my life?)

Pray: Oh Holy Spirit, please do whatever it takes to help me establish my spiritual foundation.

CHAPTER 3

REAL CHRISTIANITY

"There is a disaster which has already been under way for quite some time. I am referring to the calamity of a despiritualized and irreligious human consciousness."
Alexander Solzhenitsyn

I have a confession to make. Sometimes I don't want to go to church, and I feel like a hypocrite when I am there. There I said it! When I feel this way, I usually feel guilty. Then I wonder what's wrong with me. But, I have come to realize that I am not the only one. There is nothing wrong with me. Well, there probably are a lot of things wrong with me, but not in this regard – not for feeling this way.

Once when I was having breakfast with my pastor, I told him I felt like a "fringe-Christian." He asked, "What do you mean by that?" I could tell he was a bit shocked. I told him that I didn't fit in and that I felt like a hypocrite going to church when sometimes I didn't really enjoy it. I think it freaked him out a little when I told him that the music and all that goes on during the service irritated me. Maybe I was being too critical, but I was just being honest. Sometimes the service felt more like a performance or show to entertain people rather than a time of worship. I'm sure a lot of people come just to be entertained, but that doesn't do anything for me. He told me that he didn't see me as a fringe-Christian, but that really didn't help me much. You can't help how you feel. It comes from deep within. You can't pile up guilt about how you feel, it just is what it is. So, I continued in my frustration.

Paradoxically, during this period of time, I grew closer and closer in my personal relationship with God. Each day I spent time reading my Bible, praying and then asking God what He wanted to teach me from what I had read. Then I took the time to wait on the Lord and listen to what God had to say. The Holy Spirit spoke volumes. It was awesome! I kept a journal just to write down the important points I read and what He told me about them. But, I still didn't want to go to church.

Then one day, a friend of mine sent me a book entitled *Searching For God Knows What,* [1] by Don Miller. Don is a Christian writer. I liked the book so much, I bought and read his first book, *Blue Like Jazz.* [2] Those two books were like the Rosetta Stone to me. Don had a way of articulating all that I had been feeling and had felt for so long. I was comforted knowing that I was not alone. I came to realize that we were both simply searching for reality in our spiritual walk, and many times in church we weren't getting it.

Once, during an interview, Don was asked to defend Christianity. He told the interviewer he couldn't do that, because Christianity was too many different ideas or realities to too many different people. For example, if you were a boy who had been repeatedly molested by a Catholic Priest, how could you defend that type of Christianity which was perhaps the only form of Christianity you ever knew? One of my best friends is Latino. He told me that he never felt comfortable in the churches he went to because he never felt welcome. How can you defend that spirit of discrimination or persecution? If you were a young girl in a Christian school and were ridiculed by an insensitive teacher, how could you defend that representation of Christianity? Once, when I was on a mission trip in Nicaragua, I noticed that most of the children there were not of Indian descent which is what I was accustomed to in the other Central American countries. When I asked why, I was told the Conquistadors killed all the Indians! How can you defend that type of Christian behavior?

Don told the interviewer that he didn't want to defend Christianity, but that he wanted to tell people about Jesus. In essence, Don helped me to realize that from the days of the Apostles, the early Christians were trying to represent Jesus to those they came in contact with daily. And over the last 2,000 years there have been many so-called "Christians" who have misrepresented Jesus and what He taught. This realization helped me a lot. I concluded that all I had to do was to look at how Jesus conducted Himself with people and endeavor to do the same, always recognizing that I can only do this with the help and power of the Holy Spirit working within me.

Second, I relearned a very important truth. ***God has not called me to be the judge of anyone.*** He is the righteous Judge, not me. My job is to love, not judge. This knowledge was a tremendous relief. Judging is a lot of work and takes a lot of energy. I also realized that I don't have the ability to change anyone. Only the Holy Spirit can do that. My job is to love others and pray for them and leave the rest to God.

Young people from our church compete with other churches in what they call "Bible Bowl." The young people who train for this are intense. They study hard memorizing a section of the Bible and practicing for the competition. One Sunday our Bible Bowl team was summoned to the front of the church, and our pastor showed the large trophy they had won for placing first in the competition. Everyone applauded vigorously and shouted their approval. Somehow that did not sit right with me. It felt like our team had used the Bible to beat up on another church's team, and we were proud of it. I told my pastor about this, and he told me it wasn't like that. I still couldn't escape the feeling.

Someone sent me an email once that contained a list of bloopers that had been printed in church bulletins. One spoke of a church's basketball team that was going to play the team from another church called Christ the King. The announcement said, "Come out and watch us kill Christ the King!" Bible Bowl sounded like that to me. My youngest daughter competed in Bible Bowl, and she told me that my comments were harsh. She felt it was a good way to learn a lot about the Bible and that she enjoyed the competition. Maybe I'm just sensitive or judgmental about this.

Jesus had a lot to say to the religious leaders of His day who knew a whole lot about the Scriptures but less about how to apply their knowledge correctly. Bible Bowl is probably a great thing as long as the kids don't get too proud about their knowledge. I can see that if their leaders show them how to use their knowledge in the right way it can be beneficial. However, as I look around, one of the most prominent problems in the church is a proud, critical spirit. Everyone seems to be judging everyone else who doesn't believe exactly the way they do.

Once I traveled to Nicaragua and Guatemala with Pastor Steve Beam, Founder and President of Missionary Ventures, International. He explained to me that, throughout history, the Church evangelized using four ways:

1. War – The Crusades are an example of this - "Confess Christ or die!"
2. Manipulation – "We will feed you if you become a

Christian."

3. Extortion – "If you don't become a Christian, you will go to hell and be punished forever!"

4. Conversion and Abandonment – This happens when an evangelistic crusade comes to town, people hear the Gospel preached and respond to it. The problem occurs if there is no follow-up and no discipleship training. Those who responded quickly fall away. The next time they are approached with the Gospel message, their response is, "I tried it, and it didn't work for me."

Steve pointed out that when Jesus gave the Great Commission, He told His disciples to not just "Go" but to "Go and make disciples." He explained that we now have a phenomenon he called the "Christianity Paradox." Christianity has done so many good things such as bringing health care to many nations by establishing hospitals, setting up orphanages and schools. In India for example, people were formerly superstitious and saw disease as curses placed on them by angry gods. Karma prevented the idea of mercy. Christianity helped to change a lot of this. On the other hand, people in the third world now watch our television programs and see all the indecency and immorality. Some Islamic groups refer to the United States as The Great Satan and see that we permit abortion and pornography. They say we promote the Gospel of Materialism. It is easy to see how people can get confused.

It seems that, rather than just extending a loving hand to those around them, many Christians have an agenda. They always seem to be constantly pitching their beliefs like a vacuum cleaner salesman. If you don't jump on board with what they are selling, then you suddenly find yourself on the outside. This condemning attitude is illustrated by a car bumper sticker I saw recently: "Dear God, Please Protect Me From Your Followers!"

I found myself wondering what it would have been like to live when Jesus did and what I would have experienced just watching Him. So, I re-read the Gospels, asking myself what Jesus was like, trying to get a picture of how He specifically related to different kinds of people. One of the first things I noted was that crowds of people always flocked to Him. Sure, He was performing miracles, but it had to be more than that because they hung around for long periods of time to hear His teaching. I think they sensed His incredible love and compassion. When you love people unconditionally, people just naturally respond. Then I had to ask the hard question, "Why aren't people flocking to me?" The obvious answer was that I wasn't loving others unconditionally. Rather, I was approaching them with my agenda.

Jesus was criticized for hanging out with the undesirables of society. For example, He ate a meal in the home of two tax collectors, Matthew, who became one of His disciples, and Zaccheus. The Pharisees, the religious leaders of that day, criticized Jesus because these tax collectors did not live their lives consistent with the Jewish law. By accepting Matthew and Zaccheus as they were, Jesus was able to open a door to their hearts that caused a dramatic change in their lives.

Jesus criticized the Pharisees for being "lovers of money" and those "who justified themselves in the sight of men." His criticism was based upon His knowledge that they had misunderstood what His Father meant when He gave the law. Somehow they believed they were capable of keeping it. Jesus pointed out that His Father looked at their hearts. Hence, if they lusted after another man's wife in their hearts, they were guilty of adultery. Also, if they hated their neighbor, they were guilty of murder. Jesus said to them:

You are the ones who justify yourselves in the eyes of men, but God knows your hearts, for that which is highly esteemed among men is detestable in the sight of God.   **Luke 16:14-15**

As you might imagine, this teaching didn't go over very well.

Sometimes, when we read these accounts, it is easy to judge and criticize the Pharisees. But when we do this, I'm not so sure we are acting any better than they did. In the United States, it appears to me we have created a God whom we like and then worship Him. Televangelists often preach the Gospel of Materialism as evidenced by their "Name it and claim it" theology (also referred to as "Confess it – Possess it"). Their emphasis is that God wants to make you happy, and if you just believe and have enough faith, that is all you need. But this isn't what the Bible teaches, and when the theory doesn't work, people are left disillusioned, or worse, dead.

I have seen several people die while continuing to "name" and "claim" their healing. God isn't given to arm twisting. If all we have to do is ask and believe to get what we want, these people would get all the things they want and everyone else would jump on board. That isn't the kind of faith in God the Bible teaches. Real faith trusts God in the good times and the bad times. Real faith realizes that He is there even in "the valley of the shadow of death." Real faith realizes that God knows what is best for us. God's answer to our request may be, "Yes, no, or I have a better idea."

In our materialistic society, advertisers promise "things" will provide meaning, purpose, happiness and fulfillment. Most Americans live what I call the "Ladder Phenomenon." When we are dissatisfied, we are encouraged to buy a bigger house, a newer car, marry a younger woman, etc., in order to be happy, satisfied and fulfilled. But it never seems to work quite that way. After a short time, the bigger house, new car, and younger woman have lost their magic. So, what are we to do? The same thing - climb another rung on the ladder. Again, it doesn't work. You would think we would figure out we have been duped and get off the ladder!

This thinking has even invaded the Church. Several years ago, Bruce Wilkinson published the book, *The Prayer of Jabez,* which many misinterpreted. Jabez prayed to God as follows:

Oh, that You would bless me indeed – enlarge my territory.
I Chronicles 4:9-10

Jabez was asking for God's help to run His kingdom. His emphasis was not on personal gain, but on kingdom gain. Those who have misunderstood this prayer have asked for personal blessing for jobs, possessions, wealth, etc. But, this isn't what Jabez asked for, at all.

Materialism has no answers for the transcendent questions of life. The events of September 11, 2001 presented us with the senseless death of thousands. In the midst of the tragedy, we were forced to confront the potential of our own death. Tragedies have a way of clarifying what is most important in life. After the September 11th tragedy, Americans focused less on their jobs and more on their families. Some Americans also asked themselves, "What about God? If God exists, what is my relationship with Him?

Several years ago, I constructed a table to help me get a handle on the difference between religion and spirituality. The concept of religion is good. The word comes from the Latin *re-ligato* which means a rebinding. In surgery a surgeon finds a bleeding blood vessel and ties a ligature around it to stop the bleeding. The word ligature comes from this same Latin root *ligato*. Religion means a rebinding around a common set of beliefs. There is nothing wrong with this, but unfortunately, religion often becomes a substitute for true spirituality.

Let's look at the table. Religion often leads to a mechanistic approach to one's spirituality. For example, the Pharisees placed an extreme emphasis on the law - on "doing." They somehow believed that if they tried hard enough, they could keep the law and justify themselves before God. Jesus told them that they had missed the whole point. His Father gave the law to show them not their adequacy but their inadequacy. Jesus said the law was given to show them they couldn't do it themselves, and they needed a Savior to redeem them from their sin. There seems to be something inside us all that makes us believe we need to earn our salvation. We have a very hard time just accepting the fact that salvation is a free gift of God. The Bible says,

We are saved by grace, not of ourselves; it is a gift of God.
Ephesians 2:8

Jesus also emphasized that His Father was most concerned about inward character, not outward appearances. True Christian spirituality emphasizes a personal relationship with God, whereas religion often exchanges this for a relationship to a system of beliefs and a code of conduct. Having a personal relationship with God results in a dynamic change within a person and an observable difference in the way that person lives his life. The Kingdom of God reigns within him, and it changes his whole outlook governing his heart and mind.

The religious lack this dynamic, choosing rather to live their lives in their own strength. Hence, we often see very little difference between their lives and anyone else in the world. They are often trapped by the world's Gospel of Materialism. Their focus is money, power and fame. One aspect of true Christian spirituality is that when God changes you inside, you begin to look outwardly with a desire to focus on others and their needs.

THE KINGDOM OF GOD

RELIGION As the world sees it	SPIRITUALITY As God intends
Mechanics	Message
Law of the Pharisees Emphasis on keeping the Law	**Intent of the Law** The law shows us our need for a Savior.
The kingdom is Materialistic	**The kingdom is Spiritual**
"DOING" (Outward - Code of Ethics)	**"BEING"** (Inward - Character)
"Carnal Christian" Lives one way in church & another way during the week.	**"True Christian"** Lives always realizing he is in the presence of God. Lives a life of consistency wherever he is.
Reactions of the World: 1. Sees no difference. 2. No persecution. 3. Not drawn.	**Reactions of the World:** 1. Feels condemned. 2. Persecution. 3. Attracted/Drawn.
An absence of the dynamic (power) No power to live as God desires. **Superficial** Fake – Façade	**Dynamic (Power)** Power to live the quality which is like Jesus. **Deep** Real
The Kingdom of Satan ("The Prince of the Power of the Air") People want power which explains the appeal of the occult, witchcraft, etc.	**The Kingdom of God is "among you" & "within you"** The Kingdom of God is the reign of Jesus in your life.

We each need to examine our life to see if we are truly spiritual or just religious. Have you become comfortable in your religious walk or are you constantly being challenged to grow and change? Is your relationship with God deeply personal or has it become static? I can assure you, God has a lot to say to you. If you are willing, He has a lot to work on in your life. Your life can become so exciting. God wants to use you for His kingdom.

FIXING THE PROBLEM

Many of the problems we face today, we can't fix. One example is global terrorism. On September 11th, the world's greatest superpower was invaded, infiltrated and embarrassed at the cost of 3,000 lives that were vaporized by a small band of madmen who used our planes, our fuel and our freedoms to execute a suicide mission. What is a superpower? Our image of invincibility died on the fields of Viet Nam, and once again on 9/11. We can't fix that which is *outside,* only that which is *inside.* There is hope, but not in ourselves, only in God, the God who says,

Not by might and not by power, but by My Spirit says the Lord.
Zechariah 4:6

We will not win the war on the battlefields of countries like Afghanistan or Iraq, but on the battlefield of our hearts. In this great nation, our problem is that we are not *God's people called by His name* (II Chronicles 7:14). Often, you can't tell the difference between the Christians and the non-Christians. Our problem is not that there is too much of the world in the Church, but rather that there is not enough of the Church in the world! You can't live, dress and act as we do in the world and be on God's side by holding a membership in a church. In I Peter 2:9 we are called to be a *peculiar people.* Christianity does not suffer so much from its opponents as much as it does its exponents!

Part of our problem is that we are very temporally oriented. In Guatemala, the Guatemalan people focus more on heaven than most Americans. Heaven is more real to them and more of a genuine hope. The lives of the Mayan people are primitive and difficult. Their life expectancy is only forty-five years. Many women still die giving birth. Many children die during childbirth or from various infections within the first two years of life. These facts are hard for most Americans to believe, especially if they have never traveled outside the US to a developing country. This reality became obvious to me in a very graphic way last year as I was traveling through Guatemala. We drove past a casket maker's shop. What struck me was the number of very small caskets stacked in front of the shop at the road side - caskets that only infants and small children could fit into. When death is so common, heaven becomes a more important reality.

Our focus needs to be less on temporal things and more on eternal things. The Apostle Paul wrote to the Colossians saying:

Set your minds on things above ...   **Colossians 3:2**

Likewise Jesus said,

Seek first the Kingdom of God, and all these other things will be added unto you.   **Matthew 6:33**

Do you get the feeling that our society and some of our fellow Christians have missed the point? People should be able to see Jesus in us - see that God has brought us out of darkness - see that we look, act, talk and walk differently. Jesus made a way for us when there was no way. He set us free, covered our sins, took us from nowhere to somewhere and changed us from nobodies to somebodies.

God is looking for people who are real. Has anyone ever said to you, "I didn't know you were a Christian." Be honest - Ask yourself, "What is it about me that would make others want to know Jesus?" Our prayer should be, "Oh, Holy Spirit fill me so full today that everyone I meet will notice and be drawn to You."

I knew an operating room supervisor who had gone through a difficult divorce. One day when she went to her locker, there was a card there from one of her team. It read, "I watched you all year as you went through the bitter divorce. I became a Christian because of you." What a testimony about her behavior during a very difficult time. Her acts were such that they drew someone to Jesus. That's what our lives should be all about.

People are watching us. We need to be "*salt*" and "*light*" – Luke 14:34. If someone followed you around, what would your Christianity reveal? All of us have been frustrated by our inability to do the things we want to do and avoid doing the things we don't want to do. Jesus recognized this when He preached the Sermon on the Mount. The very first Beatitude dealt with our powerlessness. Jesus knew and was showing us that we can't do it alone. Jesus said:

Blessed are those who are poor in spirit. **Matthew 5:3**

I have asked a lot of Christians what they think it means to be "poor in spirit." My survey has revealed that about 90% really don't have a clue what that phrase means. This has been true even for people who have attended church their whole lives! How does this happen? How can you be in a church your whole life and not know where Jesus said to begin? Maybe this is why we see so many of the same problems of the world in the church.

To be poor in spirit simply means that when you look at what God requires of you, you respond, "I can't do it!" God knows you can't, but *you* need to recognize it, too. This is the starting point, the recognition that you cannot live the life God requires of you without His help and power. This is the essence of the Gospel, the Good News. Not only has Jesus died for you and paid the penalty for your sin, He offers to dwell in you with His Holy Spirit to empower you to accomplish all that He desires of you.

For awhile, I was the President and CEO of our medical group. Because I needed to do all kinds of things that I was not trained to do, it was perhaps the most difficult time of my life. The position required a lot of rapid on-the-job learning. I read a lot of books about business. One, entitled *The Fifth Discipline,* [3] by Peter Senge, repeatedly states: "Structure determines function." I thought about that for a long time. This is true not only for a business organization, but also for each of us spiritually. We must build a proper spiritual structure. Remember what Pastor Johnson said: "Once you get your spiritual foundation in order, everything else falls into place."

I want to emphasize that God is on your side. He definitely wants you to succeed in all the areas of your life. With His help, you can become the husband, father, employee, friend, brother, etc. you want to be and He wants you to be. Here's what He is saying to you:

The eyes of the Lord move to and fro throughout the whole earth seeking those whose hearts are completely His, that He might strongly support them. **II Chronicles 16:9**

God wants to support you. Give your heart, your entire self to Him and see what He will do!

1. Christianity is *Not A Religion* BUT a *Personal Relationship.*
2. Christianity is *Not Man Going to God* BUT *God Coming To Man.*
3. Christianity is *Not Works Based* BUT *Works Are A Grateful Response To What God Did.*

Several of my reviewers said that I was particularly hard on the established church in this chapter. This is true by intention. My goal was not to be purposefully malignant, but honestly critical with the intent that all of us who make up the Church, the Body of Christ, would personally evaluate ourselves to see if we are, in fact, part of the problem. If I recognize that I am part of the problem, then I can become part of the solution. The Bible instructs us *"to not forsake fellowship one with another."* I do attend church, and hope that by doing so, I can be a positive participant in the worship of my Lord. Other believers and the time I spend with them is very important to me. We encourage one another. As believers we are the *"Bride of Christ."* The Church is one of God's instruments for maturing believers. My hope is that what I have written will help us get our act together. In the Gospel of John, Chapter 17, Jesus earnestly prayed to His Father for unity in the Church. So too, is my desire.

FOCUS

TRUTH (What is the focus – the essential truth of this chapter?)

Real Christianity has little to do with the church I attend and everything to do with my personal relationship with God and who I am on the inside.

APPLICATION (What does this truth mean to me? How is it relevant in my life?)

If I focus on my inward growth, the outward will stem from it and become obvious to others.

ACTION (What should I do about it? How can this truth benefit my life?)

Pray: Heavenly Father, do whatever it takes to make me into an authentic, real Christian – one that is loving and non-judgmental.

CHAPTER 4

THE IMPORTANCE OF RELATIONSHIPS

It took me more than twenty years of being married to a great woman before I realized that the key to life is relationships. The word "relationship" comes from the Latin meaning to *relate, connect or associate*. Webster defines it as "a connection; being related; a connection by blood or marriage; kinship."

I told my children as they were growing up to always be nice to people. I taught them each encounter with someone else is important because people often cycle in and out of our lives. When I was a young doctor just starting out in practice, I often had the opportunity to teach nursing students. Some physicians saw this as a burden and were not very nice to the students. But, I tried to take the time to make them feel welcome and teach them whatever I could. Now, more than twenty-five years later, many of those former nursing students are heads of departments in the same hospital. On more than one occasion, they have been very helpful to me. I can't help but believe that it was because of the seed of kindness that I sowed many years ago.

Not only do people disregard this rule, they seem to enjoy being difficult, obstinate or down right nasty. In her book, *PLAN B Further Thoughts on Faith*, [1] Anne Lamott writes that her father told her the first rule of life was, "Don't be an a...hole!" That's good advice. In my experience that rule can keep you out of a lot of trouble.

I first met Russ Spicer when I was in Miami many years ago. Russ was actually from Indianapolis, but he had moved to Miami to work with Pastor Jim Bricker who started the Vineyard Church there. I had the opportunity to attend a medical meeting in Miami and took my son with me. Jim suggested we go snorkeling, and that is when I met Russ. We became fast friends, and when Russ moved back to Indianapolis a couple years later, we connected on a regular basis. Russ understands the importance of relationships in life. Here is an episode in his life he shared with me.

My wife and I took a vacation to the Pacific Northwest in 1995. We visited Seattle, Vancouver and Victoria, British Columbia. Laura wanted to go to an attraction called Butchards Gardens, located just outside of Victoria. The idea didn't appeal to me at all. Frankly, I could care less about looking at flowers and plants all day. I let it be known that I was reluctant about going to the park, but to no avail. As our car approached the gate, the attendant asked for 28 dollars. I almost lost it!

We paid the admission fee and went inside. As I was mumbling about the price to see a bunch of dumb flowers, I looked across this sunken landscape that was truly the most unbelievable sight I had ever seen. I couldn't get over the beauty. I thought these colors must be the brightest reds, pinks, violets, yellows, blues and greens on the face of the earth! I was overwhelmed, to say the least.

My wife could see my excitement and gave me that "told you so" look. I said, "You were right - good call on the Butchards Gardens." I told her that I would have paid 56 dollars to see what I was now calling the "Garden of Eden." Later, as I was looking out from a peak overlooking this valley of beauty, I said to myself, "This is what heaven must look like!" I kept repeating in my mind, "This is the most beautiful thing I have ever seen!"

My thoughts were interrupted by a message telling me that there was something in front of me that was much more beautiful to God than this garden. The sunken garden had a stone path weaving throughout the valley. From my high perspective, the path looked like it had little ants crawling in a row. The ants were actually people walking along the path and looking at the scenery. What was most beautiful to God in the garden was and will always be the people. God's favorite thing in the whole universe is people. On this day in Butchards Gardens, I was again made aware of this truth. This was an impression that I will never forget.

Jesus said, "Love God with all of your heart, soul, mind and spirit, and love others as yourself." People matter most. If we would think about others as if they were our actual brothers and sisters, we would love them very much. We need to realize that it is only by circumstances beyond our control that they are not our actual brothers and sisters.

In the Midwest, we are periodically hit by tornados. When the affected people are interviewed, I have always been interested by what they say. Over and over again I hear them describe how they lost their house and all their possessions, but without exception they go on to say, "But, thank God I still have my family." In the midst of such a tragedy, what is of most importance - their relationships - becomes crystal clear.

My wife is a nurse who works in palliative (end of life) care and helps patients deal with end-of-life issues. She says no man on his death bed wants to see his car! Men want their family and friends with them. Think about it. If you lost everything, what would you have left? What is really important?

RELATIONSHIPS REQUIRE TIME

Dr. Scott Peck wrote a book entitled *The Road Less Traveled.* [2] In it he speaks about the deception of "quality time." Parents who are completely overwhelmed by their jobs and all that is going on in their lives tell themselves that they are going to schedule quality time with their children. Dr. Peck points out the fallacy of this when he states that quality time comes out of quantity time spent with your children. In other words, you can't "schedule" quality time with your child. Rather, quality time or those precious moments parents relish, come from quantity time spent together.

I sometimes wonder why some couples have children at all. I guess it is because they think it is the right thing to do or something they are supposed to do. But when they do have children, they never spend any time with them. They never seem to enjoy them. Children have to be more than just a hobby, or you shouldn't have them.

In my seminars on relationships, I often use the following illustration. Imagine if you went out on a date with an attractive young woman, and you both had a great time. The woman just knows that you will call her, but as the days and weeks go by, she doesn't hear from you. She figures she misunderstood what happened on the date, and you didn't enjoy your time together as much as she did. One year later to the day, you call her again and request a second date. She is surprised, but accepts. On this second date, you both have even more fun than on the first date. She knows that this time you will call her. But you don't. She is disappointed and confused, but after a few weeks, she goes on with her life and forgets about you. Then once again, a year later, you call and ask for another date. Reluctantly, she agrees to give you one last chance. The third date goes even better than the first two combined. She is absolutely convinced you will call her this time. But again, you disappoint her by not calling.

A few months pass, and your mother is in the beauty salon. As she speaks to her beautician, she tells her that her son (YOU) are going steady with a beautiful young woman whom he (you) intend to marry. The girl's mother just happens to be sitting in the chair next to your mother! She overhears the conversation which she subsequently relays to her daughter. Her daughter is shocked! She can't believe that you think you two are going steady. Honestly, it's surprising that she agreed to a third date! What's wrong with this "relationship?" It has everything but time. Without time there is no relationship.

HOW ARE WE RELATED TO GOD?

Of all our relationships, the most important one is our relationship with God. Sin separated us from God, but Jesus' blood restored our relationship. It's only through His blood. Many people struggle with the concept of a Triune God. It is helpful to understand the nature of the Trinity so that we can draw closer to God. How can God be one, yet three? There is one God, yet three divine eternal manifestations. Think of water, which exists as a solid (ice), a liquid (water) and a gas (steam). No analogy is perfect, but each one helps us begin to comprehend the vast nature of God. Phillip Keller, in his book, *A Shepherd Looks at the 23rd Psalm*, [3] gives a good description of our Father, Jesus, His Son and the Holy Spirit. He calls our Father the "Originator, the author of all that exists and the Master Architect." Jesus is the "Artisan, the Creator of all that exists." The Holy Spirit is the "Agent, who presents facts to our mind and gives us spiritual understanding."

JESUS WANTS TO SPEND TIME WITH YOU!

One Sunday, our pastor, Doctor Gary Johnson said, "All God wants is a relationship with you." He pointed out that in all our relationships, we communicate by talking and listening to each other. But, it seems that in our relationship with God, we so often pray (talk to Him), but fail to take the time to listen. God has many things to tell us, if we would only listen. I suppose we don't listen for several reasons. We don't know we are supposed to listen or that we can. Or perhaps, we don't know how to listen to God. Or maybe the biggest reason is that we don't spend time with God, let alone listen to Him.

Pastor Gary went on to quote Psalm 62:1 – *"My soul waits in silence for God only ..."* I studied this verse, reading various translations of the Bible and commentaries about it. One said, *"Only in God is my soul quieted (at rest)."* Another said, *"In God alone there is rest for my soul."* And still another, *"Leave it all quietly to God, my soul."* He challenged each of us to take time each day to enter into the presence of God. He suggested we find a quiet place that would become a sacred place where Jesus could come. Jesus often went off by Himself to find a quiet, solitary, even desolate place where He could pray to His Father. He went to places where no one was making demands on Him. He often did this very early in the morning.

Gary told us how spending time with God requires diligence and discipline. He used Jesus' example to emphasize how we would, like Jesus, need to do three things each day:

1. Carve out the time → Jesus often got up *"very early in the morning, while it was still dark."*

2. Just do it! → Jesus had to *"get up."* It takes discipline to make the effort and stick to it. Go to your private, sacred place where there are no interruptions. Make this the highest priority of your day.

3. Be diligent in listening → Listening should be preceded by Bible reading and prayer, but don't just stop there. The most important aspect of your daily time with God is yet to come. Enter into God's presence.

So, I accepted Gary's challenge. I started getting up 30 to 60 minutes early. While I drove to the hospital, I prayed. When I arrived, I parked in a far corner of the parking lot. I would read my Bible or sometimes study a particular topic. Then I would pray briefly and prepare to listen to God. My prayer was often like this:

"Dear Jesus. This is the most important time in my entire day. It says in Psalm 46:10, *"Be still,"* which in Hebrew means to loosen my grip, relax and let You be in charge. I know that all You want is a relationship with me. I also want this very much. It says in Psalm 62:1, *'My soul waits in silence for you . . .'* So now, I wait in silence before You. What do You want to say to me? What do I need to hear from You?"

Then I sat in silence with my eyes closed. It was a time of peace and incredible relaxation. Thoughts came to my mind, often about what I had read. Then suddenly, a thought came that somehow I knew was from Him, specifically for me. I do not know how to explain it any better than that. People often speak of the "still small voice of God" that speaks to their heart. It is not an audible voice that you hear with your ears, but one that you hear with your heart, your spirit. For God is Spirit, and He communicates with us Spirit to spirit - to our heart. As I listen with my heart, God speaks to my heart. He speaks to the very essence of who I am, created in His image. God speaks from His heart to mine. Through this I learn the heart of God.

Sometimes I was struggling with a particular problem. I would come to Him and petition, "God, my heart is breaking over this issue. I desperately need to hear from You today!" I was amazed at how He answered and spoke to me.

One morning I was really struggling with an issue - the kind of issue that bugs you so much that, even when you try to think about something else, it forces its way back into your mind. It ends up controlling you. I prayed to God and told Him that I really needed to hear from Him regarding this issue and what I should do about it. After I read the chapter of Scripture He directed me to, I looked at it, and said, "You have got to be kidding! How in the world will that help? How can You speak to me from anything in that chapter?" Quite frankly, I was upset, but I know that God loves it when I am honest with Him and just pour out my heart. So, reluctantly I waited in silence.

I began to meditate on some of the verses I had read. All of a sudden as I meditated on a particular verse, He spoke to me. From a verse that had not meant anything to me came the answer I so desperately needed. I couldn't believe it. Then, to further confirm that He had indeed spoken, when I got out of my car and walked to the hospital only one hundred yards away, two doctors stopped me to talk. Both of them gave me unsolicited encouragement regarding the very issue I was dealing with! Only God can do this. As I have continued to wait on Him and listen, my intimacy with Jesus has grown. Our relationship has surpassed what I had ever anticipated.

Another verse that tells of the benefits of waiting on God was spoken by the prophet Isaiah:

Those who wait upon Me will renew their strength ...
Isaiah 40:31

The word "wait" used here in Hebrew means to remain inactive - in anticipation of something. The waiting always carries with it an expectation. It is an excited anticipation. So too, when we are experiencing difficulty in the midst of a trial, we can choose to "wait" on Him with this anticipation and excitement, knowing that He is working out everything for our good. Our suffering will not last forever, and it will produce the result that He has in mind.

Scott Veerkamp shared his account of how God showed him the difference between success and significance in Chapter 1. Listen to how God subsequently showed him how He wanted to spend time with him.

After my incredible conversion experience, I was blessed by Todd Anderson, whom God sent to come along side me to disciple me. I learned the principles and precepts of God's Word for godly living. Early on in my Christian walk, I discovered that my Spiritual gift and calling was to evangelize the lost.

After walking with the Lord for a few years, I found that I enjoyed my new life of forgiveness and freedom. My marriage, children and business were undoubtedly blessed, and I truly found myself "living the dream." By God's amazing grace, I continued to rank in the top 10 Remax real estate agents in Indiana year after year. At the age of 35, I was asked by the elders of our church to serve as an elder.

In September of 2005, I remember getting ready for work one morning. I said to my wife, "Babe, I really feel like I am at the top of my game. I am serving as an elder, we are healthy and happy and business is great. I am really feeling good about where I am going."

By that time in my journey with God, I had developed "a routine" in my relationship with God. Let me share with you the spiritual list of things that I was doing very faithfully.

1) *Praying - not just with my wife and children, but praying over them every morning before school and every night before bed.*
2) *Going to church regularly. (Sundays, elder meetings, ministry meetings, evangelism meetings, etc.)*
3) *Conducting my business in a very moral and godly fashion.*
4) *Evangelizing the lost at every opportunity possible as God put these people in my path.*
5) *Praying with people at the drop of a hat when a need was identified.*

The list illustrates the fact that by all accounts I was doing all the right things. The only problem was that at the top of the list something essential was missing. **Somewhere along the way, I am not sure how or where, in my walk with God, I replaced my relationship with Him with a religious to do list.** *I am not sure how it happened, but somewhere in my journey, I forgot my first love. In the beginning of my Christian walk in 1993, I truly didn't care about anything except spending time with God and everything else seemed to always work itself out. At some point, I got too busy with all of the businesses that I had started, all the real estate that I had bought, all of the ministry commitments, etc. I was too busy to stop and have time with God.*

Back when I was working on my real estate license, my teacher told the class if we were doing any volume of business at all, we could expect to be in court at least a couple of times a year – that was just the nature of the business. If her statement had any truth to it at all, then I must have really been protected by God. Because in the 15 years of conducting real estate transactions, I had only been in court twice, and neither time was the dispute directed at me.

One day in November of 2005, I received certified mail in an envelope about the size and weight of a telephone book from the Metropolitan Indianapolis Board of Realtors (MIBOR). It was a formal complaint against me from an investor client that I had sold a home to. In the complaint, I was falsely accused of selling property that was not worth as much as I said it was worth. The investor said some of the most wicked things about me that could be imagined. In addition to MIBOR, he also sent the package to: Indiana State Attorney General, the Grand Jury Investigators Office of Indiana for Mortgage Fraud and Real Estate Corruption, Remax of Indiana, Remax International and Channel 6 Call For Help.

I spent the next two months rebutting all the false allegations to each one of these institutions. One by one, they were dismissed. During this time, I was overwhelmed by all of the businesses I had gotten myself into. I was already stressed from not having enough time in the day to get everything done, and now I was completely engulfed in this dispute, too. What hurt the most was the personal blow that came from the words that this investor said about me.

I woke up one Thursday morning at approximately 3 AM, gasping for air, clutching my chest and telling my wife to call 911. I told her that I thought I was having a heart attack or a stroke or something. I told her that there was something wrong because I couldn't think

76

right. After getting to the hospital and all the tests, I was told that I had suffered from a severe anxiety attack. It was so severe I found myself on the couch for the next 4 months. I was totally unable to work or even function normally. Psalm 23:1-3 says, "The Lord is my shepherd, I shall not want. He **makes** me lie down in green pastures; He leads me beside still waters. He restores my soul. He guides me in the path of righteousness for His name's sake." I would not have imagined that my "green pastures" would have been my couch, but it most definitely was.

It would be impossible for me to put into words the dark place where I found myself. I felt so helpless and separated from God! I continually cried out to the Lord for relief, and all along the way, just when I would feel as if there was no hope, God, with His mountain of mercy, would show me His kindness with one sign after another. I remember one day when I was feeling so hopeless, I even asked God to take my life. I remember seeing a picture of Scripture in my doctor's office that said, "I lift my eyes to the hills - where does my help come from? My help comes from the Lord the Maker of heaven and earth." (Psalm 121:1) I was reminded and comforted of whose I was - and how in control He is.

As the result of this experience, I became convinced that we can look the part and even convince ourselves that we are who we are supposed to be - based on what we do. **But, the truth is, there is nothing we can do that will replace our devotion, quiet time and our communion time with God.** (Exodus 20:5)

I would like to challenge you. As you consider the information in this book, do a bit of authentic self evaluation and make the necessary changes needed. The Ancient Path is God's way which is clearly revealed in His Word. He knows what's best for our lives. (Hebrews 12:6-8)

I challenge you to look back over your life. Weren't the worst times where you learned the most about yourself and God? Weren't they what made you stronger? If you listen carefully to athletes, you will often hear them say their success is the result of one or more injuries. The very thing that should have defeated them is what made them the strongest.

WHAT CAN YOU EXPECT?

A couple years ago, I was visiting my brother-in-law in Bath, England. On Sunday, we attended an Anglican church. As we sang one of the hymns, I was moved by the following words:

The Holy One is here. Come, bow. His glory shines all around. His power is moving in this place. He comes to cleanse and heal, to minister grace. **The Anglican Hymnal, Hymn 53**

As I spend time with Him daily in silence and in the Word, I am nourished, sustained, spiritually filled, strengthened, given peace and internally quieted. I am built up and receive the "rest of God." Isn't this what we all need in order to live out our lives daily? Jesus is the "Bread of Life." He is the "Word made flesh." We need the hope and strength to go on, which only God can provide from our relationship with Him.

THE KEY TO LIVING THE CHRISTIAN LIFE.

Cease striving (be still; stop) and know (recognize) that I am God. **Psalm 46:10**

It's all about control. God says to each of us, "Give Me control. Let and permit Me to be God - to be God in your life. Relax." Why is it so hard for us to just relax in our relationship with Him and to let Him take control? This is the key that opens the door to an incredible life. We all have the key. God has given it to us. But, so many never take the key and open the door.

THE NATURE OF SALVATION

God has the solution to the problem of sin which separates us from Him. He developed a way for us to be delivered and saved from the curse that was brought upon all mankind as a result of sin. Remember that sin is the main deterrent to our relationship with Him. All of Scripture is really a love story, in which God continually shows us that He is doing everything He can to restore us to a relationship with Him.

What does it mean to be saved? Think of a man on a cruise who is standing on the edge of the ship. Suddenly, when the boat pitches after hitting a wave, he is thrown overboard. He is floundering in the water and if not rescued, will drown. The man is saved from the sea and death when someone throws him a life preserver attached to a rope and pulls him back to safety. In our lives, whether we realize it or not, we are all drowning in the sea of sin. It is God, the Father, who throws us His own Life Preserver by sending His Son, Jesus.

As is so commonly thought, salvation has nothing to do with living a good life or doing good works. That theology is at the core of all other world religions. Only in Christianity is salvation free. If we are genuinely saved, a change in our life will be evident. We should be bearing fruit (good works) as a result of our gratefulness to God. The man drowning in the sea who fell off the cruise ship did not pay for the life preserver to be thrown to him, it was thrown as a free gift. All he had to do was reach out and grab hold. So too, our responsibility is to reach out to the gift of eternal life, our Life Preserver, Jesus Christ, and hold on for dear life. There is nothing that we can do to deserve salvation. We can never become worthy of it, and we can never pay for it.

One afternoon during my residency, I was seeing patients in my clinic. A gentleman in his late fifties came in for his appointment. I had taken care of him for about two years and treated him with chemotherapy for a lymphoma (a malignant condition of the lymphatic system). He had responded very well and was in complete remission. My relationship with him was a bit peculiar in that the more he swore and used profanity during our conversations, the more I knew he liked me and felt comfortable with me. We had become quite close.

On this particular day, he seemed depressed for unclear reasons. The Holy Spirit prompted me to ask him if he went to church. He explained that, over the years, he had been a bartender, cheated on his wife, used profanity, abused alcohol … the list went on and on. I asked him if what he meant was that, because he had done all of those things, he felt unworthy to come to God. He replied, "Yes." I told him I had great news for him! I explained how Jesus had come not to condemn him, but to save him. I told him Jesus had come and died for him just the way he was, as an adulterer or a drinker. I told him how much Jesus loved him just the way he was, in the midst of his sin, no matter how bad or ugly his sins appeared to him. As I spoke these words, I saw giant tears first well up in his eyes and then flow down his cheeks. The Holy Spirit had pierced his heart with the truth of Jesus' immense love for him, and he was overwhelmed.

In that treatment room we prayed together, and Jesus became real to him. Jesus became a part of his life, and naturally his life changed. I never heard him swear again and NOT because he consciously tried to stop. No. God had changed him from within, and he was reborn. He had received a spiritual "heart transplant" and now loved God and was in fellowship with Jesus. They had established a relationship. He lived to please God, and the old tough-guy facade was no longer necessary. He knew who he was - a child of God. Jesus was his Savior and Lord, and he was covered with the blood of Jesus. When God the Father looked at him now, he was holy because his sins had been wiped away! His wife had been a Christian for many years and had prayed continually for her husband's salvation. She was overjoyed that God had heard and answered her prayers.

"What really happens at salvation?" When we reach out and grab onto Jesus, our Life Preserver, there is a mystical imparting of God's divine nature into us. The Holy Spirit permeates us. This is God's promise to us, and this is really the essence of eternal life. Many people mistakenly think that eternal life occurs only when we die and subsequently go to heaven. But Jesus said:

I came that they may have life, and have it abundantly.
John 10:10

This is exciting news. With the very presence of God, i.e. the Holy Spirit within us, we actually begin to experience eternal life now!

Did you ever stop to think, "What did I receive from Jesus?" From a medical perspective, I thought about this for a long time. I came to the conclusion that what I received from Jesus was a "new heart!" Have you ever thought of it that way? That you have had a heart transplant? The prophet, Jeremiah, stated what our problem is:

The heart is more deceitful than all else, and is desperately sick. **Jeremiah 17:9**

The solution is a new heart!
1. Romans 10:10 - *"For with the heart man believes ..."*
2. Ephesians 3:16-17 - *"May He grant you out of the rich treasury of His glory to be strengthened and reinforced with mighty*

power in the inner man by the Holy Spirit - indwelling your innermost being and personality. May Christ through your faith actually make His permanent home in your hearts!"

Have you ever asked Jesus to dwell in your heart? How does the Holy Spirit do this? How is He operative in our day to day lives?" Paul, writing to the Church at Rome stated:

The Spirit Himself testifies with our spirit that we are children of God.   **Romans 8:16**

The works of the Holy Spirit in our lives are numerous. Once saved, as we look back, we realize it was He who *drew* us to Jesus. He *showed and convicted us of our sin.* When we reached out for Jesus, it was the Holy Spirit who *bound us* to Jesus in a "mystical union." He *promised never to leave nor forsake us.* He *provided us comfort.* He *gave us wisdom and understanding* concerning God's truths. He continually *leads us* and *guides us* as we lean on Him throughout our lives. And He *gives us* power to overcome temptations. Later, I will discuss in more detail the work of the Holy Spirit and show you ways that you can connect with the Holy Spirit to live a more powerful and productive life.

I had lunch one day with my good friend Charles Lake, who is Pastor Emeritus of the Community Church of Greenwood. We were speaking about the nature of salvation. He shared with me that many years ago a pastor lamented how many people in his church had gotten saved, but he was disappointed by the fact that he saw little or no change in their lives. Charles pointed out that the problem was that in his preaching on salvation, he neglected the importance of repentance. The Bible stresses the requirement for repentance when we come to God. The word repent means to turn around and go in the opposite direction. For example, if you are a thief, when you come to God, you must repent of your sin of stealing. That doesn't mean you just say you are sorry. It means that you intend to stop stealing, to turn around and go in the opposite direction. Repentance simply means that when you come to God, you are serious about your sin. In repentance you are saying you want to change, and that with God's help, you believe you can change from doing wrong to doing right.

I was fortunate to be reared in a Christian home and be loved by both my parents. Even though I was brought up a Christian, it was not until the age of twenty-six that I seriously committed my life to God. In response to this, God sent the Holy Spirit to dwell in me. From that point on, the Bible had a tremendous impact on me. It was no longer a dull and lifeless book.

I am reminded of when I first saw the movie *The Never-Ending Story*. In this movie, a young boy is looking at various books in an old bookstore. The old man who tends the store tells him he can read any book in the store, except for the one on the corner of the front counter. Naturally, the boy wants to read only that book. The boy grabs it when the man is not looking, or at least when he thinks the man isn't looking, and runs out the door. As he reads through the book, he feels that somehow the characters are pulling him into it. Eventually, he gives in and is drawn into the book, and actually becomes one of the main characters in the story. He becomes responsible for saving the princess and her kingdom.

This is very much the way the Bible is. I believe the Bible can be the most dangerous book you ever read, because it is unlike any other book ever written. All other books were written by men for men. But the Bible states that it is the inspired Word of God. That is, men were literally inspired by God to write down the words in it. As a result, it is a book written by God to men. As you read it, the Holy Spirit speaks to you and at times may begin to draw you into it. You can become one of the main characters in it if you will open up and allow the Holy Spirit to pull you in. It is an incredible concept when we comprehend that the very Holy Spirit of God desires to come and dwell in us, to empower us to live effective lives. He wants to be in relationship with us in a most personal way. I believe that this has tremendous health implications for our spirit, soul and body.

Have you committed your life to Jesus and asked Him to come into your life to be in a relationship with you? If not, why not do it right now? What have you got to lose? As I have said to my children, "Who loves and cares for you more than God?" On a number of occasions, I have ministered to patients who have almost no concept of who God is. After I give them a brief explanation, I lead them in a very simple prayer: "Dear Jesus, I don't even know who You are. I only know what this doctor has told me. If You are real like he says, please reveal Yourself to me. Come into my heart and change me right now. I want to become what You desire, but I need Your strength and power. I commit my life to You now. Amen."

God loves an honest prayer. Don't let anything stop you from coming to Him. No sin is too great. His blood covers them all and washes them away. One of Satan's tricks to prevent you from turning to God is to convince you that you are not worthy, because your sin is so great it can never be forgiven. But, that is nothing more than a lie. It is totally untrue. Wherever you are in life and whatever you have done, God simply says, "Come." It's that easy. So don't let anything stop you. I encourage you not to wait.

FOCUS

TRUTH (What is the focus – the essential truth of this chapter?)

My relationship with God is the most important thing in my life.

APPLICATION (What does this truth mean to me? How is it relevant in my life?)

I need to spend time alone with God every day.

ACTION (What should I do about it? How can this truth benefit my life?)

Read something in the Bible every day (even if it is just one verse). Then pray: Oh Holy Spirit of the Living God, please tell me what this verse means to me today.
Then sit quietly and listen.

PART II

UNDERSTANDING WOMEN

CHAPTER 5

MEN & WOMEN: WHY DID GOD MAKE US SO DIFFERENT?

THE INNATE DIFFERENCES BETWEEN THE SEXES

It has been my privilege to train a number of medical students, interns and residents over the past thirty years. One observation I have made is that, for the most part, young men are clueless when it comes to understanding women. This is so blatant I sometimes wonder how any of them went on to marry successfully. I suppose that in most cases when they did succeed in marriage, it was because they got connected to a good woman who mentored and trained them well. As long as they weren't too macho and had a teachable spirit, they got by.

I also found, almost without exception, these young men were very interested in learning whatever I knew about the opposite sex. They listened intently, and many applied the principles I gave them with, at times, extraordinary results. So let me share some of the things I told them.

God has placed specific differences between the sexes for very good reasons in order to accomplish His purposes. Science has caught up with what we have observed for centuries – that the sexes are indeed different. I constructed a chart, which appears later in this chapter, to show some of these differences which I will explain. But, before I do, I want to emphasize that these differences in no way make one sex superior or inferior to the other. Rather, they allow us to be perfectly complimentary when we are united in marriage. Also, please be aware that this discussion forces me to create certain stereotypes that many readers will find they can not relate to. These stereotypes generally fit for most men and women, but certainly not all. For example, if as a man you find that you have some tendencies that are typically feminine, don't panic and think you have a gender identification crisis. This is normal. God created each of us uniquely. No stereotype will be completely true for everyone.

Physiologically, we know that the brains of men and women

function quite differently. Men tend to use primarily their left cerebral hemisphere, which makes their thinking linear and very logical. This type of thinking has been compared to an old fashioned adding machine. If you ask a man a question, he will reply with an answer. If you then go on to question him about how he got that answer, he will tell you exactly how he arrived at the answer. He can explain how his mind went from A to B to C and then to D until he finally arrived at answer F. This so-called "left-brain" thinking explains why men are sometimes said to have a "one-track mind." I don't mean by this that men are always thinking about sex, although it is a very popular track they travel on.

In contrast to men, women have the capacity to work out of both their right and left cerebral hemispheres, because they have excellent lateral communication (back and forth from right to left) across a structure called the corpus callosum. Hence, their thinking process is different. When you ask them a question, women often give you a very quick answer. But if you ask them how they know that, they may not always be able to tell you why. While, at times, the process may be unclear to them, it is not illogical. Women's brains are said by scientists to function more like computers. If you pose a question to a computer, you get an answer very fast. But if you ask the computer how it got that answer, it can't tell you. It answered based upon how it was programmed. So it is with women's brains. This ability is why women have such good intuitive skills. They sense things to be one way or another. Please don't misunderstand what I am saying. I am not saying that women are pre-programmed to behave in certain ways instinctively and that they don't know how they think. They are certainly not robots. But the fact is that women do think differently than men, and when men and women, who think in different ways, marry, a powerful combination is created.

When my wife tells me something about another person and I ask her how she knows, oftentimes she can't tell me. It is just an intuitive feeling. But she is usually right. In contrast to the Left-Brained thinking of men, women think more globally, and they are capable of thinking on many levels simultaneously. For example, many women pride themselves at being good at Multi-Tasking. Being a good multi-tasker requires global thinking.

When I was the CEO of our medical corporation, I was in charge of recruiting new doctors to join the group. Without exception, I always scheduled a dinner meeting so my wife could meet each prospective recruit and their spouse, if they were married. After the dinner, I would ask my wife if she had any reservations about the doctor. My intuitive skills are almost nonexistent, so I learned to listen and to depend upon what my wife intuitively sensed at these dinners.

The linear thinking (Analytical Reasoning) of men compared to the intuitive thinking (Global Reasoning) of women, has led to men being classified as fact-oriented and women as feeling-oriented. This is why men are said to go through life led by their head and women by their heart.

Many years ago there was a TV show entitled *Dragnet*. Time and time again, Officer Joe Friday would go up to a house, ring the doorbell and start questioning the woman who answered the door about a crime. The woman would launch out into a very detailed account of what she had seen. Then Officer Friday would give his patented response, "Just the facts, Ma'am. Just give me the facts."

Because of their linear thinking, men have the capacity to separate things in their environment from who they are. Many women find it difficult to do this. A woman is often connected to her environment and becomes a part of it. For example, when we go on vacation, my wife always has to make the bed and clean up the house. "Why are you doing that? Who is going to see it?" I ask. I have come to realize that that is not the point. She is connected to the house. As far as she is concerned, if the house is dirty or unkempt, she is dirty and unkempt. If a woman's home is messy, she is messy. It is something a man generally can't relate to. Similarly, if our son is sick, my wife is sick. She is more subjective and cannot separate herself from our child. I can be more objective and look at the situation and say, "Honey, the doctor said our son will be fine as long as he takes the medicine." Usually a husband will be at peace with this, but a mother, although encouraged by both the doctor's and her husband's comments, won't truly be at peace until her child is well.

Just because men use predominantly their left cerebral hemisphere does not mean their right hemisphere is not working. You can access the right hemisphere of men with stories, anecdotes, music and jokes. These venues allow them to activate their emotions and intellect simultaneously. For example, I read that the year after the movie *Bambi* debuted, only half as many deer were killed during the hunting season. The explanation given was that many men took their children to see the movie, and it had an impact on them. After seeing the movie, a deer was no longer just a deer, it was Bambi! Who says men are insensitive?

Men, by nature, tend to be more aggressive than women. They are the "defenders" and "protectors" of the family. Women, on the other hand, are much more relational than men. This plays out well in a marriage, as he is wired to protect and defend his family. He will lay down his life for his wife and family. I love the movie *Robin Hood*. In one version Kevin Costner plays Robin Hood. Toward the end of the movie, he is defending Maid Marian from the Sheriff of Nottingham. After he successfully kills the sheriff by throwing him out of a castle tower window, Maid Marian says to him, "You came back for me?" She is obviously surprised. I love his response, "I would die for you!" This is the classic male protector role. I remember seeing it in high school as one young boy would seek to defend his girlfriend from another boy. However, I seriously doubt if the latter was always selfless.

Because of a wife's relational skills, she is the one who affirms and supports her husband. I am convinced that most wives do not understand the power of their words over their husbands. When I speak to women's groups on this subject, I try to make them realize that they have the power to either make or break their man. If a wife tells her husband that he is better looking than some movie star, he will believe it, even if he knows it's not true. A man desperately needs affirmation from his wife. This need is so deep, he will believe almost anything she tells him. When a woman finally realizes this, she is in a wonderful position to build her husband up and help support him in all he does for her and their family. As such, his identity is rooted in her. He gets his confidence from her. She helps him nourish and fulfill his vision.

MEN "Left Brain"	WOMEN "Right-Left Brain"
"Old Fashioned Adding Machine" (Logical Linear) **Logical & Provable** (The Process Is Evident)	**"Computer Brain"** **("Women's Intuition")** Excellent Lateral Communication Quick Answers That Are Right - The Process May Be Unclear
Fact Oriented **Men Access Their Feelings** **Through Their Right** **Hemisphere** **(Very Responsive To Stories/** **Anecdotes)** Word pictures activate simultaneously the emotions and the intellect. They experience the words. e.g. - Bambi	**Feeling Oriented**
Aggressive (He Will Lay Down His Life For Her - Wired For Defense & Protection)	**Relationship Skills** (Wired To Support & Affirm - She Holds Him Up & His Identity Is Rooted In Her Strength)
Not Highly Verbal (Noises/ Short Phrases) "Just give me the facts, Ma'am."	**Language/Communication** **Skills** (Talk More/Complete Sentences) Emotional and nonverbal communication. Women speak 2 times as many words daily.
Mathematical Precision **Analytical Reasoning**	**Global Reasoning**

Men are much less verbal than women. On average women speak about twice as many words a day as men. One psychologist has said that this can lead to a problem in communication because when he comes home after work he is done talking and she is just warming up! But, as I will point out in the next chapter, men can use this difference to their advantage and fulfill a very important need in their wives.

Imagine for a moment a four-year-old boy playing by himself in the back room of your home. If you listen, what you will hear is just noise. He will utter a lot of short phrases at best, but usually you just hear outbursts of noise as he races his cars or plays with other toys. Little girls at the same age, however, are speaking in complete sentences to their dolls, stuffed animals and even imaginary friends. You see, men and women are wired very differently when it comes to linguistics. Therefore, this profoundly affects how we communicate.

WHAT MEN & WOMEN LIKE TO DO

When I was a young boy, our family moved from Buffalo, New York to live in Fort Wayne, Indiana. Every summer we traveled back to Buffalo to visit my grandparents. I learned at a very early age that men and women view going on vacation from different perspectives. My father knew the trip was about 800 miles and that if we averaged 50 miles per hour, we could "conquer" that distance in 16 hours. He disliked stopping for any reason, even to go to the bathroom. My mother viewed things differently. She liked to stop periodically and "smell the roses." Back then, the only interstates were in Pennsylvania and New York. My mother loved the rest stops on the New York State Turnpike. Looking back, I now realize that the designers of those rest stops knew what women liked. After you got your gas and went inside, you were immediately in a little gift shop. Of course, my mother loved the gift shop - not that she necessarily needed or even wanted to buy anything. She just wanted to take some time to look around. The bathrooms were in the very back, past the gift shop and the restaurant. You could not avoid the gift shop or restaurant if you needed to use the bathroom. My father despised those rest stops. Once he got so mad at the amount of time my mother was spending in the gift shop, that he threatened to cut a hole in the floor of the car so we didn't have to stop to use the bathroom! As I look back, I can understand perfectly the dynamics of the situation. He saw the drive to Buffalo as a challenge to be conquered. My mother saw it as an experience to be enjoyed. If men and women can realize this difference, a little understanding can radically change their expectations.

When men read, they usually don't sit around reading fiction like women do. No, we read magazines or books on sports or how-to books. We feed our intellects and women feed their hearts.

Most men will watch almost any sporting event. But women often don't get very interested in sports, unless there is someone they know or the relative of someone they know playing on the team. My wife has a friend whose brother is a football coach for a university in Michigan. She would drive several hours with her friend for the tailgate party and the game, and then drive back several hours. She would return home exhausted, but elated. I thought, "We had Indianapolis Colts tickets for ten years, but I don't think she ever saw even one game. She was always talking to whomever came with us! What's this sudden interest in football?" I have come to learn it wasn't football, at all. It was all about her friend and her friend's brother.

On an afternoon off, men and women approach the use of their time in different ways. She loves reading, sewing, working around the house, listening to music or perhaps spending time with her friends just talking. He more likely is off doing something like playing golf or tennis, working on the car or building something.

One of the greatest fundamental differences between the sexes occurs at the mall. Once, I gave my wife the greatest gift I have ever given her, not monetarily, but more emotionally: I offered to take her shopping on a Saturday. What was I thinking?!!!! We went downtown to "buy a dress." The stores opened at 10 AM, and I made sure we were there promptly at ten. I knew that the IU football game started at 1 PM, and I wasn't taking any chances. The first store we went into was Talbot's. She immediately saw a dress that she liked and tried it on. It was awesome, and I thought, "This is great!" But, she was reluctant to buy it without looking around. I am a patient man, so I said, "Fine, honey. Just take your time looking around." I knew enough not to rush or force the issue. She tried on several other dresses, but none looked as good as the first one. I said, "Let's just buy the first one." She still wasn't sure. She wanted to look in some other stores. So, off we went. I was, of course, discouraged by this, but tried to hide my disappointment.

About 11 AM she said, "Why don't we stop for coffee and talk?" I thought, "You have got to be kidding! We haven't bought a thing and you want to stop for coffee?" So, we had coffee and talked. I still had a while before the game started. Sometime later, after we looked at kids clothes (which were not on the list of what we were supposed to be looking for), we stopped for lunch during the first half of the game. I thought, "I'll catch the second half." At 4 PM the game was over, and we returned to Talbot's and bought the very first dress. Then we drove home. She was so thrilled by the wonderful day we had had together and her new dress. I was an emotional basket case.

As I reflect back, I now understand the dynamics of the situation. I learned that women "shop" whereas men "buy." We go to the mall with a purpose. We go to buy a shirt or a pair of pants. Once we find a suitable shirt or pair of pants, we buy it and get out of there. Women don't do that. Women want to look around. My wife had to see every dress in the mall to know that the dress she bought was the "right one." You see, women "shop" very much like men "fish." A man can go out in a boat all day, never catch anything, and still have a good day.

When my wife was eight months pregnant with our second child, we went on vacation to Florida with another couple. My friend is a big fisherman, and we went to the shore at dusk to fish. My wife, who had never fished in her life, came to watch. It was one of those times when the fish were really biting. She asked if she could try it. We baited a hook for her and helped her cast out the bait. Within thirty seconds, she got a hit and reeled in a nice fish. She was really cute with that big belly. The pole bent at about the same curve as her belly. She was screaming with delight the whole time. She repeated this about four more times, each time reeling in a fish within about thirty seconds. On the sixth cast, she waited about a minute and nothing happened. She turned to us and asked, "What's wrong?" Both of us laughed so hard, we ended up on the ground. If she couldn't "catch" a fish every thirty seconds, she got bored. From these experiences, I learned that men "fish" like women "shop."

Sex is probably the one area where men can really benefit by understanding how men and women differ. When it comes to sex, men are compared to "Microwaves" and women to "Crockpots." Neither is right or wrong, nor is one better than the other, it's just the way we are wired.

I was speaking to a MOPS (Mother Of Preschoolers) group one night about these differences between men and women, hoping to give them some insight as to why their husbands behaved the way they did. I explained to them that any normal male in the USA who met an attractive woman would usually mentally see himself in bed with her within thirty seconds. 'That's disgusting!" they all said. You see, most women don't think that way. I asked them, "How would you like to live with that curse?" I got no sympathy! I went on to explain that, barring ethical and moral constraints, any male could have sex shortly after meeting an attractive woman, thoroughly enjoy the encounter, but never really think much about it again. It would be fun, like shooting hoops. The problem is that women don't see sex that way at all.

Sex for a man is what has happened in the relationship the few moments before the sexual experience. However, for a woman, sex is the physical expression of all that has happened in their relationship for perhaps the past three months or longer. Sex for women is not primarily physical like it is for a man. To her it is a combination of the emotional, spiritual and physical all rolled up into one.

As a result of this and the fact that very few men realize it, it causes problems if a man cheats on his wife and then comes to his wife to repent. Invariably the man will say, "Honey, it was just sex. It didn't mean anything!" What that is really saying to her is, "Honey, whenever we made love, it didn't mean anything. It was just sex." You see, it just doesn't work for her.

Several months ago, I went into our Patient Services area to discuss what we needed to do regarding several patients. As I entered, one of the women was talking to her husband who had called to inquire about the upcoming night's activities. He said to her, "What are my chances for tonight?" She responded that if he made the dinner, his chances would be very good. His response was, "Well, I guess it's not happening tonight!" I thought to myself, if my wife had said that to me, I would go out and buy a cookbook and come up with something, anything to make it happen.

We talked about how men and women are so different. Then I challenged them to come up with twenty-five reasons why their husbands wouldn't be getting sex tonight. So, here is what they came up with.

25 REASONS WHY IT'S NOT HAPPENING TONIGHT!

1. Wasn't last night, last week or last month enough?!!!
2. You don't have an appointment.
3. When you use slang terms to describe our intimate moments, you ain't getting it!
4. When you pollute the air with bodily functions, it ruins the mood.
5. I really do have a headache.
6. Acting like Austin Powers is not attractive (e.g. – "Grrr . . . Baby").
7. Because you didn't make dinner.
8. Because the dogs are watching.
9. Because *Survivor* is on.
10. I have to get up early.
11. The noise will wake the kids.
12. Because just walking in the room is not enough.
13. It's that time of the month again.
14. I have another headache.
15. Dirty jokes are not foreplay.
16. Which part of "No" did you not understand?
17. The sink is full of dishes.
18. Because I really am asleep.
19. No, really I do have a headache, and no, sex doesn't make it go away!
20. You are not on my "To Do List."
21. Remember when you threatened to take away my credit card?
22. "Do you want to go for a ride?" is not a sexual proposition!
23. Underwear with characters, stains, holes or sayings are not attractive.
24. Remember what you said when I asked if my butt looked big in these jeans?
25. Last, but not least, I do have a headache.

You may find that these points provide some useful insights into your sex life, or lack thereof. The women made some very valuable points. I suspect if we paid attention to them our wives would have fewer headaches.

WHAT MEN LIKE TO DO	WHAT WOMEN LIKE TO DO
Vacations	
• Enjoys conquering 500 miles per day	• Enjoys stopping to "smell the roses" → historical markers, rest stops, etc.
Reading	
• *Popular Mechanics* • How-to magazines	• Harlequin romance novels • *People* Magazine
Love	
• Stores a dictionary definition of love	• Stores and expresses the feelings of Love
Sports	
• Watches any game	• Interested in a game only if she knows a player or a player's wife
An afternoon off	
• Memorizes batting scores • Watches sports for hours • Builds something	• Loves an afternoon devoted to art, fine music, scrapbooking, shopping, volunteering, chatting with friends, reading, etc. • Loves to sew or knit
Malls	
• He "buys"	• She "shops"
Fishing	
• He "fishes"	• She wants to "catch"
Sex	
• Men are like microwaves • Sexual touching • Sex is the culmination of what went on in the last few minutes of their relationship	• Women are like crock pots • Nonsexual touching • Sex is the culmination of what went on the past several hours, days or even months
Parenting	
• God's judgment	• God's mercy

When it comes to parenting, the difference between men and women is very important. Usually, the man represents the judgment of God and the woman represents the mercy of God. That balance is necessary in representing two very important aspects of God, our Father. However, it does not stop there. Both analytical and global reasoning are important in running a household. When one of our daughters was in high school, she told us one Friday night that she was going with a friend to visit her girlfriend, Shelly. I didn't think anything of it. However, about thirty minutes later as my wife and I sat watching a movie, I looked over at her and saw her weeping. I said, "Honey, what's wrong? Are you in pain?" "No," she said, "Our daughter lied to us. She didn't go to Shelly's. She went to her boyfriend's house." "How do you know that?" I asked. "I don't know. I just know!" she replied.

Now, this boyfriend was not exactly on my top ten list. She knew we didn't want her to see him. "Give me the phone!" I said. "What are you going to do?" she asked. "I'm going to call her boyfriend's house." "You can't do that!" she exclaimed. "Yes, I can - I'm her father!" I said emphatically. When I called her boyfriend's house, his father answered, and I asked, "May I speak to my daughter, please?" I said it in such a way that I implied I knew she was there. He responded, "Just one minute." In the back ground, I heard my daughter say, "Tell him I'm not here!" "He knows you are here," said the father. When she finally came to the phone, I told her she had twenty minutes to come home and not to speed. She returned home like a little puppy knowing it had done something wrong. How did my wife know what was going on while I was clueless? It's that intuition thing. Thank God for it!

My very talented editor Julie is quite brutal with her red pen (she calls it being diplomatic). When she first read this chapter, she sent me an email saying,

I think 85% of what you've included in this chapter is very good and presents excellent information for your audience of men. The other 15% had me squirming in my chair. I understand what you're aiming for, and am ever so grateful to see a man who 'gets it' in terms of what makes women tick, but I think there is still some inaccurate stereotyping present. Stereotypes are often used because they hold elements of truth, but there's also some danger involved, because they perpetrate ways of thinking that are really damaging. Men and women allow these ways of thinking to interfere with the process of seeing the other sex as what they are first and foremost – individuals.

I'll use myself as an example, and focus on the table explaining what men and women like to do as one example of what I mean. I hate to shop, and have more of the male approach you describe – get in, get what I need and get out. I find shopping stressful. Give me time, and I will not be knitting or sewing (though I took classes in both as a child and can see that sewing, for a woman, is indeed "building something"), but sitting on the couch reading a good book. I do NOT read Harlequin romances, though. I tried reading one of those once and nearly flung it out the window; it irked me so. I've only bought two issues of People magazine in all of my 46 years – when the cover story was something that interested me. I know romance novels sell big, but most of the women I know read books from the New York Times bestseller list, mysteries and science fiction. I watch only snatches of sports on TV, usually the finals or playoff for the World Series, the World Cup or the Super Bowl. This fall I rooted for the Tigers, and not because I knew anyone on the team. It was because I lived in Detroit while in college. I wouldn't mind going fishing, though, and as a kid discovered that cubes of cheese are great for catching bluegills. If you said I wasn't the typical female, you would be right. But there is, perhaps, a greater variety of characteristics and behaviors among women than we are often given credit for. I'd hate to think we're passing down inaccurate stereotypes about women to the next generation of men. Mostly, I'd like men to see women as individuals first, women second.

Julie also pointed out that there are generational issues to deal with. Both men and women change with each passing decade. For example, women today are much more physically active than they were in my mother's day.

I was at a neighborhood get-together several months ago, and we were discussing some of these differences between men and women. One of the women there said, "Michael, remember when you came and spoke to our ladies' church luncheon?" I did remember, but it had been seventeen years before! She went on, "You spoke about how men are different from women. That really helped me. There was something my husband did that always bothered me, which he still does. I used to think he did it intentionally to irritate me. But, as I listened to you, I realized that he didn't do it intentionally to upset me. That's just the way he is." I was amazed by how a little information can bring such understanding and comfort. One time I heard Gary Smalley say that women think their husbands lay awake at night thinking of ways to strain their marriage. No, these things just come natural to us!

GOD'S PERFECT PLAN

God's plan is for balance in the family. The second chapter of Genesis states, *"the two shall become one flesh."* We only see God reflected in the two together. God created them male and female and called them *"Adam."* God's design was for the differences to form **complimentary** people for marriage. In a marriage we see things from two different perspectives. We need to recognize how valuable this is. In marriage we are mutually interdependent. Because God created men and women so dissimilar, we definitely see life quite differently, from different perspectives. One problem is that a wife thinks her husband sees the world like she does. If she sees a problem in the marriage relationship, she thinks her husband does, also. She needs to recognize that this is seldom the case. So too, a husband needs to realize that his wife does not see the world as he does.

In his book, *"Wild at Heart, Discovering The Secret of A Man's Soul,"* [1] John Eldridge states, "Deep in his heart, every man longs for a battle to fight, an adventure to live, and a beauty to rescue." This marvelous and timely book asks the question, what happened to real men? He describes how society's expectations for men, contrary to the way God made us, have changed, frustrated and angered us, and most of us don't know why.

Then God said, 'Let Us make man in Our image (likeness), according to Our likeness; and let them rule over the fish of the sea and over the birds of the sky and over the cattle and over all that creeps on the earth.' God created man in His own image, in the image of God He created him; male and female He created them.

Genesis 1:26-27

When God created male and female in His own image, we see in Him both a masculine and feminine side. So, the innate differences between the sexes reflect these two sides of God. As we have seen, by nature boys are aggressive compared to girls. They play war games designed to kill. Little girls play house and dress-up – much more

100

civilized games. Things don't change when we grow up. My wife took up golf a few years ago. She was content to gently stroke the ball down the middle of the fairway. However, she would come home astounded by the men she witnessed playing. "They hit the ball so hard and seldom straight. You never know what fairway their ball is even on!"

As men we are victims of our testosterone. I played tennis competitively for twenty five years. There were days I really didn't care where the ball went; I just had to hit the heck out of it. It was therapy. Many women don't seem to understand this. But this aggression, if controlled, is a significant advantage for men. You need aggression to fight battles.

When I became the CEO of our medical corporation, we had some real problems. Some very difficult and painful decisions had to be made. Everyday it seemed like I was in the midst of a fire. But, I not only liked the fire, I loved it! After three and a half years, once the problems had been dealt with, I resigned my position, suggesting one of my partners who is less aggressive take over. My partners asked, "Why don't you want to continue?" I explained that I was what they needed as a leader three and a half years ago, but I was not what the organization needed now. I told them that I need fires, and if there weren't any fires, I would start them! I reassured them that I wasn't going anywhere and would still be there to give my full support.

I believe that women do want their knight in shining armor. However, once they get him, they don't always know what to do with him. Sometimes women try to make men more like themselves. There is nothing wrong with a little domestication so that we can live in a socially acceptable way. But, we are not women; we are men. Several years ago everyone seemed to be wearing the WWJD (What Would Jesus Do?) bracelets. I thought to myself, "A lot of these men don't have a clue as to what Jesus would do in some situations!" Do they really understand what was going on when He physically threw the money changers out of the Temple? Do they really understand what He said repeatedly to the Pharisees? He was not nice. No, rather He was defending His Father's truth with boldness. That's the Jesus I love. I can't wait until He returns. It's going to be totally awesome. Look how Scripture describes Jesus' return:

And I saw heaven opened, and behold, a white horse, and He who sat on it is called Faithful and True, and in righteousness He judges and wages war. His eyes are a flame of fire, and on His head are many diadems; and He has a name written on Him which no one knows except Himself. He is clothed in a robe dipped in blood, and His name is called The Word of God. And the armies which are in heaven, clothed in fine linen, white and clean, were following Him on horses. From His mouth come a sharp sword, so that with it He may strike down the nations, and He will rule them with a rod of iron; and He treads the wine press of the fierce wrath of God, the Almighty. And on His robe and on His thigh He has a name written, KING OF KINGS, AND LORD OF LORDS.   **Revelation 19:11-16**

Here is Jesus returning as our Warrior-Messiah-King. His eyes like fire define His passion. If I am on the wrong side, I would not want to look into those eyes. His secret name implies a divine, secret mission, known only to the Father. We are not told if the blood on His robe is that of the enemy or his own blood shed at Calvary. I tend to favor the former. His sword symbolizes divine judgment. Jesus is passionate about His purpose and calling. So too, God wants us to be passionate defending our wife and family with honor and integrity. They are our focus in life. Procreation affords us the opportunity to raise up Godly children.

I love the movie *Braveheart*. It's my all time favorite. My wife can't watch it because she says it's too gory. Whenever I am flipping channels and come across it, I have to watch it again. I can't tell you how many times I have seen it. There is just something inside me that makes me watch it over and over. Wallace's determination to see Scotland free resonates within my heart. I believe that God put that desire within me. It is one of the ways men differ from women.

Every boy wants a sword. Once when I returned home from a trip to Guatemala, I brought back a large decorated machete for my fifteen-year-old son. My wife went through the roof. "Are you crazy? He could hurt someone with that thing!" she said. I explained to her that I would instruct him on how to properly use it. I told her that I felt he was old enough to be responsible with it. Why would I buy him such a "dangerous weapon?" Because I want him to grow up to be a man, that's why. I know what his heart's desire is and how God made him. He loved his machete and never hurt himself or anyone else with it. I also taught him how to properly and safely use a chain saw. A father needs to teach his sons the skills a man will need. Some are potentially very dangerous. That's life.

Men love adventure and the associated challenges. Several years ago, our family went skiing in Colorado. My wife and daughter enjoyed weaving back and forth down the slopes in total control and almost never falling. In contrast, my son and I always seemed to find ourselves on slopes that we probably shouldn't have been on at all. Once, I couldn't find my son on one of the trails. Suddenly, I heard him yelling. I skied over to the side of the mountain and looked down. There he was lying in one of the safety nets! He had taken the turn too fast and over he went. By the end of the day, we were both exhilarated by the dangers the mountain had presented. My wife didn't even want to listen.

Within every man is the desire to defend and save his woman and maybe any woman. Earlier I mentioned the part in the movie *Robin Hood* where Maid Marian, trembling, says incredulously, "You came back for me?" Robin responds, "I would die for you!" That pretty well sums it up.

As men, if we understand the differences between men and women and why God made us the way He did, this understanding will help us understand the women in our lives. This understanding will help us to avoid a lot of difficulty the majority of men seem to experience with the opposite sex. And even better, it will help us to become the men and husbands God desires.

FOCUS

TRUTH (What is the focus – the essential truth of this chapter?)

God intentionally made my wife and I quite different. She thinks and communicates in dissimilar ways than I.

APPLICATION (What does this truth mean to me? How is it relevant in my life?)

I need to live with my wife in an understanding way. I want to learn more about what makes her happy or sad and her likes and dislikes.

ACTION (What should I do about it? How can this truth benefit my life?)

   Pray: Oh Lord Jesus, I want to be the best husband I possibly can be. Please help me to grow in my understanding of my wife. Help me to respond to her in considerate and loving ways.

CHAPTER 6

BECOMING THE HUSBAND AND FATHER GOD WANTS YOU TO BE

Make Your Wife Feel Guilty and She Will Love You For It!

THE PROBLEM & THE SOLUTION

The problem that we have in America today is that men don't understand what real love is.

Several years ago, I was driving alone to give a lecture. I was listening to WFMS, a country music station in Indianapolis. The station has a call in show at night called something like, "Loving, Lying, Laughing & Leaving." People call in to tell their significant other how much they love him or her, how much they are sorry for something they have done, how much they don't want to divorce, etc. You get the picture. If you call in with a question about a relationship, other callers can give their advice. One night a woman called in to say she was having an affair with a married man. He had promised to divorce his wife and marry her, but it wasn't happening after SEVEN years! Several men and women called in to tell her the guy was a jerk and was just using her and stringing her along. Her response was, "But I love him!" Give me a break! Love really is blind sometimes. On another night the DJ asked the question, "What is love? Call in and let me know what you think." So, I listened as I drove for one and a half hours. Disappointingly, I did not hear a definition of love that even began to approximate the Biblical definition of love. All the definitions were based upon feelings. But feelings change. We can't always control how we feel. If love is truly just a feeling, we are all doomed when we marry. We will all end up in divorce court.

The Bible defines love as an act of one's will. It is a conscious decision to do something. Real love is not just a feeling but a definite act of our will. We decide to love our wife, and we make that commitment. That's why it is possible to make wedding vows and keep them. If love is just a feeling, how could we ever commit? Our feelings change from day-to-day. How could we ever take the marriage oath based upon our feelings? Sometimes I tell my wife or she tells me, "I don't like you today, but I still love you!" We understand the difference between how we feel and our commitment to each other. When I married my wife, the oath I made to love her in good and bad times was made first to God and secondly to her. I made that oath as a conscious decision knowing that how I intended to treat my wife would not depend on how I felt, but would be based on my commitment. Interestingly, I found that as I "loved" her, even when I did not feel like it, my feelings towards her changed. I subsequently "felt" like I loved her. The biblical principle is right actions produce right feelings. This approach allows me to honestly say that I have loved and liked my wife more each of the thirty-two years of our marriage than the previous year.

Men seem to possess a dictionary definition of love, whereas women store and express the feelings of love. As husbands if we can understand how our wife sees love, it can help us relate better to her and respond to her as God desires.

John Haggee and his wife have written a wonderful two part book entitled *What Women Want In A Man & What Men Want In A Woman.* [1] I heard John say that success in a marriage is not about finding the right person, it is about being the right person. Dr. James Dobson, Founder and President of Focus on the Family, said, "Marriage is never perfect, but it's a perfect part of the Lord's plan."

Many men don't seem to understand what God has defined as their role in the home. Our society has so distorted this role that men are just doing what comes naturally, and that's not working. In fact, I blame the men in this country for the women's liberation movement. I honestly believe that if men had treated women, and in particular their wives, as God intended, there never would have been a feminist movement. From physics we learn that every reaction produces an equal and opposite reaction. The feminine reaction to men's actions led to the feminist movement.

To make matters worse, men have abdicated their leadership role in the home. Many have left their homes because of divorce. This tragedy plays out in disastrous effects. Young boys desperately need the mentoring that only a male can provide. Without fatherly mentoring, young boys often grow up headed for trouble. Studies have shown that the majority of men in prisons lacked a father figure in their home. The presence of a father is necessary to rein in the "young bulls" of a family and keep them headed in the right direction.

The solution to these problems is that we must understand what God means by love and what He expects of each of us as the leader in our home. Various studies have demonstrated a number of benefits from marriage. Children who grow up in two parent homes are on average healthier. Children of divorce are less likely to graduate from college and achieve high-status jobs, and they are twice as likely to have their subsequent marriages end in divorce. Married men earn 10% to 40% more income than single men of the same age and educational background, and they are healthier and live longer. Domestic violence happens less frequently among married couples compared to those who cohabitate. A number of studies have shown that living together before marriage actually increases the chances of divorce by 50% to 80%. Unfortunately, our nation now has the highest divorce rate in the world. So much for the American dream! The disintegration of American families through divorce is the biggest problem we face in this nation, because the stability of the family supports every other aspect of our society. The stability and the strength of our nation depend on the family, which is the fundamental social unit in our culture.

A very interesting article was published in the *Indianapolis Star* in 2005 entitled "Do Parents Matter? It was written by Stephen J. Dubner and Steven D. Levitt, the authors of *Freakonomics: A Rogue Economist Explores the Hidden Side of Everything.* [2] The authors investigated how much parents should congratulate or blame themselves for their children's accomplishments. They examined the data from the Early Childhood Longitudinal Study, which tracked the progress of more than 20,000 children in America from kindergarten to fifth grade. I found the results of this study very interesting because it debunked a lot of commonly accepted ideas about what leads to a child's success. Here are the issues they found:

What Matters	What Doesn't Matter
Parents are highly educated.	Regularly watches TV
Parents have high incomes.	Mother didn't work between birth and kindergarten.

What Matters	What Doesn't Matter
Parents speak English at home.	Parents regularly take the child to museums.
Mother was 30 or older at the time of the child's birth.	Child attended Head Start.
Child's parents are involved in the PTA.	Child is regularly spanked at home.

Hence, watching TV does not turn a kid's brain to mush and those trips to the museum don't seem any better than going to the grocery store. What does seem to be very important is that parents who are well-educated pass on their smarts and work ethic to their children. The authors concluded, "So it isn't that parents don't matter. Clearly, they matter an awful lot. It's just that by the time most parents pick up a book on parenting technique, it's too late. Many of the things that matter most were decided long ago – what kind of education a parent got, how hard he worked to build a career, what kind of spouse he wound up with, and how long they waited to have children . . . When it comes to early test scores, it's not so much what you do as a parent, it's about who you are." Many years ago I heard Dr. James Dobson say, "You must be what you want your children to become." He was right then, and he still is.

Some men find themselves thinking divorce is their only option to make them happy. In most cases, this is not true. A research study published by the Institute for American Values in New York interviewed individuals who reported being unhappily married. Some separated, others divorced and others remained together. When interviewed five years later, two-thirds of those couples who stayed together said they were actually happier. The study also found that those who divorced to escape the pain of a bad marriage, often found themselves in emotional and psychological difficulties over which they had no control. Only 19% of those who divorced said they were happy five years later. Dr. Linda J. Waite, a sociology professor at the University of Chicago who wrote the study, concluded that "the benefits of divorce have been oversold." [3]

Let me begin by speaking in general about what I believe our relationship as men to women should be. Several years ago, I came up with my number one rule for success. For men who want to be successful in all they do in life, I recommend this rule:

DOC ELMO'S RULE FOR SUCCESS

Make as many women as happy as possible everyday of your life, and you will be a successful man!

I told a patient of mine this rule once, and he scoffed at it. So, I said, "Ok. Go out and make as many women around you each day as miserable as possible. Then see what happens." He immediately grasped the obvious! We are all surrounded by women almost every day of our life. Some work for us, others work with us and some may be our bosses. It doesn't matter. The principle remains the same. Seek, to the best of your ability, to make them all as happy as possible. If women like you, they will not only work with you, they will work for you. This support is critical for success. You can not afford the macho attitude. So, determine to get rid of it. If you don't, it will cost you their support. Married men inherently understand this principle much better than single men. Once you have lived with a woman, you find out how the world really operates!

Women instinctively know how this works. When my daughter, Kelly, was just three years old, I asked her to do something. She said, "No." I replied, "What do you mean, no? I'm your father." "Yes," she said, "but you're not the boss of this house." I thought to myself, "Well, I'll play this game." So I asked her, "If I'm not the boss of this house, who is?" She immediately responded, "Mom is the boss of this house!" Then I asked, "Well then, who am I?" I will never forget her answer as long as I live. She put her hands on her hips, stuck out her little chest and said, "You are the king!" Gosh that sounded really good. I am the king. That was more than twenty-three years ago, and I still haven't exactly figured out what the king does. But I am the king, by golly! I'd been had by a three-year-old.

What I eventually learned from this encounter was that my daughter knew and saw me as the king, the leader of the family, but when it came to the day-to-day running of the house, that was my wife's domain.

HOW TO BE A DYNAMITE HUSBAND

After reading and studying innumerable books on the subject of marriage and love, I came up with some basic rules about how anyone can become a dynamic husband. These rules are time-tested. Many young men I have instructed over the years have successfully implemented them. If you apply them, I can give you a personal guarantee that these principles will deeply enrich your marriage.

I always tell my children that the "R" in the word "Relationship" stands for "Respect." Respect is the common thread that undergirds all these rules.

RULE 1 - *GIVE YOUR WIFE UNDIVIDED TIME DAILY.*

The first thing you must do when you come home each day is simply ask your wife, "Honey, how was your day?" Then you must do something that is difficult and unnatural. You must give her your undivided attention. Don't have the TV blaring in the background and don't be reading the newspaper. You must look at her intently and really listen to her. Rule 1 requires Rule 2 to be effective. They are linked together.

RULE 2 - *NEVER, EVER OFFER ADVICE OR SOLUTIONS UNLESS SHE SPECIFICALLY ASKS, "WHAT DO YOU THINK?"*

Rule 2 is the most difficult, yet potentially most rewarding, of all the rules. As you are listening to your wife, *you must not interrupt her*. Just listen! If you do not completely understand what she is saying, you can ask short questions that affirm you are listening and want to know more. You might ask, "Tell me more about that." *Under no circumstances should you ever offer advice* unless she says to you, "What do you think?" But don't be surprised if she never asks! Most women do not need their husbands to solve their problems. They are quite capable of solving their own problems. Unlike men, they often work out the solutions to their problems by talking to others about them. Remember that women need conversation more than men do. By inquiring about her day and allowing her to just talk, you are fulfilling a great need that she has.

When I first stumbled on to these first two rules, I went home and immediately asked my wife how her day had gone. The next twenty minutes were very painful for me. She listed one problem after another that needed fixing, but not once did she ask for my advice on how to fix even one of the problems. Meanwhile, I was making a mental list of all the issues. Suddenly, at the end of the twenty minutes, she came over to me, kissed me on the cheek and said, "You are such a wonderful husband!" Then she left the room. I sat there stunned. "What just happened here?" I thought to myself. I was an emotional wreck. She hadn't asked for my opinion once. We hadn't solved or fixed even one problem! "What a waste of time!" was my initial thought.

As I considered what had transpired, I realized that I had fulfilled a great need she had just to allow her to talk about the problems. She didn't need me to fix any of them. As I continued to do this day after day, I eventually began to enjoy listening to her. It's similar to eating some foods – they are an acquired taste. So too, listening was a skill I had to acquire and as I did, I actually began to enjoy listening without having to interrupt and give my two cents. I realized that she would deal with most of the problems, and that if she needed my help, she would ask for it. I also realized that, just like the head of an organization, I needed to be aware of the issues facing the family, even if I did not solve them personally.

By simply following Rules 1 & 2 everyday, you can dramatically transform your marriage in a very short time. I always tell young married men that the first two rules will get them 90% of the way. If you aren't going to pay attention to them, you might as well forget about the rest.

Think about it. How much time do you usually spend each day actually talking to your wife? I know spouses talk a lot, but often times there is not much listening going on due to all the distractions around us. We are all just too busy for each other! Sad, isn't it? When was the last time you shared your dreams with your wife or let her tell you hers? Do you even know the details of what her daily life is really like? As husbands, we need to know.

RULE 3 - <u>NEVER DEVALUE OR CRITICIZE YOUR WIFE IN PUBLIC. ALWAYS HONOR HER!</u>

Overall, I tend to be reasonably laid back. I am aggressive in certain ways, but I have found ways to channel this aggression effectively at work or in sports. However, as I previously shared, I have one potentially dangerous weakness. I can not stand to see a man criticize a woman, particularly his wife, in public.

Have you ever been in a restaurant when suddenly a conversation at a nearby table becomes louder? The man raises his voice and levels blistering, demeaning comments towards his wife or girlfriend for everyone to hear. At these times, I have the most difficulty. Such behavior is never right. If he has something to say to his wife or girlfriend, he should do it in private and not bring all of us into it!

Nothing is more uncomfortable than when you are out with another couple and the other man belittles the woman he is with. He may not say anything really bad, but his comments are not kind. It not only makes everyone uncomfortable, it does two other things. First, he wounds the woman, and second, he demonstrates his small nature and insecurity. I have always told my children that when someone belittles them it is only an attempt to make themselves look bigger.

Once when one of my daughters was in grade school, she had to ride the bus to school. An eighth grade boy started regularly picking on her, and it upset her. I told her why he was doing this. "He is just trying to make himself look bigger in front of the other kids at your expense. If he were really self-confident and self-assured, he would not need to act that way." After explaining the psychological dynamics of the situation, I gave her something to say the next time he confronted her. A few days later she came home all smiles. "Dad," she said, "I told that boy exactly what you said, and it shocked him so bad, he just turned around and sat down without saying another word!" What was the response I had given her to say? It went something like this, "If you really possessed any sense of self-esteem and self-confidence, you wouldn't have to pick on kids smaller than you just to make yourself look bigger!" The truth is sometimes a powerful weapon. He never picked on her again.

So to be a real man, NEVER criticize your wife or girlfriend in public. Rather, always seek to make comments that elevate her in front of others. You will not believe the power of even small positive comments spoken in front of others that affirm your most significant other. You will consistently score big points by doing so. Positive affirmation will pay big dividends in your relationship.

You don't have to stop there, either. I daily seek to affirm as many women around me as possible. Many times I have commented to a woman how nice her dress looks or that her perfume smells wonderful. Somehow, they know I am not hitting on them. I just truly want to compliment them.

RULE 4 - *NEVER LET THE COURTSHIP DIE- ROMANCE HER!*

There is an old Irish joke about one couple who has been married for over thirty years. One day the wife asked, "How come you never tell me that you love me?" He responded, "I told you I loved you when we got married. If anything changes, I will let you know!"

Never take your relationship with your wife for granted. I realize that most men are not by nature romantic, but there is hope. With all the young men I have mentored, I have found that even those who don't have a romantic bone in their body can still find ways to be romantic. They just need a little guidance. When these young doctors or medical students have been on my gastroenterology rotation, I have often given them romantic assignments. For example, "I want you to go to the store and buy your wife a romantic card and give it to her for no reason at all. You can just give it to her, or you may want to get creative and put it somewhere where she will discover it. Sometimes I tape one to the rear view mirror of my wife's car, secretly slide it into her purse or my favorite, I tape it to our kitchen fan with a ribbon and turn the fan on low. She comes into the kitchen to see her card flying!"

A card given for no specific reason, viz. no occasion like a birthday, anniversary, etc., sends the message, "I was thinking about you and how much I love you. I just wanted you to know." Sometimes, I suggest that a young man go to the grocery store and buy his wife some flowers, again for no reason at all. "Isn't the fact that you love her reason enough?" I ask. Most wives love it when you do something around the house without being asked or nagged. So, find something on the "Honey Do List," and "Just Do It!"

Since the majority of men are not particularly romantic, at least in a spontaneous sense, I created a few suggestions to help. So, give some of these a try.

DOC ELMO'S 25 WAYS TO BE ROMANTIC
(Non-obligatory, Optional Romance)
Reviving Chivalry
(Women love a real gentleman)

1. Give her a card for no reason at all. Hide it in a unique place like her purse, under a pillow, in her car, in the refrigerator, under her dinner plate, etc. Consider making your own card.
2. Buy her flowers for no reason at all.
3. Give her a day of your time, but let her decide the agenda.
4. Surprise her with a box of her favorite candy. Chocolate is usually a safe bet.
5. Take her to the opera or some other social event you know she would enjoy.
6. Go out dancing.
7. Write her a letter or a poem. If you can't write your own poem, find one and give it to her.
8. Know all her clothes sizes – buy her a blouse, a dress, or some other item, and give her permission to take it back if she wants to exchange it for something else.
9. If you travel a lot, give her a rose everyday you are gone. If you don't travel, then bring her home a flower each day for several days to make a bouquet.
10. Celebrate your anniversary for twelve days leading up to the big day by giving her a card or little gift each day.
11. Tell her how much you love her three times in one day.
12. Give her a gift certificate to her favorite store.
13. Offer to give her a foot massage.
14. Buy her some candles.
15. Subscribe to her favorite magazine for her.
16. Surprise her with a night out. Arrange for a babysitter, then tell her you're going out on a certain day, but don't tell her where.
17. Cook dinner for her and the family, and clean up the kitchen.
18. Fix something around the house she has wanted you to fix for a long time.

19. Take her for a moonlit stroll.
20. Make a list of all the reasons why you love her and present it to her with a surprise night out or romantic dinner.
21. Give her a gift certificate for a pedicure or a massage.
22. Compliment her in public. Brag about her.
23. Remember that men are motivated and empowered when they feel needed, and women are motivated and empowered when they feel cherished. Find ways to show her how much you cherish her.
24. Watch a romantic movie together that you know she loves.
25. Go on a typical date like you did when you first met. Go some place where you used to go and talk about how fond you are of those memories.

These are just a few of the many things you could do. You can even read books on how to be romantic that will give you tons of ideas. If you really want to surprise her and score big points, plan a surprise dinner or get-a-way for a day or a weekend. Be sure you are planning it around things she would like to do, not what you want to do, like going to a game! It may cost you a few bucks, but I have come to realize, there is no better way to spend your money than by investing in your most important relationship.

RULE 5 - *PROVIDE SECURITY FOR HER.*

I have learned that women hate surprises when it comes to finances and the home. When I speak of providing stability and security, I am not just talking about financial support. A husband should also seek to provide the spiritual and emotional stability so necessary in the home, as well. Many men seem to think that their job is primarily to provide the financial support for the family and achieve the American dream. What I have found, however, is that most women would rather have a husband who makes less money and is around the house more, playing with the children in the evenings. A wife often senses the proper balance in the home much more so than her husband. Usually, just when I feel as if I have established the proper balance in my life between work and family, my wife comes to me and says, "You're doing it again!" I know exactly what she means. I have become over committed and need to eliminate a few things. I depend on her to point this out to me, because I know I have this tendency to get over involved in many "good causes." They may all be good, but as far as priorities go, none of them are as important as my family.

A wife needs her husband to be predictable. That means he must be completely honest with her. A husband must NEVER lie to his wife. She must know you are 100% trustworthy at all times. Remember that lying comes in two forms. You can lie about something you have done (a lie of commission) and you can tell a half-truth (a lie of omission). If your wife asks you why you are late for dinner and you say, "I had to stop by the office to pick up some papers," you am not entirely honest. Maybe you did go by the office to pick up some papers, which took some time, but the real reason you were late was because you met up with the boys for a drink. That is a lie of omission. You only told part of the truth, and omitted the rest.

Your wife needs to know that you value her above all else on earth and that she is number one in your life. She needs to hear you tell her this, and even more importantly, she needs to see you demonstrate this truth by your every action.

RULE 6 - *PROVIDE WAYS FOR HER TO UTILIZE HER TALENTS.*

One of the most important verses in the Bible is I Peter 3:7 where it states:

You husbands in the same way, live with your wives in an understanding way, as with someone weaker, since she is a woman; and show her honor as a fellow heir of the grace of life, so that your prayers will not be hindered.　　　　　　　**I Peter 3:7**

This verse is one of the most misinterpreted verses in the whole Bible. I want to point out that the phrase *"as with someone weaker,"* which is also translated *"as a weaker vessel,"* does not mean that women are necessarily weaker than men. As husbands we need to recognize that our wives may have less physical strength than we have, and as a result, give them the needed assistance and protection. However, we must also recognize that they have full equality as fellow sharers in the grace of God.

I like to think the phrase *"a weaker vessel"* means that she is precious, and I should value her highly. What do you do to protect something precious? You place it on a pedestal and surround it with a protective covering of some sort. You enclose it so that people can see and appreciate it, but not touch or harm it in any way. That is how God wants us to behave with respect to our wives. We are to treat them with the utmost of respect, as the most precious person in our lives. As such, we are instructed to live with our wives in an *"understanding manner."* What does that mean? It means that we are to seek to learn about our wives daily. We must continually ask, "What does my wife like to do?" What makes her laugh?" "What are her skills; what is she good at?" "What does she not like?" "What is she not good at doing?"

I am always trying to learn more about my wife. By learning more about her, I am able to support her in doing those things she is most talented at doing. For example, one of the things that drew me to my wife was her benevolent spirit. She has the biggest, most giving heart of anyone I know. When I first met her, she was a critical care nurse. I observed that if you were her patient and you were dying, as long as she was at your bedside, death didn't seem to matter. She has a special gift from God for understanding and providing comfort, even in the face of death. Later in our relationship, she had an opportunity to work as a nurse in palliative (end of life) care. I realized that this would be a perfect fit for her, and I strongly encouraged her to pursue the opportunity. She interviewed and was hired for the position, and as a result, many people have been blessed by her work.

Sometimes we pursue things that are not a good fit for us. I need my wife to help me recognize this. We can help each other steer clear of those things which will only frustrate us. None of us enjoy trying to do those things that we are not suited at doing.

A most important aspect of I Peter 3:7 that we cannot ignore, is the comment, *"so that your prayers will not be hindered."* In other words, if we don't live with our wife in an understanding manner, then we can't expect our prayers to be answered. Have you ever thought of that? Have you ever realized this? Now you do, and you can do something about it.

RULE 7 - *BE INVOLVED WITH THE KIDS.*

It is very important that fathers be involved in the lives of their children. Parenting takes a LOT of time. As fathers we need to demonstrate our commitment to our wife and children. We do this by giving them our most valuable commodity: our time. I remember sitting in the blistering sun for hours watching my son play baseball and my daughters play softball. There were hours and hours of dance, gymnastics and basketball games. Learn to enjoy these because they are only for a season, and then they are gone. Having dinner together is very important, in my opinion. That is where all the meaningful conversation occurs regarding the day's activities. My wife always held dinner until my work at the hospital was done. Many times we ate supper at seven or eight o'clock, but we always ate together. If the children got hungry, she gave them a snack. By doing this, she demonstrated to our children how important it was for us to eat together.

For several years, my wife chose a different Kentucky State Park for us to go to on vacation. We swam in the lake and/or pool, hiked in the forest, played games at night and ate all our meals together. We have many fond memories of spending these times together. As husbands we need to find ways for our family to share times like these together and build, as my good friend, Jeff Cardwell, says, "Memories of a lifetime."

Once, when I had a speaking engagement in Paducah, Kentucky, I took a few extra days off, and we all went on vacation to Kenlake State Park. My son had just learned how to dive off the diving board. I sat by the pool trying to read. Every thirty seconds I heard, "Hey, Dad. Watch this!" He would purposefully wait until I stopped reading and looked up to watch him do another dive. Then he would ask, "How was that one?" Psychologists say that the number one thing kids want from their parents is to "Watch me!"

A woman is never happier than when you make your children happy and laugh. Find ways to be involved with your children, having fun and making them laugh. Women are also happy when a husband takes over a share of the caretaking of the children.

RULE 8 - *BE THE SPIRITUAL LEADER IN YOUR HOME.*

Jesus was the ultimate example of a servant leader. Think about it. He set aside His glory for a time to come down to earth as a man. His only agenda was all about us. In Ephesians 5, the Apostle Paul tells us we are to love our wife like Jesus loved the church. What did

Jesus do for His church? He died for it! Are you prepared to die for your wife? More importantly, are you prepared to live for your wife? We are likely more valuable to her alive than dead. I will have much more to say about spiritual leadership in Chapter 7.

RULE 9 - *REMEMBER THAT SEX IS 90% COMMUNICATION & 10% PHYSICAL.*

While men are looking for sex, women desire affection. Affection can be many things. Unfortunately, often when a man touches his wife, she immediately thinks he wants sex. Now where in the world would she get such an idea? Perhaps your previous actions have trained this response. Whenever you touched her in the past, you were thinking about heading off to the bedroom. Men need to learn the value of what is called NST, or Non-Sexual Touching. NST can be just holding hands, hugging, rubbing her back, putting your arm around her waist as you walk together, etc. Every husband needs to develop NST in order to satisfy his wife's need for affection. Once you have done this repeatedly, *without sex in mind*, you will find out how much your spouse appreciates it, and sex will likely be better too. A wife needs to sense her husband's affection. It provides her with security and great comfort in your relationship.

In the morning before I go off to work, I have developed the habit of finding my wife and gently holding her. Then I pray for her, our children and the needs of the day. I have been amazed how something this simple has strengthened our relationship. She has told me how much this means to her and that she appreciates my effort.

Remember, for your wife, sex is all about what has been happening in your relationship. It is simply the physical expression of all that has been going on previously. Many men, in their excitement, want to rush to the "main event." If men could learn to take some time, it would make a huge difference in the end result for both of them. Also, we need to learn to live with our wife in an understanding way sexually, as well. We need to find out what she likes and what she doesn't like. Our goal should be first to please her. When you are willing to give and seek to please her, you will be amazed at how much more you will come to enjoy the experience. It is the old principle of giving and receiving, in action.

Not long ago, I was speaking to a young, newly married man

who implied that he believed sex would probably be great the first few years of marriage and then trail off. I told him I did not believe that, nor was it my personal experience. I explained that my wife and I had been married for over thirty years and when you are with a woman that long and you have experienced many things together, you grow together. The sexual experience is focused on pleasing one another. The end result can be quite amazing.

RULE 10 - *GOD CREATED WOMEN TO BE QUEENS!*

As husbands we are to treat our wife with the utmost of respect and love her even if it costs us our life. Not only is she equal to us in God's eyes, but we are to place her on a pedestal. Let your wife know she is your queen and that you are proud of her.

Harold Schubert is a financial consultant who came to the US with his wife from Chile. Their marriage was tested in a variety of ways. This is the story he told to me.

I was born in Chile in 1942. My grandparents had left Germany prior to the rise of Nazi Germany and settled in Chile. While growing up and going to school, I worked on the family farm.

When I was twenty seven years old, I married Sylvia on May 10, 1969. I thought to myself, "This has to work." I knew that for us it would be a life long commitment. We moved into our new house the following year. I had gone off into the forest to cut trees for lumber. I spent a year building the house with my own hands. Unfortunately, the Communist/Socialist Party came to power shortly thereafter, and one day I read in the newspaper that the Schubert Farm was now owned by the government. Our family had lost everything! These were the infamous land and industry reforms of socialism where property and businesses were taken from the owners by the government and given to the workers. Demonstrators blocked the entrance to our farm 24 hours a day, and we needed a police escort to come and go. We fought what had happened for six months, but to no avail.

So in May of 1971, we packed up and left. We had to sell even our wedding presents and came to the United States with only two suitcases and $2,000 in our pockets. When we arrived in Bushton, Kansas, Sylvia spoke some English, but I spoke none. We had to go back to square one. Previously we had been heirs of a farm and industry, now all that was gone. Sylvia went to work at Penney's in the *catalogue department, and I went to work on a farm. After a year and a half, I got a job in the factory of the Fuller Brush Company. Over the next five years, while working in the factory, I eventually became a supervisor. I also began to work part time in financial services, and became a registered financial representative and insurance salesman. Today I am a registered securities' principal.*

I asked Harold if he and Sylvia were ever bitter about all that had been taken from them. He responded that he had become a Christian as a teenager, as the result of German missionaries. Sylvia had accepted the Lord before him. They started dating at one of the youth camps. He spoke of how their Christian foundation helped them through their tough times. They always had devotions and prayed together every morning.

With his farming background, Harold compares marriage to things he remembers while working on the farm. He told me that a pair of untrained oxen will always try to go their own way. Once yoked together they learn to pull in the same direction. In the same way, the yoke of marriage (the commitment to one another) helps a couple to get together and work as one.

He told me that building a marriage through hardships is similar to the way a blacksmith forges steel. He recounted a situation about a hitch that had broken repeatedly, despite having been welded several times. Finally, the broken pieces were taken to the blacksmith. The two pieces of metal were heated, pounded and reformed into just the right shape. Once hammered together at close to the melting point and fused together as one in the fire, they were never to come apart again. A marriage often experiences stresses beyond what individuals can bear alone, but the perfect "fusing" will always come at the Hand of the Master.

ENCOURAGEMENT
THE POWER OF YOUR WORDS

"The thing I hate about an argument is that it always interrupts a discussion."   G.K. Chesterton, Writer

I believe there is tremendous value and power in words, particularly the words of encouragement. Words can cut very deep. They can produce tremendous harm or tremendous healing. A very interesting paper appeared in the *British Medical Journal of Clinical Research* in 1987 entitled "General Practice Consultations: Is there any point in being positive?" The author, K.B. Thomas, evaluated twenty patients with symptoms not attributed to any particular ailment. The physician gave either a positive or negative response to the patients. Sixty-four percent of the patients who got a positive response got better within two weeks. Only 39% who got negative responses improved. [4]

The Bible encourages us to be careful with what we say and to focus on saying what is most appropriate in every situation.

Let your speech always be with grace, as though seasoned with salt, so that you will know how you should respond to each person.
Colossians 4:6

As my children were growing up, I remember the various coaches they had in sports. My son was exposed to several different coaches while playing summer baseball. Some coaches always seemed to take the game much more seriously than I thought was appropriate. I felt they were trying to live out their lives vicariously through their sons. They coached from a negative perspective. I wondered if it wouldn't be better and more effective to encourage these young boys, to point out those things they were doing right, rather than always focusing on their particular mistakes. After all, weren't they just children? Didn't we expect them to make mistakes? Isn't that how they were supposed to learn? Shouldn't they be benefiting from their mistakes, rather than being ridiculed for them?"

Several years ago, while attending a medical meeting in southern Arizona, I had the opportunity to play tennis in a men's and women's doubles round robin. The tennis pro who supervised the event told us that we would play for two hours and rotate partners every twenty minutes. During each twenty minute session, each person playing would accumulate one point for each game won. In the first few rounds, I could not help noticing that many of the players were quite good. Obviously, they had played a lot. Others may not have been quite as experienced, but seemed to holding their own. However, there was one unfortunate young woman who was clearly having trouble. She was almost in tears. No one wanted her as their partner, but we had no choice in who our partners were. The rotation was random.

As I watched her playing on the court next to me, my heart went out to her. I silently prayed, "Oh Lord, I would love to have her as my partner so that I could encourage her." On the very next rotation, we were *randomly* assigned to be partners. I approached her and said, "It doesn't look like you are having a very good day?" She looked at me and could only nod affirmatively. We were to play against two men who were very good players. I told her, "I can see from watching you that you have good strokes. I think the problem may be that you are not always in the best position on the court to hit the ball. Would you mind if I helped show you the best positions to be in strategically so that you will have the greatest opportunity to hit the ball?" She readily agreed.

As we started to play, the first few balls she hit went everywhere. Each time, I simply said something to encourage her, like: "That was a great swing; don't change anything," "I like what I see," "Just watch the ball, and keep doing what you are doing." I could tell that the men playing against us had already counted on winning and racking up a bunch of points. After a few minutes my partner took a swing at a ball and hit a most amazing shot, winning a point for us. I praised her to no end, telling her that I knew this would happen, it was only a matter of time. As you can imagine, her whole disposition changed. She was now having fun and enjoying the game. She was listening to my coaching, standing in the right place and hitting the ball with more confidence.

At one point, I whispered to her, "Those guys over there really want to win this whole tournament. They know that the faster they play, the more points they can accumulate. Why don't we have some fun? Let's talk to each other between points and laugh a lot like we are having a great time." She smiled in agreement. What happened over the next fifteen minutes can only be described as a small miracle. I have played tennis for over 25 years, and I have never experienced anything like it before or since. As we continued to play, the men became upset by two things. First, my partner started hitting some great shots and winning points. Second, they couldn't seem to get us to play quite as fast as they wanted. That made them angry. The angrier they got, the worse they played. The worse they played, the more games we won. That made them even angrier! In the end, not only had we held our own, *we actually beat them!* They were furious. My partner was ecstatic! I thought, "Wow! Look what a few words of encouragement can do!"

As far as my partner was concerned, it did not matter in the least what happened in the remaining rounds. She had beaten the best. It made her whole day. I suppose I should have felt guilty for manipulating those gentlemen, but I didn't! I hoped that in time, as they analyzed what had happened, they would come to the realization that their attitudes caused their own problems. Their uncontrolled anger had resulted in a lack of focus. When you lose your focus in tennis, you stop watching the ball, and the game is over!

As men we need to realize that our words are very powerful to the women in our lives. Whether it is your wife, daughter, mother, girlfriend, secretary, or another woman, choose your words very carefully. The Apostle Paul in his letter to the Church at Ephesus stated the following:

Let no unwholesome (literally "rotten") word proceed from your mouth, but only such a word as is good for edification according to the need of the moment, so that it will give grace to those who hear.
Ephesians 4:29

I love to cook. Cooking has become a very enjoyable and useful hobby for me. Of all the various spices and herbs available to season food, salt is the most important. If I could only have one seasoning, it would definitely be salt. Think about it. Without salt, food is insipid. Insipid means that food has no taste; it's bland. I quoted Colossians 4:6 which says, *"Let your words be seasoned like salt so that you will know how to respond in each moment."* (my paraphrase) So, Paul is saying that the words we speak have the capability of being salt in the lives of those around us. We can provide "taste" or encouragement to those we associate with, or the opposite if we are not careful with our words. As Christian men, we need to speak words that will build up those around us, rather than tear them down or hurt them.

The words we speak have the most powerful effect on our children. When they are young, they are the most vulnerable. Think back to your childhood. All of us can remember things our father said to us that we will never forget. Psychologists, who have studied this, speak of how important the presence of a father and his words are when a child is growing up. I once heard a psychologist say that the most important thing that determines what a sixteen-year-old girl does or does not do in the back seat of a car is the relationship she had, or did not have, with her father from birth to four years of age. If her father conveyed to her that in his eyes the sun rose and set by her, he gave to her the most important gift of her whole life. From that point on, how she sees herself in relation to men is determined by that relationship. That is what gives her self-esteem.

Psychologists speak of how boys are wounded by their fathers. None of us had perfect parents, nor will we be perfect parents. But as a young boy is growing up, he desperately longs for affirmation from his father. At the age of about four, a young boy starts to cut the apron strings and begins to pull away from his mother. If a mother does not understand why her son is doing this, she will be hurt by the rejection. She needs to be supportive of this separation. He will still run to her for comfort in the event of injury, but he inherently seeks the mentoring of his father.

It is the father who will show him what being a man is all about. Along his path to manhood, he will repeatedly look to his father to answer the questions, "Am I good enough to be a man? Am I strong enough?" He looks to his father for times of adventure with some aspect of danger. During these times, his father helps assure him that he is good enough and strong enough. If however, the father is an abusive alcoholic who constantly berates his son, the boy will grow up not believing in himself.

When my son was little, I used to get down on the floor and wrestle with him. He loved it. As he got older, this interaction took on different forms. In grade school and high school, he loved to play basketball. We used to play a lot of one-on-one. As he got older, he got taller and quicker. There was a lot of banging around in those games. The day came when he beat me. It was for both of us a momentous event. Now that he is in his twenties, we still enjoy doing things together. Every couple of years, we take a trip together - just the two of us. We decide where we are going and some places we might like to visit, but that is about it. We never make hotel reservations ahead of time. When the day arrives, we fly off to our destination city, get a rental car and begin our adventure. My wife always asks, "Where are you going?" I say, for example, "Southern Arizona." "Where are you staying?" "I don't have a clue," I respond. My son and I love the uncertainty and the freedom of not having to be somewhere at a particular time.

Sometimes we see if we can find the cheapest flea-bag motel in a town to stay at for the night. We love to hike, especially up – the higher the better. My wife hates heights. Once in Zion Canyon in Southern Utah, we had climbed to the top of one of the peaks. It even had a chain anchored to the side of the mountain to hold onto so you wouldn't fall off. But when we got up there, that wasn't good enough. There was another pinnacle in the middle of the area that we climbed, and we had someone take our picture. I had my cell phone and called my wife. "Honey, you won't believe where we are!" I said. "I probably don't want to know!" was her response. I continued, "We are sitting on top of this stone pinnacle, and when we look to our right it is 1,500 feet straight down, and when we look to the left it is about 2,000 feet straight down!" "Be careful," she said, "I want my son back alive." One time I rented a four-wheel drive vehicle and had my son drive me all over the back country. There were times that he wasn't sure he should drive into an area, and I reassured him it would be fine. Those were experiences of a lifetime that neither of us will ever forget.

When my oldest daughter was ten years old, I was asked to come to Tampa, Florida and speak to the Florida Dietetic Association. I was to fly down on a Friday morning and return that afternoon. The more I thought about it, it seemed like such a waste of time to go all the way to Florida just for the day. So, I arranged to take Monday off from work too, and I told my wife I was taking our daughter with me. She sat in the back all dressed up as I gave my lecture, and we spent the next three days visiting various sights in and around the Tampa area. When we returned, my wife asked, "How was it?" I told her, "It was one of the best times of my life!" My daughter and I had such a good time together. It was almost magical. That trip really impacted me, and I realized how valuable an experience like that can be for a child.

After that I started to take one of my children on trips with me at least every two years. It was so much fun planning where we would go and what we would do. I came to realize that the message these trips gave to each of my children was, "I love you very much. You are very special to me, and I want to spend this time only with you." Traveling one-on-one has been one of the most significant things I have ever done with my children.

Whether spending money on vacations or just staying home, all of us as fathers need to find ways to carve out time to be one-on-one with our children. Once, I took one of my daughters who was six years old to Brown County State Park for the afternoon, just doing things she wanted to do. Another time, my youngest daughter who was in high school, took me to lunch at a restaurant downtown and then we toured a small art gallery. These times were very precious to me, and I will never forget them.

Once I heard a psychologist say that fathers should always date their daughters. This made a lot of sense to me, so I started taking my daughters out to dinner one at a time. They would get all dressed up, and we would go out to a nice restaurant. This was another way I was able to communicate to them how valuable they were to me. During these relaxed times together the conversation was often rich. I learned so much about my daughters. Another advantage of dating your daughters is that it demonstrates to them how they should be treated. When young men come into their life, they will know what to look for.

I wonder how many parents realize the profound impact their words have on their children. Several years ago, between flights, I was eating in a small airport restaurant. In the booth next to me was a young boy whom I estimated to be about ten years of age. He was sitting next to a woman whom I presumed was his mother. Sitting across the table from them was a man who may have been the boy's father, but was more likely (from the little bit of conversation I overheard) the woman's boyfriend. During the forty-five minutes I sat there eating, not once did I hear either the woman or the man say a single nice or supportive word to the boy. By contrast, frequent negative, inflammatory comments were made to him. I thought to myself, "No child deserves this," and I wondered what happens when a child continues to be exposed to this on a daily basis. Is this why we read in the newspapers about a sixteen-year-old who takes a gun and shoots his parents?

As a father, you must be aware that the words you say to your son or daughter are of immense value if good, and very damaging if bad. You possess the ability to wound your child. Some of the wounds he or she will carry into adulthood and maybe for a lifetime. Each wound carries with it a damaging message. For example, a woman who was sexually abused by her father often has thoughts like, "I'm not worth anything. I deserved for it to happen." Hence, the love she never received from her father, she attempts to obtain from one pathologic relationship after another.

Similarly, the daughter of an alcoholic who witnessed her mother verbally and physically abused, often goes on to marry an alcoholic. That's how she was mentored, or worse, what she thinks she deserves. Divorce produces wounds in children from which many never recover. Children often believe that they were the cause of the divorce. If only they had been better children, maybe mom and dad would still be together. The loss of a father in the home is a devastating blow to a young boy. Who will mentor him to manhood? A single mom can be a great mom, but she will never be the masculine mentor her son needs.

The messages of wounds many times lead to disruptive behavior. Adolescent violence is often not the problem, but rather a symptom of the problem. The violence is a cry for help and attention. It may be a response to anger. A youth that joins a gang may do so for protection and for a sense of belonging. The gang may be the family he never had.

I would recommend that you find ways to praise your sons and daughters at every opportunity.

THE ANCIENT PATH & MARRIAGE

Gary Johnson is the Senior Pastor of Indian Creek Christian Church in Indianapolis, where my wife and I are members. He had this to say about the Ancient Path and marriage.

Godly ancestors have provided for me an ancient path, and for nearly 30 years of marriage, I have discovered that it is a good way in which to live. Grown children often inherit something from their aging parents when they pass from this life. That inheritance takes many forms, ranging from that which is material in nature to that which is intangible. Though I received some of my parents' possessions at the time of their passing, the portion of my inheritance that I consider beyond earthly value is that of an ancient path. Each of my parents bequeathed to me a value that has blessed my marriage and family in extraordinary ways.

My father was a common man. He worked his entire life in a factory as a maintenance worker. My dad started working in the factory while still a high school student and retired from the plant 35 years later. During that time, I continually observed how he stayed. My parents were married for 55 years before my mother died. My dad stayed with his one and only bride. When my dad passed away at the age of 76, he died in the very house he had lived in since he was a 7-year-old boy. He stayed in the very same neighborhood - and house - his entire life. From my dad, I inherited a priceless gift—the value of staying. An ancient path worth following is one that calls me to stay. Like my father, I have every intention of staying - of putting down the deepest of roots in my marriage, my family, my ministry and in the community where I live. This sense of commitment to stay runs contrary to the values of our American culture. But as I have chosen to walk in this ancient path, I have experienced a good and restful life.

My mother was an uncommon woman. She was an only child, and her mother died while giving birth to her. When she was five, her father died a violent death. Her grandmother raised her. The week my mother graduated from high school, her grandmother died. Shortly after marrying my father, my mother cared for an aging uncle who had given her away in marriage. He died while living with my newlywed parents. Then, my mother gave birth to a little girl, who died within hours of her birth. So, by the age of 22, my mom experienced the profound loss of five of the most important people in her life. She could have become a most bitter individual, lashing out in anger against God. Yet, she never did. My mother was most uncommon in that she always looked for the good in difficult situations.

When, as a boy, I would complain, she would be quick to point out to me that there were others in life with far greater problems. From my mom, I inherited a priceless gift - the value of looking for the goodness of the Lord. An ancient path worth following is one that calls me to see the goodness of the Lord in the land of the living (Psalm 27:13). Like my mother, I am determined to echo the words of a classic hymn, "Morning by morning, new mercies I see." Within my marriage and family, as well as in my ministry, I counter painful difficulties with this different perspective, one that sees God's goodness in life. When I choose to walk in this ancient path, I experience a good and restful life.

When we work hard to leave our children an inheritance, it is essential to leave them an inheritance beyond value - an ancient path to follow.

FOCUS

TRUTH (What is the focus – the essential truth of this chapter?)

Real love is not a feeling. It is an act of my will, a determination that I make.

APPLICATION (What does this truth mean to me? How is it relevant in my life?)

Since loving my wife does not depend on how I feel, I can choose to love my wife. Therefore, I can focus on How To Be A Dynamite Husband and even if I am not romantic by nature, I can do romantic things to please my wife.

ACTION (What should I do about it? How can this truth benefit my life?)

Pray: Holy Spirit, empower me to do all the things necessary to be a romantic, dynamic husband.

CHAPTER 7

THE ABDICATION OF LEADERSHIP

"Glory is fleeting, but obscurity is forever."
Napoleon Bonaparte, French Emperor

What do I mean by "abdication?" To abdicate means to shirk one's responsibility or to walk away from it. That is exactly what I believe many men have done in their lives, especially with respect to their wives and children. This chapter is not just about leadership, it is about spiritual leadership. God has placed us in our homes to be spiritual leaders. We must lead, but we must do it in the right way. The problem is many men have never been taught how to lead effectively. Perhaps their only mentor was a father who was alcoholic, abusive or just never around. They didn't have the proper instruction on how to be a husband and father. The good news is that the past doesn't have to stop them or any of us from being the leaders that God desires and requires.

Some time ago, one of the women in my office gave me a copy of an email she had received. It went like this:

"Men are like
  Laxatives – they irritate the crap out of you.
  Bananas – the older they get, the less firm they are.
  Weather – nothing can be done to change them.
  Blenders – you need one, but you're not quite sure why.
  Chocolate Bars – sweet, smooth and they usually head right for your hips.
  Commercials – you can't believe a word they say.
  Department Stores – their clothes are always ½ off.
  Government Bonds – they take soooooooo long to mature.
  Mascara – they usually run at the first sign of emotion.
  Popcorn – they satisfy you, but only for a little while.
  Lava Lamps – fun to look at, but not very bright.
  Parking Spots – all the good ones are taken and the rest are handicapped."

Although this was sent out in jest, the reason that it is so funny is because there is so much truth wrapped up in it. I guess as men we need to ask ourselves some questions:

1. How much do we really irritate the women in our life?
2. Have we let ourselves go physically as we have aged?
3. Are we really unchangeable?
4. Is our focus always on sex?
5. Are we untrustworthy? Basically, are we liars?
6. Do we always walk around sloppily dressed?
7. Do we ever grow up?
8. Are we incapable of handling feelings and emotions?
9. Are we only satisfying to our wife for a little while and unable to meet her needs sexually?
10. Are we stupid?

Although these statements are exaggerations, is this really how women see us? How could this view have occurred? As I mentioned before, I believe the entire women's liberation movement was the direct result of men not treating women the way God instructed. If every woman had been treated like a queen in her home, I doubt we would have seen the movement. It is now up to us to change how we are perceived by the opposite sex. I believe we can do it, one man at a time.

LEADERSHIP IS CRITICAL

"Great moments are born from great opportunities."
Herb Brooks, 1980 Olympic Hockey Coach

Most men have had the opportunity to play on a sports team of some sort. Certainly the quality of the players on these teams is very important, but the coach is critical. It is impossible to have a great team without a great coach. A great coach recognizes that as he stands on the sidelines, he needs a good leader on the field of play. Someone has to lead. During difficult times, players look to their leader.

At this point, it would be helpful to define leadership. Although I could give you a dictionary definition, I would prefer to give you a more pragmatic one. John Maxwell is a former pastor and prominent author. He calls himself the "Pastors' pastor." He has written many excellent books on leadership. I have heard him say over and over,

"Leadership is influence," and "A leader who thinks he is leading and turns around to realize no one is following, is not leading, but just out taking a walk." Many people in organizations have titles that identify them as leaders, however, many of them have nothing more than the title. They do not have the respect of their employees, and therefore, are just out taking a walk. On the other hand, some employees without any specific title are often the main influencers in an organization. These are the ones who have employees' respect and ear. As they speak, others listen and move in the direction they have indicated.

Leaders have to earn the respect of their employees. When I became the President and CEO of our medical corporation, the employees were surprised. It happened quite suddenly. I am sure there was some apprehension about what the new leader would do. I am sure some wondered if I was up to the task. Over the weeks and months that followed, I had to gain their respect by my actions. They needed to see I was a man of integrity. I had to prove that my walk always followed my talk. I had to show that I was consistent and true to my word.

Eventually they did what I requested, not because I was the CEO, but because they respected me. I became a leader of influence. Leaders are not always liked. Sometimes you have to choose whether you will be liked or respected. When you find yourself in that situation, I suggest you always choose respect. I have seen leaders who did everything they could to be liked by their employees. In the end, the employees liked them only because they lacked respect for them and could take advantage of them.

One day I flew to Chicago to spend the weekend with one of my daughters. While there I received a call from Jeff Cardwell from the People Helping People Network. Hurricane Katrina had just hit New Orleans, and Jeff was organizing a relief effort. He asked if I would lead the medical part of the team. Fortunately, Indianapolis Gastroenterology & Hepatology, my medical group, agreed to let me go and represent them. We boarded the Motorcycle Drill Team bus loaned to us by the Marion County Sheriffs' Department and headed south to Slidell, the community on the north side of Lake Pontchartrain, across from New Orleans. The last hour and a half before we crossed into Louisiana was eerie.

There were no lights except in houses that had generators. Trees that had blown across the interstate, blocking it, had been cut by chain saws and pushed up along side the highway by bulldozers. It was like driving through a black tunnel. We arrived at 11:00 PM in a blacked out town under marshal law. We went first to Slidell Memorial Hospital, from which we had received calls about patients dying. Our bus and the five semi-trailers that had joined us along the way were met by the police, who wanted to know who we were and what we wanted. We had our own SWAT team members with us. They were all dressed in black uniforms and sported more guns than I had ever seen in my whole life! They said, "We'll handle this."

Once they explained to the police who we were, the police deputized our officers and let our medical staff go to the hospital. Never before had I approached an ER and been met by National Guardsmen with AK47 automatic rifles! "Who are you and what do you want?" they asked. Once we explained who we were, they let us speak with the doctors. Fortunately, things weren't quite as bad as we had been led to believe, but they certainly could have been better. Most of the patients had been successfully evacuated. The ones that had remained toughed it out with a skeleton medical staff. The next morning we headed into New Orleans, a trip that took forever. Interstate I-10 was closed because the bridge had been partly destroyed. We finally got there four hours later. What I saw was unlike anything I had ever witnessed. I have led over twenty-five mission trips to South and Central America, into very remote places, but I had never seen devastation like this.

95% of the inhabitants had fled. The only people still there were those who had refused to leave or had returned to try and claim any remaining items from their homes. We stayed in a seminary dormitory. The head pastor there met every night with one of the council women, who in turn met each day with the Mayor of New Orleans. I had the opportunity to sit in on one of the meetings and spend time with the pastor, observing all he and others were doing to help. It was painfully clear that although he was doing everything he could, the situation lacked leadership at the governmental level, both in the mayor's and governor's office. As a result of this situation, I became convinced that, in life, leadership is critical! Whether in a home, at work, in an organization or in a community, leadership is essential. In medicine without leadership, patients die. We are very fortunate that the death toll as the result of Hurricane Katrina was not significantly higher.

SERVANT LEADERSHIP

*"The ability to lead your family when under pressure is critical.
Will you worsen the crisis by heating it up with anger, confusion,
negativity and impatience? Or will you maintain composure
and a sense of humor? Whether people will respect you
or not will depend on your response."*
Michael F. Elmore, Physician

By His servant leadership, Jesus demonstrated the power of sacrificing self for the one we love. Contrast this with the so often "What about me" attitude so many individuals have in their marriages. Imagine what it would be like to live giving yourself completely to another. That would really be treating your wife like a queen! Just think what her response to that would be. Do you think she would be totally devoted to this type of love and commitment? Imagine how secure she would feel to be joined to a man who let her know everyday, by his actions, the importance of their marriage. His actions would say, "Honey, I want to do everything today that I possibly can to make you happy. I'm not going anywhere no matter how bad things get; I will be right here by your side and with our children." These are the kind of men we need. Men who live for their wives and family.

In Chapter 6, I presented the idea that sex can get better and better throughout the years of marriage. This is true because in a healthy marriage the husband and wife grow together, rather than apart. As time passes, you experience many good times and some bad times. You bond together as you progress through these experiences, and your bond becomes stronger and richer. As a result when you make love, it is the physical expression of all that you have experienced together. My approach to sex changed as the years passed. Initially, sex was all about my gratification. But as I grew more and more in love, I found myself wanting to please her more and more. Sometimes as we made love, I would be praying, "Lord, let her experience all the enjoyment that is possible." As I sought to please her more, she did the same for me. The Song of Solomon is an amazing and quite graphic love story. If you have never read it, I would encourage you to do so, using a good study Bible. As you read the story, read all the study notes, and you will find out all that is really going on in that book! I believe that this is the kind of love God wants all couples to experience.

Jesus was all about meeting needs. The Church is His bride, and He did everything for her even to the point of giving His life for her. Likewise as husbands we are expected to meet the needs of our wife. But what are these needs? When I got married, my wife didn't come with an instruction manual describing how to properly care for her. I suppose this book is an effort in that regard.

One of the best books I have ever read is entitled *His Needs, Her Needs, Building An Affair-proof Marriage,* by Willard F. Harley, Jr. [2] He describes how the most basic needs in a marriage tend to be the following:

MEN	WOMEN
1. Sexual fulfillment	1. Affection
2. Recreational companionship	2. Conversation
3. An attractive spouse	3. Honesty & openness
4. Domestic Support	4. Financial support
5. Admiration	5. Family commitment

Dr Harley points out that these needs are listed in their usual order of importance, but this order may not be the same for all men or women. For example, I enjoy sex, but it is not my most important need. For me the admiration of my wife is of the utmost importance. The important thing is for those of us who are husbands to recognize the needs of our wife and then to do our best to meet them. Dr. Harley sees these as basic needs within a marriage, and if these basic needs are not satisfied, the marriage is in jeopardy. For example, my wife's most important need is conversation. If I don't provide the time for this within our marriage, I jeopardize our marriage, because I am forcing her to go outside the marriage to meet this need. If she starts having significant conversation with a man at work, then her most important need is being met by another man. This is a very dangerous situation.

One of the most useful concepts Dr. Harley shares in his book is what he calls the "love bank." He describes how we all have a love bank for everyone we meet in life. The love (i.e. coins) that is placed in the bank is not necessarily romantic. Think about it. With everyone you meet, each encounter results in you either depositing or withdrawing coins from the love bank you have with them. Some people in your life always seem to be withdrawing coins and never making any deposits. These are the people who suck the life out of you. You would really rather never see them again. Their accounts with you are always overdrawn. Then there are other people who you always like to see. Each encounter is good, and they are always depositing coins in your bank.

When you first met and began to date your wife, you both made deposits in each other's love banks. After a while, enough coins had been deposited that you decided to go steady. More coins were deposited, and you got engaged and then married. The problem all too often is that, once married, the strains of life appear, and you start withdrawing more coins than you are depositing. After a while, the couple says, "We just fell out of love." They see no alternative but divorce. How sad. Their marriage could have been saved if they only understood the dynamics of what happened. If they divorce without understanding what happened, they are likely to remarry only to repeat the same cycle again.

Now you can understand how dangerous it is to have your wife's conversational needs met by some other man. With each conversation, the man is depositing coins in the love bank that your wife has with him, and she is depositing coins in his bank. This is not romantic initially, but once enough coins are deposited, it often progresses to a romantic event, leading to an affair. Only you, as her husband, can prevent this. Hence, it is critical that we each understand the needs of our wife and seek to meet them.

In Chapter 5, I spoke about the innate differences between the sexes. It is important for husbands to recognize that our needs are different from those of our wives. Sometimes we think, "Why is that so important to her?" We need to understand that it is, and we must deal with it! We aren't going to change her. God made her that way, just as He made us the way we are. Everyone quotes the Golden Rule as how we should live. But I believe there is an even better way. When I was responsible for the running of our medical corporation, I frequently found myself in situations where I didn't have a clue about what to do. I subscribed to a business book club trying desperately to educate myself. Each month I received two book summaries thought to be on the cutting edge of the business world. One of the books I read was entitled *The Platinum Rule,* a book designed for sales people who wanted to be more successful. [3] The basic premise of the book is that the Golden Rule is not good enough in the business world. It is not good enough to treat people the way you want to be treated. They are not you. They may not want to be treated the way you want to be treated. So, you must use the Platinum Rule, which states that you first figure out how someone wants to be treated and then treat her or him that way. I think this makes perfect sense for a marriage. My wife has different needs than I have. I need to apply the Platinum Rule and first find out what her needs are and then meet them. I thought that if Jesus were in my shoes as a husband, that is exactly what He would do.

NEEDS

In order to properly understand leadership, it is important to understand the concept of needs. All of us have needs. Abraham Maslow is famous for establishing the theory of the hierarchy of needs, which states that all human beings are motivated by unsatisfied needs. Certain lower needs have to be met before the higher needs. Maslow used his theory to explain human behavior. For example, he believed that war and violence are a direct result of human needs not being met. He described general types of needs. First, there are physiological needs such as food, water, sleep, sex and shelter. Only when these needs are satisfied can we go on to think about other needs. Next, is the need for safety which involves establishing stability and consistency in an otherwise chaotic world. For this, the security of a home and a family are very important. If a wife is living with an abusive husband, she is prevented from moving to the next level of needs because of her constant concern for her safety. She is driven by fear. Many people who live in our inner cities desperately need law and order, and fear to even walk the street in their own neighborhood. They are stuck at the level of needing safety.

I have seen this on medical mission trips in developing countries. People there are often times more religious or more open to the Gospel message, which promises a safe place *after they die!* Heaven is much more real to them than to people in the USA and, because of their living conditions, they long to experience this promise sooner rather than later.

The next need is for love and belonging. Human beings have a desire to belong to groups - family, a church, a club, a gang, etc. We all need to feel loved and accepted, and all of us need affirmation from others. Then there is the need for esteem, which exists in two forms. First, is self-esteem which comes from completing or mastering tasks. Second, is the esteem we derive from the attention and recognition of others. Big houses, fancy cars and expensive designer clothes are all ways of saying, "Hey, look at me!" Wanting admiration often relates to having a sense of power. An expensive home in a prestigious neighborhood communicates, "Look what I have accomplished and what I can afford."

Maslow called these needs "deficiency needs." We are obsessed with meeting these needs, and satisfying these needs is healthy. However, these cravings can result in evil behavior if the path to gratifying the needs is blocked in any way. For example, the healthy need for a teenager to be accepted may lead abnormally to heroin addiction or other aberrant behavior, as the teen tries to function "normally" in certain segments of society. Young boys are often lured into street gangs to have their basic needs met and to receive safety (protection), love (however distorted) and esteem (acceptance).

Once these deficiency needs are satisfied, Maslow believed that humans then focus on a desire to become everything that one is capable of becoming. This maximizing of one's potential he called *self-actualization*. Rick Warren's best-selling book, *The Purpose Driven Life,* speaks to this issue. [1] Finding one's purpose in life is a high priority for humans. We need continual personal growth and learning. Maslow believed self-actualization to be a continual, ongoing process. Some describe their purpose in life as a "calling." A musician must create and play music. An artist must paint. A writer must write. Many such people can't always articulate why they must do these things, they just know that inside they are driven to do so. Others take up environmental causes and commit their lives to them.

Maslow's theory radically changed the classical views of psychology. His ideas were a breath of fresh air to the depressing determinism of Freud and Skinner, that saw man as a mechanism driven by the Id or long forgotten past experiences. However, one glaring deficiency in Maslow's hierarchy of needs is the lack of anything related to spirituality and God. We are spiritual beings created in God's image, and there is within us another need or void that can only be filled by God. We inherently need the love, grace, mercy and acceptance of our Creator. We also sense that our life has a deep spiritual purpose that can only be achieved by God's divine direction.

From a Christian perspective self-actualization is described by the term *progressive sanctification*. By accepting Christ as our personal Lord and Savior and by turning control of our life over to Him, He puts the Holy Spirit within us. Our body becomes the "temple of the Holy Spirit." It is the working of the Holy Spirit within us that gives us the power and ability to live as God wants and directs. This takes the self-actualization process to a whole new and exciting level. Imagine. Now you have God, the Father, your Creator, actually directing every step of your life through the Holy Spirit. He not only guides and directs, He promises to be with you in the tough times of life, right by your side. He even goes a step further and promises that for those of us who are called by His name, i.e. Christians, He can work good out of every potential "bad" situation.

And we know that God causes all things to work together for good to those who love God, to those who are called according to His purpose. **Romans 8:28**

If God be for us, who is against us? **Romans 8:31**

Jesus was our example of servant leadership. The Apostle Paul directs us in his letter to the Ephesians:

Therefore, be imitators of God . . . and walk in love, just as Christ also loved you and gave Himself up for us, an offering and a sacrifice to God as a fragrant aroma. **Ephesians 5:1-2**

Paul goes on to instruct men who are husbands:

Husbands, love your wives, just as Christ also loved the church and gave Himself up for her. **Ephesians 5:25**

This was a demonstration to us by Jesus of how we should love our wife. We are to be so devoted to her that we would die for her, if necessary. I have heard men say that they would readily die for their wife. Maybe that is true, but my response is, "You are not any good to your wife dead. God wants you to live for your wife now while you are alive!" Paul speaks to this in verse 28:

So husbands ought also to love their own wives as their own bodies. He who loves his own wife loves himself.

Ephesians 5:28

Did you ever stop to think about why God made man from the dust of the ground, but when He created woman, He made her from the rib of Adam? I believe that this is highly significant. It says to me that a man can never again be complete without his wife, the rib taken from him. She was created to satisfy his loneliness, to make him complete. A woman has the natural God-given desire to have a great relationship with her husband. She intuitively knows what a great relationship looks like. As men we have to learn this from our wife. If you don't believe this, ask your wife how your relationship could be better. You might be surprised by all she has to say!

God knew the profound effects a union like this could have. Moses wrote in Genesis:

For this cause a man shall leave his father and his mother, and be joined to his wife; and they shall become one flesh.

Genesis 2:24

This principle is often referred to as the principle of "leaving and cleaving." Many marriages are strained and even destroyed because husbands and wives don't understand what this means. Let me share an example. After my wife and I married, there were times when her parents would call and ask her if we could attend a family function or do something with them. At other times my parents would call me to ask the same thing. Both my wife and I wanted to please our parents, and so we often committed to do what they wanted, which often resulted in the other of us being upset when we both scheduled our respective family events at the same time. It produced so much turmoil that we finally agreed that neither of us would commit to any function without first discussing it with the other. That sent a clear message to our parents. After that when they would ask if we could do something, my wife responded, "I would love to, but I need to speak with Michael first to see what his schedule is." I did the same when my parents called. This sent the message to our parents that we were no longer individuals. We were now married and functioned as one.

The Bible addresses this when it says that a man and a woman "leave" their parents in order to "cleave" (be bound to) each other. It does not mean that my parents stop being my parents, but it does mean that they no longer occupy the same priority they once did. Now my priorities are: God first, then my wife, next my children (when they come along) and then my parents. By understanding this principle couples can save themselves a lot of grief!

QUALITIES OF A LEADER

"A great leader is not necessarily one who does great things. He is the one who gets the people to do the greatest things."
Ronald Reagan (1911 – 2004), U.S. President

Husbands must lead in a variety of ways. But what do women want in a man? Let me list the types of leadership that I think we should provide.

1.   Spiritual Leadership - A wife wants her husband to take the lead and to be the spiritual leader in the home. God wants us to be men of faith and so does our wife. If you were to ask my wife when our relationship changed before we got married, she would not hesitate for one moment. She would immediately respond, "It was when we prayed together for the first time."

2.   Submissive Leadership – What do I mean by a submissive leader? It sounds like a contradiction, doesn't it? Unfortunately, there has been a lot of faulty teaching in the church about how wives are to submit to their husbands. Some of the teaching is what I call "Doormat Theology." Doormat Theology teaches that a wife must submit to her husband, no matter what, in all situations. However, this is not what Scripture intends. It undermines a woman and how God created her. If a husband asks his wife to do something that is contrary to God's Word, she must not submit. For example, if she is pregnant, and he demands she abort the child, she must not do that. If her husband suggests going to a particular party that involves wife swapping, she must not submit. What the Bible does teach is mutual submission.

... be subject to one another in the fear of Christ.
Ephesians 5:21

As husbands, we submit to the needs of our wife. If she has a need, we, by nature, should seek to meet that need. This may involve helping with the children, preparing a meal, cleaning up the home, etc. Remember, you are a team working together to accomplish the same goal. A true leader never sees any job as beneath him. He will do whatever it takes to get the job done.

3.   Committed Leadership – A wife wants to know and be assured that her husband is going to be there for her. She needs to be certain he isn't going anywhere. Henry Ford was asked on the 50th Anniversary of Ford Motor Company what the key to his success had been. His response was, "Stay with the same model." That is good advice for a husband, too! When you marry a woman, you make a wedding vow. I always explain to couples preparing for marriage how that vow is made only secondarily to one another. It is made primarily to God. The wedding vow can be called an oath, and it can also be called a covenant. In the Bible, God speaks of the Covenant of Marriage.

We don't use the word covenant much anymore. This is unfortunate, because God calls us to be men of covenant. God is looking for men of integrity who will be loyal and faithful to their wives and children and not desert them. Too many men are tripped up by extramarital affairs that destroy their marriage. Remember, the grass may look greener on the other side of the fence, but when you get over there, you still have to mow it. Speaking from a gastroenterological standpoint, I would phrase it slightly differently: "The grass looks greener on the other side of the fence, but when you get over there, you realize that's where the septic system is!"

God's relationship with us is defined by a covenant. He signed the covenant with His own blood; that's how serious He was and is about it! He never changes, and He is fully and for all times committed to us. This provides us with incredible comfort, the same type of comfort we should be giving to our wives. The concept of covenant in the Bible is that when two parties enter into covenant, from that point on they are inseparable. So too, in marriage we covenant with each other that we are now inseparable. Our lives are bound together as long as we are both alive. More importantly, and not as well understood, we yield our will to the other.

I believe that the greatest gift a father can ever give to his children is for them to see his devotion to their mother. Such devotion creates a secure environment of incredible value in the lives of children. One morning I was driving my youngest daughter to school. She was in fourth grade. She asked me, "Dad, are you and Mom getting a divorce?" I was shocked, and almost drove my truck into the ditch! "Why would you ever think that?" I asked. She responded, "Because all the other kids' parents in my class are getting divorced." We need to work extra hard in today's culture to reassure our children of our commitment to our family.

4. **Paternal Leadership** – Men need to realize that in everything they do, they are a mentor to their children. Many years ago, before we had established medical schools in the United States, when a young man wanted to become a doctor, he searched for a physician to mentor him. He became his mentor's disciple. He bound himself to his mentor for however long it took to learn all he needed to become a physician. He watched everything his mentor did and emulated him. So it is with our children. God gives us our children for eighteen years, plus or minus a few. They are bound to us. They watch us very carefully. That is why we must be what we want our children to become. When I studied parenting, I learned that 90% of the time when my children disobeyed, it was due to some behavior I had taught them. If they cursed the cat, I had to ask myself, "Where did they learn that?" Rarely, perhaps 10% of the time, I had not taught them that behavior. As a father, this realization is very humbling. Being a father is very serious business and has profound effects on the future lives of our children. A father is also the disciplinarian in the home. It is his job to keep law and order. As their father, he should demonstrate both the justice and the mercy of God. I believe that being a father is the hardest job in the world.

David Michel is a retired pharmaceutical representative. He shared this experience with me about his life and trying to be the best father he could be.

I was attending Vincennes University in Vincennes, Indiana, when I met Janet. She was still in high school and working at a local restaurant. We dated a few times, and we went to her Senior prom. Two years later, we were married. That was 38 years ago. We first lived in Terre Haute, Indiana while I finished my degree at Indiana State University. I taught school for a year, and then we moved to South Bend, Indiana where I accepted a position with Abbott Laboratories. A few years later, I was offered a district manager position in Chicago. The position would have meant more money and prestige, but I turned the offer down, feeling that it was more important not to relocate since our children were young. I worked for Abbott for thirty years before retiring.

In the last five years prior to retirement, I noticed how the pharmaceutical business changed. Many physicians would no longer see pharmaceutical representatives in their offices. What once inspired and drove me, no longer did. I had enjoyed most the dialogue with physicians. Now that was gone. I began to sense that God had something else in store for me. Although I was successful at work, it was not satisfying and lacked significance.

The church we attended seemed to focus on a lot of "doing." It seemed that to be a good Christian meant church attendance three times a week and being present at all the church's activities. I was disillusioned.

Trying to be a good father, I had family devotions every morning before the children left for school. One morning as I read from a devotional booklet, I noticed my son, Brett, who was in 6th grade, was not paying attention. I came down hard on him. Brett started crying and ran off to school. I felt terrible. So, later that morning, I called the school and arranged to take Brett out of school for a short time. We went to McDonald's® to talk. I asked Brett for forgiveness. The fact that his father would go to the trouble of taking him out of school to ask for forgiveness really impacted Brett. Brett still talks about it today.

After that I threw the devotional booklet away and simply asked, "What has been going on in your life?" Then we would discuss it in the light of Scripture. That seemed to go a whole lot better.

When Brett was in high school, I caught him in a lie. Brett and some other boys had been sneaking off drinking alcohol. I confronted him and talked with him. Brett actually felt better once it was in the open. He promised not to do it again. Two years later when he went off to college, Brett wrote a note to me saying, "Dad, you don't have to worry." He knew I cared.

Now retired, Dave was right. God did have something more in store for him and Janet. They are now involved with mission activity in Central and South America, and each day is packed with success and significance.

I met Larry Lane in 1967 when we were both students at Indiana University. We became best friends, and I was privileged to be his best man when he married over 35 years ago. Larry writes this about the influence his father had in his life.

I was blessed to have a father who was an ordained minister and

145

a teacher by example. I believe that one of the most important traits a father can possess is consistency with regard to what he says and does. One of the most valuable lessons that my father taught me was the joy of serving. One very cold snowy winter night when I was 5 years old, my father received a call from a rural farmer. His wife was very ill and wanted to be baptized before she died. Without hesitation, my father said he would be there as soon as possible. My father requested that I go with him, since he had not seen me for a week. My mother wrapped me in an army blanket to keep me warm, and we started our trek. We arrived at the farmer's house after dark with less than a quarter of a tank of gas and bald tires. With her husband's help, my father baptized the woman in the bathtub, and she was helped back to bed. My father held her hand, read Scripture, shared words of comfort and prayed. The farmer left us for about an hour, probably to take care of the cattle. The farmer's wife died that night with my father comforting her and continually holding her hand.

On our way back, my father noticed that we had over a half tank of gas and that the traction on the snowy road was greatly improved thanks to the two new tires from the farmer's car. I asked my father why the woman died and why the farmer called him instead of the doctor. He told me that answers to these types of questions only come from God. He told me to remember two things: God will always take care of you, and tonight we were blessed in serving the Lord. For the past 50 years, this example has been a constant reminder to me in serving the Lord.

It is my hope and prayer that my example will have a similar impact on my son. Ask yourself, "What kind of example am I leaving for my son?"

5. Provider Leadership – This includes being a financial provider, but is not limited to that. I have seen many husbands who come home, eat supper, plop down in front of the TV, read the paper and then, eventually, go to bed. They think that because they bring their paycheck home on Friday, that is all they need to do to be a good provider. But, being a good provider also means providing for the other needs of the family. This involves many things. Every husband should make the time to have a date night with his wife, at least once a month. Once a week is even better. A father needs to spend time with his children helping with homework or playing games. Your wife and children need to know that you care about them.

6.   Defender Leadership – Maybe if you had lived in the Wild West during the 19th Century, you might have needed to defend your family from Indians or thieves. But, that is unlikely today. A man is now called upon to protect his family from different and more subtle types of attack. The most dangerous to your marriage and to the stability of your family is the attack of infidelity. Not only must you protect your wife from such attack, but you must protect yourself. I mentioned earlier in this chapter about how important it is for you to meet your wife's needs so she does not have to go outside your marriage to have her needs met. How do you protect yourself from infidelity? This is of critical importance, and a very real danger. King David did not do what he should have been doing as a king, which led him into adultery and committing murder. The Bible states that David *"was a man after God's own heart."* If that were true and it happened to him, then the message is clear. It can happen to you and me if we are not careful. I don't presume to have all the answers, but I will simply share what I do know. First, by being the husband God wants you to be and doing all you can to meet your wife's needs, she will likely in return seek to meet your needs, too. Remember, if you want to receive, you must first give. That is the Biblical principle. Next, protect yourself from temptation. As men we are naturally attracted to women. When we look at women, you know where our thoughts go. The fact that these thoughts pop into our minds is not wrong. It is what we choose to do with them once they occur. We must train ourselves not to dwell on sexual thoughts.

7.   Romantic Leadership – The husband needs to take the lead in nurturing the courtship. Always romance your wife. And, I mean everyday of your life! It is the simple, thoughtful things that women appreciate the most. They speak volumes to her about your love and devotion to her. Before you leave the house in the morning, find her. Give her a hug and a kiss. Pray for her. Sometimes I don't let go of my wife until she laughs, and she pushes me away. She says, "Will you just go to work?" But, I know she loves it. Give her a call during the day to let her know you are thinking about her. Find out how her day is going. I can tell when something is bothering my wife. On those days, I tell her that I will continue praying for her throughout the day. Next to God, she is your number one priority. Demonstrate that to her everyday by your actions.

8. Encourager Leadership – We all need support, but I believe this is particularly true for married women, because of all they do. Wives are great "Multi-Taskers." They not only take care of the kids, they take care of us and everything else. An encouraging husband seeks to find out those things that are stressors for his wife and encourage her. Your loving support as her husband is an incredible gift to her. You don't necessarily need to do anything regarding the things that are stressing her out. You just need to be there with and for her. I believe that if you have the gift or talent of being an encourager, you, by nature, make people believe they can do something they have never done and don't believe they can ever do. Whether you have that gift or not, God calls all of us to encourage our wives.

9. Humorous Leadership –This one may surprise you. But, when women are asked what they want in a man, one of the things they always say is, "I want a man who makes me laugh." What is it about laughter? Why are comedy movies such a big hit? As a physician, I believe that laughter is important to our health.

A joyful heart is good medicine, but a broken spirit dries up the bones.   **Proverbs 17:22**

Laughter lifts our spirit and temporarily frees us from the heaviness of our day-to-day burdens. As a gastroenterologist, my work entails performing a lot of endoscopy. Many patients who come for gastroscopy (examination of the esophagus, stomach and duodenum) or colonoscopy (examination of the colon) with an endoscope (a flexible instrument with a small TV camera attached to the end so that the lumen of the intestine can be visualized) are fearful of the exam. Their fear is not hard to detect. I try to lighten the mood before each procedure by telling an Irish joke. My theory is that it is hard to be terrified when you are laughing. My goal is to get every fearful patient laughing prior to their procedure.

We all need humor in our lives. I believe that it is essential that we laugh everyday – the more the better. Many times when I am in the office seeing patients, I wander into the various departments and tell them a "Murphy" joke. My wife says I have an alter ego, and his name is Murphy. Some people in our office actually call me Dr. Murphy. Murphy loves to tell jokes and have a good time. One year at the office Christmas party, the staff gave an award for the Most Humorous person in the office. Murphy won! Our day-to-day work often beats us down, that's why I think we need to take periodic breaks and laugh. It is difficult to define what makes a joke funny. It just is. I believe this is a special gift that God gave us that is unique to humans. Our brains are hard wired for humor. I don't see cows laughing in the field, except, perhaps, in a "Farside" comic.

10. Financial Leadership – One of the primary reasons for divorce is financial tension in a marriage. My good friend, Harold Schubert, who is a financial consultant and one of the reviewers of this book, pointed out to me that couples fight more over their finances than anything else. So, in order to protect your marriage, you must adhere to sound financial principles. I am not a financial expert, but I have received a lot of good advice over the years. I would like to thank Harold for his input in this section.

"Every family has the choice of keeping up with the neighbors or with the creditors."   – Author Unknown

Many Americans are confused about what real wealth is. Wealth has nothing to do with how much you spend, the car you drive, the home you live in, or any of the other financial barometers that give the impression of wealth. Real wealth is what you have accumulated. Unfortunately, many American households have accumulated very little and, quite the opposite, are deep in debt. What is your net worth? Recognize that your net worth does not correlate with your income. You may make a lot of money, but if you don't save anything and build equity, you may have no net worth at all. You may look great and still be poor! One way to measure your net worth or wealth is to see how long can you go without a paycheck? Most people live paycheck to paycheck, spending everything they make without saving. If they lose their job, they are in real trouble.

Most Americans are spenders, not savers. Don't get trapped into a lifestyle of excessive spending to purchase all the toys of life. Many young people today want everything their parents have, but they want it now, not after a lifetime of working for it like their parents did. How do these young people get everything? They buy everything on credit and end up financing their entire future on debt. They don't have any idea how much the debt will actually cost them. The interest they will pay on what they have purchased will cost them a small fortune, much more than if they had saved and then purchased what they wanted.

Here is my prescription for financial success.

DOC'S RULES FOR FINANCIAL SUCCESS

1.   **Always Tithe** → Never deprive yourself of God's blessings on your life and your family.

2.   **Never Spend What You Don't Make** → Let interest compound and work for you, not against you. Don't live above your means. If you are an excessive spender, you will end up buying a lot of things that you will have to spend time taking care of and maybe insuring. This is the additional cost of possessing these things. Spenders usually end up needing more and more money to pay off the credit that ends up owning them. How do they do this? They work harder and end up spending less time with their families. Their families have everything but their husband and father. What is more important to your family, you or the things you buy your family? Don't get trapped into impressing others.

3.   **Eliminate Debt** → Only borrow to purchase appreciable items (those that increase in value over time) like your house. The only exception should be a car, which you might need for work and for your family. If you are in debt, pay off the smallest bill first, then apply those extra dollars to pay off the next smallest bill, and so on.

4.   **Establish an Emergency Fund** → This is mandatory, not optional. Everyone has times of financial difficulty. To be a good steward for your family, you must be prepared for bad times. Accumulate enough in this fund to live for three months if you lost your job.

5.   **Save 10% to 15% of What You Make** → There is an old saying I've heard over and over: "Always pay yourself first!" Think about it. If you decide to save 10% of your salary, but you wait until after you have paid all your other bills, there is nothing left. The same is true for your tithe. You must pay God first, then pay yourself next, based on what you determined to save. Then pay everyone else. Think of your paycheck as a cash register. Where are you in line to get paid?

Put God and yourself at the front of the line. If you don't save money, then you will have nothing to invest. Find an accountant and financial advisor you can trust and who have a good reputation. Building your net worth takes sacrifice and planning.

6.   Pay Off Your Credit Cards Completely Every Month → If you can't, then get rid of them! If you owe a lot on your credit cards, start by eliminating all but one card. That way you will have only one monthly payment. Next, develop a plan to pay off the card as quickly as possible.

7.   Own Your Own Home – Don't Be Owned By It! → Never buy a home that is more than you can afford. A good rule of thumb is to never buy a home more than twice your annual income. Otherwise ,you will end up working to support your home. Buy smaller than you can afford, then work to pay off the mortgage early so you can build equity. Then you will be in a position to trade up. The more you pay for your home, the more the property taxes and homeowner's insurance will cost you. Also, if you live in a fancy neighborhood, you will be influenced by your neighbors to drive a more expensive car, and to live a more extravagant lifestyle. By buying an affordable home, you will have income to save to build your wealth. Avoid paying rent if at all possible. You are just throwing money away. In contrast, when you have a mortgage, you can write off the mortgage interest on your taxes.

8.   Invest In Yourself – Get As Much Education As You Can While You Are Young and Unencumbered → It is much easier to devote yourself to your studies and focus on your education when you don't have a wife and children. Be realistic about your potential future earnings and don't over-borrow for your education.

9.   Develop a Budget and Stick to It → A credit card is not a budget! Practice deferred gratification. Do you spend your money based upon what you have decided ahead of time? If you don't, then you don't have a functioning budget. Focus on saving and investing first, then use the leftover money to live on. Most people try to do just the opposite, and there is nothing left to save and invest. Do you know what you spend every year for food, car maintenance, clothes, and other essentials? How can you write a budget not knowing?

10.   Establish a Good Credit Rating → A good credit rating makes it possible for you to get the best interest rate for a mortgage. Build a good credit history by always making your credit card and mortgage payments on time.

11.   Save For Retirement Starting With Your First Job → Always take advantage of your company's retirement plan, especially if it offers a matching program. The sooner you start saving for retirement, the faster your money will start compounding tax-deferred for your future.

Young people mistakenly think they will have plenty of time to save for the future. Wrong! It is not a matter of *time* but of *timing*. For example, if you start working at age 25 and save $2000 per year for just 10 years and then don't save another dime, 40 years later at age 65, you will have $211,000 in your retirement account (at an 8% rate of growth). Your money grew eleven-fold. But if you start working at age 25 and wait until you are 35 to start saving and you save $2000 per year from age 35 to age 65, you will have only $124,000 in your account! That is only two-fold growth. The cost of waiting in this illustration is $87,000.

The message is clear – start saving for retirement as early as possible, so your money can compound for you tax-deferred. Remember, there is an old person in all of us. Who will care for you when you are old? Will you have saved any available resources? You can't depend on Social Security – it won't be nearly enough.

12.   Protect Your Assets → All you have saved and all the equity you have built up can be lost if you do not have the proper insurance. The following are types of insurance you should consider to protect your wealth: health, home, auto, liability (with an umbrella policy) and extended care facility insurance.

13.   Never Give Your Children Too Much → We all want the best for our children. But there is a right and wrong way to give. There is an old saying: "If you give a man a fish he will eat one meal; if you teach him how to fish, he will eat for a lifetime." So, focus not on giving your children fish, but on teaching them how to fish. For example, don't give them money directly, but rather help to fund their education. But don't pay for all of it. If you do, they will have no financial involvement in their education, and they won't appreciate it.

If they have to pay for part of it, they will appreciate it and work harder. In the end, they will be more successful. Support your children in a way that encourages them to become independent.

14. Have A Will → Always plan for the future. One day you will die. It may be sooner or later, and you must be prepared for the sake of your family.

Harold told me that a successful money formula has three components:
1. A plan to save.
2. A way to control your living expenses (that is called a budget)
3. A solution for debts.

He pointed out that this plan will not work if any one of these ingredients is missing. I suggest that you look at each paycheck in the following way.

Total Earnings (gross pay)
Pay your tithe.
Pay your taxes.

Working Money (the money left over after paying God and the government)
10% for Saving & Investments
70% for Living Expenses
20% for Debts & Emergency Fund

In the end, real wealth has more to do with family, happiness, good friends, finding significance in life and your reputation than it does with the money you accumulate.

YOUR KINGDOM

"The future must be seen in terms of what a person can do to contribute something, to make something better, to make it go where he believes with all his being it ought to go."

Frederick R. Kappel
Former Chairman, American Telephone & Telegraph

At the beginning of this chapter, I shared the story of how my oldest daughter, when she was very young, told me that I was not the "Boss of this house," but that I was the "King." If you are the King of your Castle, what does your kingdom look like? Are you the type of king that is an abusive tyrant obsessed with demonstrating your power over your subjects? Do those in your house walk around in fear of you? Or are you a benevolent king that loves his subjects and seeks to serve them by doing good for them? Do your subjects love and respect you for who you are?

Take some time to think about the kingdom you have created. You might ask the Boss what she thinks.

FOCUS

TRUTH (What is the focus – the essential truth of this chapter?)

Leadership in my home is everything – it is critical!

APPLICATION (What does this truth mean to me? How is it relevant in my life?)

If I can recognize the needs of my wife and meet them, then I will not put my wife and my marriage in jeopardy.

ACTION (What should I do about it? How can this truth benefit my life?)

Pray: Dear Lord, help me to love my wife like Jesus loved His church. Teach me to be a dynamic servant leader to my wife and family.

CHAPTER 8

THE PURPOSE OF WORK

Sometimes in life it is easy to be overwhelmed by the selfishness, greed, corruption, narrow-mindedness and intolerance that we see, but I believe that one man can make a huge difference. I challenge you to raise the bar for those around you by your vision, courage and wisdom.
Michael F. Elmore, Physician

Men gain their identity from their work. That's the way it is. If you don't believe it, just observe the conversation that occurs when several men who have never met get together. If you have ever been in this situation, the first question you are usually asked is, "What do you do?" What you do identifies who you are.

This is unfortunate, because who we really are is based upon our relationship with God. My true identity is that I am one of God's children, one of His sons. I am a joint heir with my Brother Jesus who is my Savior and Lord, who gave His life for me. I was born again and adopted into the family of God. I received the Holy Spirit, and right now I am seated beside Jesus in heavenly places. God covered me with the blood of His Son, and now when He looks at me, He sees me as holy. As such, I have the right to enter into the very presence of God, because my sin has been washed away completely. This is a whole lot more significant than, "What do you do?" But we live temporally on earth, and for many men all they really have is what they do, their work.

Because we gain so much of our temporal identity from our work, the woman we marry becomes very important. I don't think most women realize that they have the power to absolutely make or break their husband. A wife who gets excited about what her husband does and fully supports and encourages him in his work is an enormous gift to him. A man desperately needs the affirmation of the women in his life, particularly his wife. If she says to him, "I know you can do it. I will be praying for you," it gives him an incredible boost. However, if she is jealous of his job and resents it, then she brings him down.

Criticism makes men feel inadequate and demotivates them. The problem of jealousy usually occurs when a man devotes too much time to his work to the exclusion of his family. Finding the right balance is critical. If a wife is not understanding of the requirements of her husband's work, and if he is honestly doing his best to achieve the balance between work and family, her criticism will drive him away. He will move away from her in their relationship. A wife with insight will praise her husband for the good work he is doing to support the family. This draws him toward her and makes him look forward to returning home.

WORK

Sometimes success is due less to ability than to zeal.
Charles Buxton, Philanthropist & Statesman

Why do you work? This may seem like a mundane question, but I believe it is highly relevant. People work for all kinds of reasons. Of course, the number one reason is that we all need to make a living. There are other reasons, however, that may co-exist. Men receive a lot of gratification from their work and their accomplishments. Their self-esteem and ego may depend on their work. If this is the case, you can see how devastating retirement can be. Work may provide a camaraderie of friends that combats loneliness and isolation. This is particularly true for single men. Work may be fun and exciting because of the challenges. Some men would rather go to work than do anything else. These men usually end up as workaholics, destroying their families and all relationships outside of work. There are some men who have earned enough money and don't need to work. They choose to work to keep busy and for some of the reasons stated above.

The bottom line is that God worked and so must we. When God created Adam, He placed him in the Garden of Eden to work:

Then the Lord God took the man and put him into the garden of Eden to cultivate it and keep it. **Genesis 2:15**

Adam was given the responsibility of governing the earth under God's sovereignty. We can conclude that work is good. We were meant to work, and work is necessary. Work obviously matters to God.

Following the fall of man and the subsequent curse that God placed on the earth, work became *"painful toil."* The norm for work would be hard, sweaty and difficult. Nothing has changed since then.

IMAGE

The advertisement for Canon cameras states, "Image is everything!" If that is true, we are all in a world of trouble. Of course, this idea fits in nicely with the "Doctrine of Materialism" that is so prevalent in our affluent society. I feel sorry for the pressure placed on teenagers now-a-days. A few years ago, I drove my youngest daughter to high school. As she walked in the front door, I couldn't help but notice the other students that were arriving. High school was never like that when I attended! The young girls all looked like models. They had the right designer jeans and all the make up. I wondered how long it took some of those girls to get ready for school in the morning. My wife always looks great when we go out, and I know what it takes.

Personally, I don't believe that image is everything – not even close! Rather, I believe, "Attitude is everything!" Several years ago, my oldest daughter had met a young man at college. My wife and I arranged to meet them downtown for dinner one night. The young man drove up in a 1984 silver Toyota Corolla. He told me his grandmother had given him the car as a gift when he went off to college three years earlier. He said that he planned to sell it because he wanted to buy a new car. I asked what was wrong with it. "Nothing," he responded. He just wanted a new car. The car only had 64,000 miles on it. His grandmother only drove it to church and to the grocery store. I told him I would be interested in buying it to have as a second car when one of ours broke down and was in the shop. He sold it to me for $800. The car ran well, but it did have a bit of rust. My wife suggested I take it to the body shop. The man there told me, "Doc, it's not worth the money to do all the body work. I suggest you just let it rust out around you!" About that same time, I took it to a service center to get an oil change. The owner of the shop, whom I knew, said to me, "You can't drive that car!" I asked, "Why not?" "What about your image? You are a doctor," he stated. I explained that I did not intend to let the car I drive define me. My life would have to speak for itself. Then I got an idea. I knew the art teacher at the high school where my children attended. I called and told him that I had this old car, and how would he like the opportunity for his art class to paint the whole car with chile peppers. I explained to him that every year I competed in the State Chili Cook Off. I wanted his students to paint my "Doc Elmo's Gastro Delights" logo on the front hood, and then to paint colorful chiles all over the rest of the car. He told me they would do it if I bought the paint. It cost me $285 for the auto paint, and the art class did a great job. The local newspaper published a picture of the art class standing by the finished product.

The car was a big hit at the chili cook off. I loved that little car so much, I drove it everywhere I went for the next three years until it started having engine trouble. So much for my image! The fact that a doctor would drive a car like that challenged a lot of people. That chili car stuck out like a sore thumb in the doctors' parking lot at the hospital, parked next to all the BMWs and Mercedes Benz's. I saw it as a way to make my anti-materialism statement. If you care to see what the "Doc Elmo's Gastro Delights" logo looks like, just go to my website at www.mckcorporation.com and click on the logo in upper right hand corner.

BALANCE

Over the past 30 years, I have noticed that patients coming into my office are overall more stressed, weary, exhausted and just plain worn out by daily living. Often, the pace at which we live our lives seems to create nothing more than a blur. Numerous activities gobble up all our time and leave us exhausted and paradoxically unfulfilled by the end of the day. As I mentioned earlier, the emphasis seems to be all on the *doing* of life, not on the *being*.

In his book *Margin*, Dr. Richard A. Swenson aptly states, "We have leisure but little rest." [1] He points out how even our weekends and vacations are occupied with so many activities that we are left exhausted by them. After a vacation, we feel like we need a vacation to recover from our vacation!

What is rest, really? Webster states that it comes from the Latin word *restare* meaning to stop, stand, rest or remain. *Restare* literally means "to stand back." Listen to the various words used to describe rest: peace, ease, refreshment, repose, sleep, inactivity, relief, tranquility, absence of motion, immobility, remaining quiet, an interval of silence. All of these sound good to me!

Unfortunately, I don't think we or our children realize how brainwashed we have become. During the nine years I was in medical school, internship, residency and finally fellowship, I spent the majority of my time studying, learning and caring for patients. My life was virtually consumed by these activities. What resulted was a state of imbalance from which it took me ten years to recover. Even when I got out into practice, I felt that every moment had to be occupied by some activity that accomplished something. Otherwise, I felt like I had wasted the time, which left me feeling guilty. When I finally realized the sad state I was in, I had to figure out how to get out of it in order to restore balance in my life. Believe me, it was not easy, and at times I still struggle with it. Fortunately, with God's guidance I have come to enjoy the *being* of life as much and usually even more than the *doing*.

To a large degree, our emphasis on work has driven this situation. When I was a child growing up in the 1950s, no one I knew worked nights or on Sundays. Now, everything seems to be open all night and on weekends, including Sundays. I know of some couples where the wife works second shift, and the husband, nights. During the day, the wife cares for the young children while the husband sleeps. When he gets up, she goes off to work while he cares for the children. He has to go off to work even before she gets home. They are like two ships simply passing in the night, never communicating. No wonder the divorce rate is so prevalent.

Why do we have to work so much? There are two reasons. First, the expectations placed upon businesses to produce and deliver have sky-rocketed compared to thirty years ago. Second, since the standard of living has increased so much over the past three decades, it now costs a lot of money to live, which usually requires both spouses to work. A significant and growing problem is personal debt. Every week I receive one or more unsolicited, pre-approved credit cards in the mail. Many individuals get caught in the "debt trap" where they have charged so much, they can't afford to even pay the monthly interest. This simply adds further stress to already overloaded and stressed-out lives.

But, the real question is, "Of what benefit is all this?" Sure we live in bigger homes with more conveniences and filled with innumerable "things," but what a price we have paid. Most people seem so busy that they can't even enjoy what they have. They find out that it not only costs a lot to purchase all those "things," but it takes a lot of time and effort to maintain them. The treadmill just keeps going faster and faster with no apparent way to get off.

I know that many people have accumulated so much stuff that their homes won't hold it all. So, they pay extra money to rent a storage facility to hold on to it. Wouldn't that stuff do a whole lot more good if it was given to poor people who could really use it?

It is worthwhile to examine why we need to rest. Obviously, when we get tired, we need to take a break and at night we need sleep. We understand the need for physical (soma) rest. But, oftentimes we fail to recognize our need for emotional (psycho) rest (rest of the soul). The many reasons that cause us to be so stressed out not only compound this need for rest, but also prevent it. I have always taught my children that relationships are the most important thing in life. First, comes their relationship with God, then with family and then with those they encounter outside the family.

I am frequently disappointed when I observe the many relational problems that people have in their families, at work and in society in general. Everyone seems to be demanding their rights and focusing on their needs with little or no thought for the needs of others. I saw a T-shirt recently that said, "It's all about me!" Not only do we recognize the problem, we seem proud of it! This attitude and the resulting turmoil rip relationships apart. The end result is that when we selfishly focus on our needs and ignore the needs of others, we become more and more lonely and separated from those around us. God has provided a better way.

PRIORITIES

The truth is that many people set rules to keep from making decisions. Not me. I don't want to be a manager or a dictator. I want to be a leader – and leadership is ongoing, adjustable, flexible, and dynamic.

Mike Krzyzewski, College Basketball Coach

Sometimes we get ourselves in trouble because we live unbalanced lives. This happens when we get our priorities all out of whack. Dr. Richard Swenson in his book, *Margin,* says that we all need "time to get much less done." He describes margin as simply breathing room and some space to enjoy what you've done.

Many people get themselves into trouble because they don't seem to understand the concept of priorities. God must come first in our life; He must be the number one priority. Our second priority is our wife and then our children. Everything else comes after that. Where does work fit into this? On average we work eight or more hours a day for at least five days a week. Our jobs are essential to provide for our family. But sometimes, we let our job take on further importance. It becomes our career, our profession. In and of itself, this isn't bad, but the danger lies in letting it take over our life to the exclusion of all else, especially our family. If you aren't sure if this has happened to you or not, just ask your wife for her opinion. Believe me, she will tell you whether you have your priorities right or not.

TIME WITH GOD

Spending time with God should be our highest priority, but it so easily gets shoved aside by the tyranny of the moment. Even in our spiritual life, we have the tendency to focus on *doing* with God rather than on *being*. I spoke about this earlier in the book, but I want to expand on this in a more personal way. We need to create times when we can just relax and *be* with God. I call these times "Holy Moments."

THE SABBATH REST & THE REST GOD INTENDS

Most Christians have no clue about what God intended when He commanded us to rest on the Sabbath. The word *Sabbath* comes from a Hebrew word meaning repose, i.e. cessation (from exertion). Scripture describes it as a holy day, and Israel was instructed to sanctify it (separate and set it apart for a purpose) as a reminder of God's divine rest on the seventh day after creation. Its observance was to serve as a sign of the perpetual covenant between Israel and God. By requiring the people to cease their work, the day became one of self-denial and dedication to God. Its purpose was to strengthen their spiritual lives. Jesus spoke of this when He stated:

The Sabbath was made for man, and not man for the Sabbath.

Mark 2:27

The Sabbath rest is seen as a foretaste of our eternal rest in heaven. Moses recorded:

And by the seventh day God completed His work which He had done; and He rested on the seventh day from all His work which He had done. Then God blessed the seventh day and sanctified it, because He rested from all His work which God had created and made.

Genesis 2:2-3

Why did God rest? I don't believe it was because He had to, or because He was exhausted and worn out from all the creating. It states in Genesis:

And God saw all that He had made, and behold, it was very good.
Genesis 1:3

Have you ever finished a big project and then taken the time to sit back to just enjoy and appreciate what you have accomplished? I think that is exactly what God did. The creation of the heavens and the earth was an incredibly important series of events to which we owe our very existence. The Sabbath rest that God commands is a time every week when we pause to remember and think about all He did in creation. In the creation, we see His profound work and the beauty of all that He made.

When I traveled through Europe, I was impressed by the fact that in every town there was a large cathedral. Even now, these cathedrals are the largest structures in the town. A tour guide once explained that during the period when these churches were built, the goal of the architects was to create a sense of awe for all who entered the cathedral. The churches were adorned with detailed sculptures in wood and stone and with marvelous stained glass windows. These sculptures and windows depicted accounts from the Bible. When the priest preached on Sunday, he would refer to one of these and tell the story and its significance. Most of the people were uneducated and illiterate. But when they returned to the church later to pray and meditate, they would look at these carvings and windows and remember what the priest had said. Some of the churches took hundreds of years to build, and remain today as a testimony to the impact that Christ has had on the world. The sense of awe within the great churches in Europe is still present. Even the great buildings we presently construct fail to hold a candle to these magnificent structures of the past.

It is this very sense of awe that I believe God intends for us to experience on the Sabbath, when we take the time to reflect on all He has done. Even the Apostle Paul wrote to the Church at Rome saying,

For since the creation of the world His invisible attributes, His eternal power and divine nature, have been clearly seen, being understood through what has been made, so that they are without excuse.   **Romans 1:20**

Paul was speaking about those who refused to believe in God and denied His very existence. We who are believers are inspired by God's attributes, power and nature when we pause to reflect on all He has done and continues to do in our lives.

It is sad that we have lost the significance of what the Sabbath is all about. All the joy of what God really intended has somehow been stripped out of the day. It should be a day when we deliberately stop to think about all He has done. This will create within us a deep appreciation for not only His creation, but also His continuing presence and attention in our lives. We don't stop because we are tired anymore than God did. At least I don't believe that is why we should stop. God commanded us to take this time and dedicate it to remembering Him and all He has done.

Even when we do come into our churches, something is wrong. Very quickly the service begins, and is carefully orchestrated to get everything in within the specified time period. Shouldn't going to church be a time where we enter into a period of not only community fellowship and worship, but also of solitude with our God with whom we have a very special personal relationship? Where is the rest He commanded? It too, has been gobbled up by the very nature of our incessant *doing*. There is no solitude, no meditation, except maybe, for a short time during communion. We must remember that He calls us to the Sabbath rest.

Out of obedience, we must submit to what He commands. After all, He knows what is best for us. I believe that if we do this, He will honor this time in our lives, and it will provide for us a wonderful communion with Him. We will begin to experience what He intends for us – a time of refreshment for our spirits, spiritual insights for our lives and an intensification of our relationship with Him. As the spiritual leaders in our homes, we must not let our families get trapped into incessant *doing*. We must help our family members experience the Sabbath for what it was really intended.

The seventh day commemorated God's resting from creation, and in the New Testament we see believers coming together on the first day of the week. This first day of the week commemorates redemption as guaranteed by Jesus' resurrection. We need to remember the words of Jesus:

Come to Me, all who are weary and heavy-laden, and I will give you rest. **Matthew 11:28**

If we examine the context in which Jesus said this, we find something most interesting. The very next two verses state:

Take My yoke upon you, and learn from Me, for I am gentle and humble in heart; and you shall find rest for your souls. For My yoke is easy, and My load is light. **Matthew 11:29-30**

This presents us with a paradox. How can putting on a yoke be easy, light, and of all things, give us rest? And how do we put this yoke on? The answer to these questions comes only from an understanding of the very nature of Jesus and what He was all about. This can best be understood through what Jesus said in the Sermon on the Mount. The third Beatitude states:

Blessed are the gentle (humble, meek), for they shall inherit the earth. **Matthew 5:5**

We mistakenly think that we will possess the earth by power, money, fame, etc. But, Jesus said quite the opposite. It is God who owns everything and He who loans it to us for a time while we are on earth. We really own nothing but are simply stewards of what He entrusts to us. Isn't it interesting that Jesus describes Himself as "gentle" and "humble." Our perception of what it means to be meek is usually that it means to be weak, which is not the meaning at all. My favorite word to substitute for meek, humble, or gentle is "malleable."

In surgery there is an instrument called a malleable. It is a piece of metal that can be bent to the shape desired by the surgeon and then placed in the wound for retraction to give the surgeon proper exposure. At any time, the surgeon can remove it and bend it into a different shape. It is stiff enough to retain whatever shape it is given.

This is how God wants us to be. He is the Potter, and we are the clay. A potter needs the clay to be neither too soft nor too hard, but just the right consistency that it can be shaped. So too, we are to be soft and pliant in the Master's hands. Therefore, the essence of being meek is to be fully yielded to God so that He can use your life as He sees fit. The understanding of the paradox is revealed in your submission. As you submit to His will for your life (the yoke), you are set free from your struggling and are free to be used by Him. In the process, we are told we will "inherit the earth." This is the rest He has called us to.

In Psalm 37, David instructs us to *"Rest (be still) in the Lord and wait patiently for Him."* Stillness is a concept foreign to present day society.

The writer of Psalm 95 calls the people to *"sing"* and *"shout"* to *"the rock of our salvation"* and to *"come before His presence with thanksgiving"* for *"the Lord is a great God."* (verses 1-3) In verses 4 and 5, the writer refers to the creation, speaking of the *"depths of the earth,"* *"peaks of the mountains,"* the *"sea"* and the *"dry land."* Then he concludes, *"Come, let us worship and bow down; let us kneel before the Lord our Maker. For He is our God."* (verses 6-7) But, he goes on to give a warning. He tells us not to *"harden our hearts."* (verse 8) He explains how the people of God had *"tested"* and *"tried"* God even though *"they had seen My work."* (verse 9) God described the people as *"a people who err in their heart, and they do not know My ways."* (verse 10) As a result, God stated, *"Therefore I swore in My anger, truly they shall not enter into My rest."* (verse 11) God was speaking of the *"resting place"* promised to Israel as their inheritance across the Jordan River spoken of in Deuteronomy 12:9. God promised to then give them rest from all their enemies. (verse 10) When it came time to cross over the river and possess the land, Joshua reminded the people:

Remember the word which Moses the servant of the Lord commanded you, saying, "The Lord your God gives you rest, and will give you this land."   **Joshua 1:13**

The writer of Hebrews quoted Psalm 95:8-11 in Chapter 3. In that chapter, he encourages us to be faithful to God and to *"hold fast our confidence and the boast of our hope firm until the end."* (verse 6) He warns us to be careful of an *"unbelieving heart"* (verse 12) *"hardened by the deceitfulness of sin."* (verse 13) It is clear that unbelief (a hardened heart) leads to disobedience if we allow ourselves to be deceived by the lure of sin. Then in Chapter 4, he speaks of *"entering His rest."* (verse 1) He tells us, *"we who have believed enter that rest."* (verse 3) In verses 4 and 5, he quotes Genesis 2:2 speaking of how God rested after the creation. Then in verses 9-11, he ties it together by stating:

There remains therefore a Sabbath rest for the people of God. For the one who has entered His rest has himself also rested from his works, as God did from His. Let us therefore be diligent to enter that rest lest anyone fall through following the same example of disobedience.

Throughout Scripture God is consistent about unbelief. Jeremiah, the prophet, speaking about the impending destruction of Jerusalem stated:

Thus says the Lord, 'Stand by the ways and see and ask for the ancient paths, where the good way is, and walk in it; and you shall find rest for your souls. But they said, "We will not walk in it."

Jeremiah 6:16

God also speaks of our eternal resting place in heaven. Isaiah spoke of this:

Then it will come about in the day that the nations will resort to the root of Jesse, who will stand as a signal for the peoples; and His resting place will be glorious. **Isaiah 11:10**

We don't have to wait until we get to heaven to begin experiencing eternal life. We can have a foretaste of it now by yielding to God and entering into His rest. Our complete surrender to the Master and our choice to put on His yoke, opens the door to our resting in Him. Those who choose to do so will live life in a way few ever appreciate. Will you choose to cease struggling and enter His rest?

TIME

We have all expressed the feeling that we just don't have enough time. I used to think that if only we had thirty hour days, it would be fantastic. Just think how much we could accomplish with the extra six hours a day. Then my wife and I flew to Hawaii on vacation.

There was a six hour time change. We left Indianapolis at 8 AM. It took us sixteen hours to reach our destination. So when we arrived at midnight Indianapolis time, it was only 6 PM in Hawaii. The sun was still shining! We stayed up until 10 PM like we normally do, which was 4 AM our time. It was at that point that I was glad that God had not made the days thirty hours long. We were both wiped out. Our bodies are not made for thirty hour days. I concluded that if we did have thirty hour days, we might get more done everyday, but we would live shorter lives. It would kill us!

The more I thought about the concept of time, I came to realize several things. First of all, although time existed when Adam and Eve lived in the Garden of Eden, it appears to me that time really didn't matter much until after the fall of man when they sinned. Before sin there really was no concept of time running out. Adam and Eve were immortal. They would have lived forever. However, everything changed when sin entered the picture. Now they were mortal and would face death – the final moment when time runs out.

God lives outside the concept of time. He created time for us. As part of His overall creation, He declared it *good.* We are the ones frustrated by time. I believe that if you have committed and fully yielded your life to God, you have all the time you will ever need. Every morning when I get up, I quote the following verse to myself and to God:

This is the day which the Lord has made; let us rejoice and be glad in it.   **Psalm 118:24**

I used to get frustrated by my inability to get as much done everyday as I thought I should. Finally, I decided to begin to give each day to God. I would often describe to God my anticipated schedule for the day, pointing out how impossible it was. Sometimes in desperation, I would ask Him to do what I came to call "the miracle of time." Yielding my day and my schedule to God totally changed everything. Let me give you just one example.

One day after making rounds at the hospital, I arrived late to my office at 9:45 AM. My office was supposed to start at 9:00 AM. I went to see the first patient. During the entire time I spent with her, all I could think about was how late I was for my second patient. How could I catch up? After seeing the first three patients, I hadn't gained any time; in fact, I had lost time spending more than the allotted time with them. I was totally beside myself. It was in that moment I made a conscious decision to stop focusing on the *doing,* the care I had to provide to each patient. Rather, I chose to focus on the *being,* the caring about each patient. Before entering the next exam room, I silently prayed, "Lord, I am sorry I got frustrated. I yield this day and my schedule totally to you. Do with it as you will. Please do your miracle of time. Amen."

As the day progressed, there was one patient that was scheduled for a fifteen minute visit that I spent almost an hour with. She needed some extra time for counseling and prayer. The fact that now I was even later would normally have really bugged me. But I was at total peace. God was in control. I knew that He had sent her that day for me to encourage and help. I continued seeing patients. It amazed me that, with the next couple of visits, the patients were doing so well their visits did not take the allotted time. Then a couple patients cancelled their appointments at the last minute. One patient never called. He just didn't show up. Somehow, almost magically, at five o'clock all the patients had been seen, and I was finished. I was amazed. By not focusing on time and my schedule, but rather on the needs of each patient, the day flew by, and I thoroughly enjoyed each visit. I finished the day with a deep sense of satisfaction.

That day was a valuable learning experience. I have had many days like it since. What I have to say to you is that God wants us to learn to enjoy the time we have each day rather than racing through our days. I believe there is a way for us to slow down time. If we will simply yield our day and our schedule to Him, He can make each day into what He wants. In the process we will enjoy each day, and we will finish each day with a sense of fulfillment and satisfaction.

My son, Christopher, worked in Chicago as the Production Department Manager for a graphic arts company that produced catalogues which were out-sourced from other companies. He was responsible for not only his department in Chicago, but 30 workers in India who did much of the page production. His department in Chicago did quality control, corrections and final proofing in preparation for printing. Here is what he had to say about a particularly difficult time.

Work was really busy. We had a deadline to produce a 1000 page catalogue each week for four weeks. As the Production Department Manager, I realized there was no way humanly possible to get these catalogues out.

I spoke with my dad who told me how he prayed what he called the "Miracle of Time" before he would go to work, especially when he knew he had a bad day coming. So, I started praying the "Miracle of Time" each day as I prepared to go to work. I was amazed at how much work we got done. Even our team of 30 in India, who usually worked very slowly and produced work of poorer quality, somehow turned in better quality work and more of it each day.

Everyday for the next three weeks, I continued to pray asking God to do His "Miracle of Time." Despite being short staffed, we stayed on track. I became convinced that God is ready to do His "Miracle of Time" if we will simply ask.

Will you yield your schedule to Him and allow Him to do the miracle of time in your life? God can change your life from always being late on your schedule, to always being on time on His.

GOOD WORKS

If you really want to do something, you'll find a way;
if you don't, you'll find an excuse.
Author Unknown

For we are His workmanship, created in Christ Jesus
for good works, which God prepared beforehand so
that we would walk in them.
Ephesians 2:10

The phrase *prepared beforehand* gives us the perspective of God's sovereign purpose and planning. God *created us in Christ Jesus,* viz He regenerated us. What is the difference between the *good works* spoken of here and our work? The *good works* are all those things that we do for others. We do them for two reasons. First, God brings about a tremendous change in us when we give our life to Him. He changes our heart so that our whole life changes. We are no longer under the bondage of self, and can begin to focus on the needs of others, not just our own. Second, as a result of all He has done for us, our grateful response is good works – the fruit that we bear.

It is my hope for each of you reading this that you will be able to merge your *good works* with your work. What do I mean by this? Everyday when we go off to work, we don't leave who we are behind at home. We are not robots, with no personalities, working on an assembly line. The transformation that God brought about within you should, in many ways be obvious to those around you. Let me give you a personal example.

After I committed my life to God, many changes occurred. I became more caring and considerate of others. My language changed, and I was less likely to swear. I was more patient and understanding. People noticed these things. Once when I entered the doctors' lounge at the hospital, the doctors who were talking suddenly ceased. They had been telling a dirty joke and knew I wouldn't appreciate it. I tell lots of jokes, but not dirty ones. When someone says to me, "I want to tell you a joke. It's not too dirty," I have gotten in the habit of saying "No, thank you." I have learned from experience that "not too dirty" means that it is too dirty for me.

Once I flew to a city in the Midwest to speak at a physicians' conference. After I gave my lecture, one of the pharmaceutical representatives was driving me back to the airport. On the way he said, "Doc, it's really too bad you have to leave so early. If you could only stay for lunch, we could go to this one amazing restaurant for lunch!" I asked, "Is the food great?" "No," he said, "They have nude waitresses!" After he said that, I purposefully paused for a moment. Then I asked, "May I ask you a question?" "Sure," he said. "What is it about me that led you to believe I would ever want to go eat at a place where there are nude waitresses?" After that, the ride to the airport was very quiet. Quite frankly, I was offended that he would assume that all men would want to do that. I wanted to make a definitive point that that was not true. Maybe I was too blunt, but I wanted to shock him a bit.

Now, I am far from perfect, and even though I have been saved and God has changed my life significantly, I still sin. Just ask my wife. My point is simply that I am very different now compared to the way I used to be.

So, who we are in Christ affects how we act when we go off to work. In this way, we merge our *good works* and our work. The two become congruent. For some reason, we seem to want to separate our personal and work life. We speak of "secular" and "sacred" aspects of our life. When we go off to work, we see it as secular. We are more likely to see our home or church as sacred. Let me ask you, "Do you think of your work as sacred?" I believe that whatever we do, there should be no distinction between the two. The Apostle Paul said,

Whether then, you eat or drink or whatever you do, do all to the glory of God.   **I Corinthians 10:31**

God wants us to see our work as a way to glorify Him. Paul wrote to the Colossians:

Whatever you do, do your work heartily, as for the Lord rather than for men; knowing that from the Lord you will receive the reward (pay) of the inheritance.   **Colossians 3:23-24**

Our work, whatever we do, is sacred and secular at the same time. There is no distinction to God. In his book, *Disciplines of a Godly Man*, R. Kent Hughes states, "You can glorify God where you are by your heart attitude." [2] Remember the story of the three stone cutters that I shared earlier? They each did the same job everyday. Only one saw his work as both secular and sacred.

Win Turner is a pharmacist and my right hand man planning and running the pharmacy on our medical mission trips. He writes this about his work experience.

Do you feel like you've been "called" to do the work you do? Like me, you may have associated that term specifically with those called to the ministry ... a pastor or priest, minister of Christian education, nun, minister of music, etc. That's the way I always looked at that term, until several years ago, when I had a conversation with my dad, a "retired" pastor (if there is such a thing!). Here is my story.

For years I struggled to move up the ladder of success as defined by contemporary society. Coming out of pharmacy school in the late 70's, I actually had an aggressive plan that targeted where I wanted to be at certain points in my life. It wasn't based on any concrete criteria. It was based only on where I thought I should be at future points along my career path. For example, I wanted to be a supervisor within 5 years, in middle management within 10 years, in upper management within 15 years ... you get the picture. I actually hit most all of those self-imposed markers along the way, although much of it had more to do with the timing of external events than it did with my own personal accomplishments. Be that as it may, as the years passed, I found myself becoming more and more cynical, stressed to the point of physical illness, and increasingly less compassionate with those patients and employees who needed it the most. Despite hitting my "success" markers, I had become miserable along the way.

A few years back, I had an epiphany - you know, one of those "ah ha!" moments. It occurred during a short conversation with my dad. I wouldn't be surprised if he doesn't even remember it. In the course of that short exchange, my dad expressed that he had been somewhat disappointed when I chose pharmacy school and had not felt the "call" to go into the ministry. However, over the years, he had come to understand that my "calling" had been to become a pharmacist. With that statement, within the context of that short conversation years ago, my life began to change.

About the same time that I had that conversation with my dad, I also became involved with medical mission teams traveling to Central America. This was the result of a back-hallway conversation at church with two doctors who had been on past trips. They invited me to go with them the following year. In a matter of a few months, not only did I start down the path of understanding that my skills, i.e. "calling," as a pharmacist could be used in a different way, but I was presented with an opportunity to act on that new understanding by putting it into practice on the mission field. Since then, my family has also become involved in medical mission work. It has become a great passion in our lives, and we have found it to be a way to use our skills to the glory of God.

You might want to take an inventory of the skills, training and experience you use each day in your work. In a new and different way, look at this as a "calling," a way to minister to those around you with compassion, fairness, forgiveness and Christian love. Not only will this offer to you a chance for a new beginning within your day-to-day work, I believe it will also open you to new and exciting ways to use your skills on the mission fields.

God wants to use you as a witness to those around you at work and wherever you go. People are watching how you behave in various situations. Your behavior in difficult times may be the reason some people will choose to come to Christ. Your life will demonstrate to them the benefits of being in a relationship with God.

Let me encourage you by my personal experience. I have found it peculiar that many of the people who criticize me in public for my beliefs are the same ones who later come to me in private with their problems, asking if I would pray for them.

I would like to encourage you to begin to see your life as God does. Ask Him to give you new eyes with which to see your life. I can assure you that you will begin to see the hand of your Father in all you do. When this happens, even work becomes exciting.

FOCUS

Everyone is necessarily the hero of his own life story.
John Barth, Writer

TRUTH (What is the focus – the essential truth of this chapter?)

My work is both sacred and secular. Through my work I provide for my family, and I demonstrate my relationship with God to all who watch me work. I will never let what I do determine who I am.

APPLICATION (What does this truth mean to me? How is it relevant in my life?)

I must balance my work and family time, keep my priorities straight, create margin in all areas of my life, and not get trapped in the demanding rut the world dictates.

ACTION (What should I do about it? How can this truth benefit my life?)

Pray: Oh God, please do your miracle of time today. Help me accomplish this day all that You set before me. I commit this day totally to You.

PART III

ESTABLISHING YOUR SPIRITUAL FOUNDATION

CHAPTER 9

CONNECTING WITH GOD

In the human species, spiritual development is the supreme law.
Alexis Carrel, *Reflection on Life*

WHO OR WHAT IS IN THE CENTER OF YOUR LIFE?

A few years ago, I read the book *Half Time,* by Bob Buford. It had a profound effect on me. I read it at the same time I was reading a number of books that dealt with men in mid-life crises. As I pointed out earlier, it is not unusual for a man to reach a point where he finds himself in crisis. He may realize he has become tremendously *successful,* but begins to question what *significance* his life has had. Buford suggests that it is reasonable to take some time to plan a strategy for the second half of life so that you will achieve the desired significance. He compares this to the half-time of a football game when a team develops its second-half strategy.

At one point in the book, there is a picture of a box with a question mark in the center. Buford explains that everyone has a box in his life, but we are only allowed to have one thing in the box at a time. Whatever is in the box is central to our life and controls it. Everything else revolves around it. If we do not consciously choose to put something in the box, then life has a way of forcing something into it for us. It is this one thing that takes precedence over everything else. Ask yourself the question, "Who or what is in my box?" Is it money, my job or my career? Is it my children, my spouse, or God? Who or what is it? Remember, only one thing can be in the box. What is in the box may change throughout your life, but at any given time, only one thing can be in the box. Who or what does your life revolve around? Be as honest with yourself as possible. If God is in the box, then your life and all of your activities will revolve around Him. What you do will have meaning and significance based upon your relationship with Him. The Apostle Paul stated:

For we are His workmanship, created in Christ Jesus for good works, which God prepared beforehand so that we would walk in them. **Ephesians 2:10**

If we are truly Christians, we need to recognize that we were created for good works. But these are not good works that we do on our own. The good works that God speaks of are those that come subsequent to our total submission to Him, allowing His Holy Spirit to work through us and accomplish all that He desires with our lives.

WHAT ARE YOU ALL ABOUT?

In this section, I will ask you to consider what you are all about. To do this, please refer to the following figure as I attempt to help you answer this question. I developed this figure for personal evaluation and to help those going through a mid-life crisis. I have come to believe that it is helpful to anyone who wants to honestly evaluate where he is in life and gain some insights that will help him go forward.

The large circle represents who you are. Inside the circle are various ovals, two rectangles and a bold box. I will begin by defining what I call your Power Base. Generally speaking, your Power Base is the result of your education and the investment of time and resources that led to your career. That career now provides for your financial well-being. Your Power Base is who you are known as and belongs in the large central bold oval. If you can't figure out what belongs there, ask your children how they answer when one of their friends at school asks them what their dad does. In my family, I am known as a doctor and my wife as a nurse. Those careers are what our time and financial resources were invested in.

Why is it important to know what your Power Base is? You won't believe how many men, in the midst of a mid-life crisis, decide to venture into another career that they have no business being in. They desert their Power Base, and when they do, it usually leads to disastrous consequences. My rule is that you should never, under any circumstances, desert your Power Base, unless you have spent the time, money and effort to develop another one. Unfortunately, many men don't do that. They just venture out, assuming that all will go well.

For example, my power base is being a physician. I mentioned previously that I like to cook as a hobby. Let's say I came to you

"Shoot for the Moon"

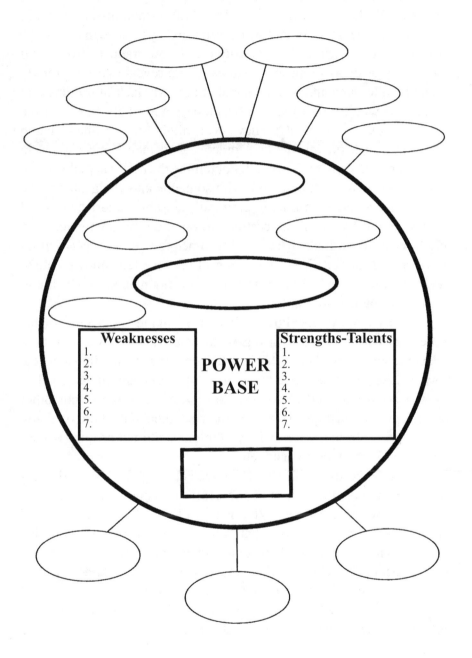

Weaknesses
1.
2.
3.
4.
5.
6.
7.

POWER BASE

Strengths-Talents
1.
2.
3.
4.
5.
6.
7.

and told you that I intended to give up my medical practice and open up a restaurant. Hopefully, you would ask me some very pointed questions like the following: Do you have any experience running a restaurant? Do you realize that 85% of all restaurants close within two years of opening? What formal training do you have in restaurant management? What culinary institute did you graduate from? Of course, my answers to these questions would reveal that I am totally unqualified to open and operate a restaurant. My lack of training and experience would mean that the business would likely fail from the start and cost me a lot of money. You might suggest that I begin by cutting back on my medical practice and take some classes in restaurant management. Then, after obtaining the necessary education, you might encourage me to work with someone knowledgeable in the business for a period of time to gain indispensable experience. If all went well and I was still determined to open up my own place, you might recommend that I partner with someone who had successfully operated a restaurant. Your wise counsel has, in effect, allowed me to develop a second power base from which I might actually be able to open a profitable restaurant.

Directly above the Power Base is a smaller bold oval. This represents who you are with regard to your family. You may be a husband, son or brother. The fact that the oval is smaller than the Power Base oval does not mean it is of lesser significance. The other ovals beside and above the Power Base represent your other significant relationships. If you are married, then in the bold oval you write "wife." In the other ovals you might write father, son (if your parents are living), best friend, etc.

At the bottom of the circle, in the center, is the box. Whoever or whatever is in the box is at the center of your life. Remember that only one thing can be in the box at a time. Everything in your life revolves around who or what is in the box. I went through this exercise with my youngest daughter when she was in high school. When I asked her who or what was in her box, she stated, "Dad, I know you would like me to say that God is in my box. Someday, I believe that He will be. But, right now my friends and school are in my box." That is about as candid as you can get. It helped me as a father to know how to pray for her.

The two rectangles on either side of the words POWER BASE are your strengths and weaknesses. I encourage you to first list what you believe your strengths and weaknesses are. Then, go to your best friend, someone close to you whom you can't fool, and ask him or her to identify your strengths and weaknesses, without showing that person what you have come up with. Lastly, if you are married, go to your wife and have her do the same. Then, show your wife what you, your best friend, and she listed. Now, have your wife help you finalize the list for each. This step is important because we don't always know ourselves as well as we think.

I remember doing an exit interview with a gentleman who had been with our organization for a few years. He had accepted a new position elsewhere. He was very competent in many aspects of his job, but he lacked some financial skills. I helped him identify his strengths and weaknesses and encouraged him in his new position to do lots of the things on the list of his strengths. But I also warned him to take an honest look at his weaknesses and try not to do those things. I encouraged him to find a good accountant who could help him in the areas where he was weak.

My good friend, Lyndon, did this exercise with his wife. What he had listed as his number one strength, his wife had listed as his number one weakness! How could this be? Actually, this is not unusual. Our greatest strength is oftentimes our greatest weakness. For example, if a doctor has compassion as his greatest strength, he will be very effective at meeting the many needs of his patients. However, his compassion may lead him to spend too much time with each patient, such that he becomes very inefficient. This could cause him to run continually late with his appointments and his business to suffer economically.

One young man I worked with asked his girlfriend to help him with this process of identifying his strengths and weaknesses. Many of her comments were very enlightening. She pointed out that he was extremely loyal, but the loyalty sometimes kept him in relationships that were not entirely healthy. His quick wit and cleverness were remarkable, but at times could be biting and hurtful. His strong opinions and firm stance about what he believed sometimes prevented him from seeing another person's perspective and made him judgmental. His caring nature for family and friends sometimes came across as knowing better what was best for them. She noted that he was extremely intelligent, which caused him to seldom doubt his capabilities, and sometimes that got him into trouble. She closed by pointing out that he had taken a risk by putting himself in the vulnerable position of asking her to judge his strengths and weaknesses, and she wondered if he would reject what he asked for by becoming defensive and angry. He appreciated her frank honesty which helped him in his personal growth and development.

Below the circle are additional ovals that represent other significant relationships in your life. For instance, one might be your relationship to your church. Take some time to identify these significant relationships. Add additional ovals, if necessary.

Also, notice that there are several ovals outside the circle at the top. These are for you to perform an exercise I call "Shoot for the Moon." In this exercise, I ask you to assume that you have sufficient financial resources and adequate time to do whatever you want. So, what would you like to do? List all the things in life you would like to do if you had all the money you needed and plenty of time. You can add additional ovals if you need to. Why is this exercise so important? I find that a lot of people would like to do a number of things in life, but they mistakenly make the assumption that these would not be possible. Taking the time to list them helps people articulate and recognize what they might like to do. Second, it is likely that doing all of the things is impossible, but many people can pick one or two things and plan to do them over a year or two. Some things on my list I may never do, but many of the others I will, even if I can't accomplish them for several years or until I retire.

An additional benefit of the "Shoot for the Moon" exercise for spouses is that it helps them plan constructively for the future. When my wife and I first did the exercise, we concluded that, if we both pursued the things on our respective lists, after a few years our lives would be miles apart. Of course, we did not want this to happen. We evaluated our lists and found a few things that were common to both. Then we made a conscious effort to focus on these items so that our lives would grow together and not apart. This does not mean she won't do any of the other things on her list. She may do some of these independently or I may choose to do some of them with her. The same is true for my list. Every few years, we repeat this exercise and make sure we are staying on track. Remember, you are not the same person you were five or ten years ago, and neither is your wife. We all change throughout our life. Some things that were important to us ten years ago are not so important now.

PRIORITIES

Now we come to a very important aspect of who we are. This is the issue of priorities. Over the years in my medical practice, I have had a number of medical students rotate through my Gastroenterology and Nutrition Senior Elective. Many of them were already married and others were preparing to marry. I have always taken some time during the elective to help them focus on their priorities. I begin by having them list how they spend their time by writing down all the things they do. Then I ask the students to list these activities in order of what they think is most important. I use the analogy of a triangular building. Each floor rests on the one below. Each floor gets smaller as one moves up to the top. The smaller the floor, the less important it is, relative to the ones below.

When the student has done this, I ask him or her to then list how the floors of the building are really arranged in their life. Usually, how the floors are arranged and how they want them to be arranged are not quite the same. We then talk about how the floors can be rearranged to set the priorities in the proper order. We all have the tendency to gradually drift away from how we want the floors to be arranged. The floors, our priorities, subtly change. That is why it is so necessary to reassess what is really going on in life at regular intervals. If we can do this in a disciplined fashion, it helps us to maintain balance in life.

Once, when I was working with one of the medical students, he first listed all the things that he did every day. Then, he listed those things he did one or more times a week. Finally, he listed those things that he did maybe once or twice a month or even less frequently. Next, he set those lists aside and made out a list of what he believed his priorities to be. He listed God as his number one priority, his wife as number two, his children as number three, and so forth. After he had completed his priority list, I asked him to compare all the activities he had listed with his priorities. He was shocked to realize that, although he had listed God as his number one priority, God did not show up on his list of activities. He had not listed prayer, Bible reading, meditation, attending church or Sunday School, or any activity in any way related to God. Until I had directed him to do this exercise, he had not realized that he gave God, his number one priority, no time at all in his life! He made a conscious decision to change this. We talked about the various ways he could do this, and he was very grateful.

Now it's time for you to do the same thing this medical student did. Complete your priority list, ranking the most important item as number one. Add the other items below in decreasing order of importance. Sometimes it is easier to write down all the things in life that are important to you on a separate piece of paper, and then rank them with regard to their importance.

My Priority List
1.
2.
3.
4.
5.
6.
7.
8.
9.
10.
11.
12.

Next, complete the following table, listing all the things you do as indicated by the column headings.

Things I Do Every Day	Things I Do Weekly or Monthly	Things I Do Occasionally Throughout the Year
1.	1.	1.
2.	2.	2.
3.	3.	3.
4.	4.	4.
5.	5.	5.
6.	6.	6.
7.	7.	7.
8.	8.	8.
9.	9.	9.
10.	10.	10.
11.	11.	11.
12.	12.	12.

Finally, compare all the things you do with your priority list. Ask yourself the all-important question, "How do my priorities compare with how I spend my time?" Are you living your life consistent with what you believe is important? If you aren't, what changes do you need to make to align your priorities and your activities?

If you are married, I suggest you have your wife complete this exercise, as well. Then look at each other's priorities and activities. You may be surprised how much you might learn about each other.

MEDITATING ON GOD'S WORD

What is meditation? Webster defines the word "meditate" as: 1) to think about; contemplate, 2) to plan, intend, purpose; to think deeply and continuously; reflect; ponder; muse. Meditation is defined as "deep, continued thought; reflection." An excellent word picture for meditation is how a cow chews its cud. The cow eats and fills up its stomach, and then, repeatedly, regurgitates it to chew on the food. This is how we are to meditate on Scripture.

Communion with God isn't something you institute. Don't try too hard. It's like sleep. You can't make yourself go to sleep. But you can create the right conditions that allow sleep to happen. We need to create the right conditions for meditation. Open your Bible. Read it slowly, focusing on each word. Listen to it. Reflect on it. If the Bible speaks of a particular person, imagine yourself in that person's place. Become that person.

It is important for us to set aside all tendencies toward arrogance and, with humble hearts, receive the Word addressed to us. Just as you don't analyze the words of someone you love, but accept them as they are said to you, you need to accept the Word of Scripture and ponder it in your heart. For example, we cannot read the story of Abraham when he is about to sacrifice his son and simply say we are glad we are not in his shoes. We *are* in his shoes! We struggle with the decision to sacrifice the one thing most precious to us. We are brought to the place in which we must give over to God our most cherished possession. Like Abraham, we come down from the mountain with the meaning of the words *my* and *mine* forever changed.

When reading Scripture, you will need to resist the temptation to skim over many passages. Our rushing reflects our internal state, and our internal state is what needs to be transformed. My sister, Linda, is a very talented writer and writes a weekly column called "The Nature of Grace," for the *Anderson Herald Bulletin*. She wrote one column entitled "Transformed," after the Scripture in Romans 12:2, which states, *". . . be transformed by the renewing of your mind."* She stated, "Sometimes I'll be 'reading,' but not really paying attention, lost in thought about this aggravation or that which I can't escape worrying over, and all of a sudden I'll have this awareness that I've just read over something that is tugging for my attention. I'll backtrack to really read the passage and my yellow highlighter will go into motion. In spite of the fact that my reading comprehension is suffering, the Holy Spirit taps me on the shoulder and says, 'Listen up! This is for you, right this very moment.'"

There is also what is referred to as *kenotic meditation.* This type of meditation comes from the Greek word *kenon,* which means to empty, or the Greek word *kenosis*, which means an emptying. An example of this emptying is when Jesus emptied Himself of His glory to take the form of a man (described in Philippians 2:5–7). Therefore, kenotic meditation is an emptying of the mind in order to pray effectively.

Many have asked, "How do you meditate?" I usually recommend the following. Begin by sitting in a comfortable chair, in what I call a neutral position. Your feet should be flat on the floor. You should be sitting upright, but comfortably so, and your arms should be resting on your thighs or on armrests. Your hands should not be touching and your legs should not be crossed. Once you have achieved a comfortable position, close your eyes and focus your attention on your breathing. Just sense yourself breathing in and breathing out. After you have done this for a few breaths, take in a deep cleansing breath and then slowly exhale. Continue to observe your breathing. Next, focus your attention on your head. Notice if there is any area of tension there. Do you have a headache, or is there tension above or behind your eyes, in your eyelids or temples, or at the base of your skull? As you recognize these areas of tension and as you continue to breathe, watch this tension, with each breath out, begin to dissipate and flow down into your body below.

Move your focus to your neck. Is there tenseness in the muscles of your neck? See it begin to flow down. With your eyes still closed and breathing slowly in and out, progressively move from one area of your body to another. It is helpful to take a cleansing breath and, as you exhale, see the finality of the tension flow from one part of your body to the part below. Move to your chest and sense the air moving in and out of your lungs. Visualize the blood being pumped from your heart to your body, and begin to recognize any tension that exists in those areas. See it drain down into your abdomen. Next, turn your attention to your arms, since some of the tension from your head and neck may have flowed into your arms. Sense your arms as being totally relaxed, almost floating, and see the muscular tension dissipate and flow out of your body through your finger tips. Now, turn your attention to your abdomen. Sense any tension or discomfort that exists, and see it begin to move down into your legs. Lastly, appreciate any tension that exists in your legs and see it flow down and out through your toes.

Usually, when I take people through this exercise for the first time, they tell me they feel more relaxed in just a few minutes than they have ever felt in their life. It is helpful when you are meditating to be in an area that is quiet and free of distractions, although it is not absolutely essential. It is not uncommon when you meditate for thoughts to come into your mind about the day's activities or problems. I encourage meditators not to be too hard on themselves in their inability to shut these thoughts out. Rather, appreciate and recognize the thoughts. Don't become frustrated by their presence. Simply acknowledge them as you continue to meditate and see them flow in and then out of your mind. Remain relaxed and return to your focus.

If you have just completed this exercise, you will have evoked the relaxation response and, with it, a concomitant change in your physiology. Your heart rate will have slowed, blood pressure dropped, respiratory rate slowed, bodily tension decreased, basal metabolic rate decreased, and the slow-wave activity of your brain increased. Participants in my class, "Achieving Your Spiritual Potential," have told me that, when they have evoked the relaxation response through this method, it has helped them cope with their daily stress. One gentleman told me that, during his lunch hour, he would sit in his car and meditate for just 5 or 10 minutes. He stated that it had a profound effect on the rest of his day. He found his overall approach to problems that occurred later in the day was much more calm and controlled.

There are, however, forms of meditation that I find dangerous. I do not encourage people to empty their minds and then open them up to anything and everything. This is a recipe for real trouble. The term "channeling" has been especially prominent in New Age circles. The question I have is, "What is being channeled?" From which source of power are they receiving information? Is it from the Kingdom of Light or from the Kingdom of Darkness? I believe channeling often results in demonic oppression and the adverse consequences commonly seen as a result. God speaks to us about the importance of active meditation (on His Word or Him) versus passive meditation. Passive meditation opens the mind to demonic forces. In contrast, active meditation opens the mind to the Spirit of God.

In 1995, an article appeared in the *New York Times* entitled "Brain May Tag All Perceptions With a Value." [1] It was written by a New York University psychologist, Dr. Jonathan Bargh. Dr. Bargh pointed out that we assign emotional values to everything we perceive. These emotional values are judgments that we assign to events. They happen in a fraction of a second. We trust these first impressions, and we are usually unaware that we are biased by them. Because of these emotional value judgments, he has concluded that none of us have the ability to be truly objective, because everything we think about arises from within our mind where emotional values have been assigned. Hence, they are all subjective.

With the use of the PET (positron-emission tomography) scanner, it is possible to demonstrate areas of increased neural activity in the brain due to increased blood flow. These areas are called neurosignatures. The scan detects an image relating to this heightened neural activity. Each of our activities and every emotion we experience has its own neurosignature. The more we participate in a given activity, the more prominent the neurosignature becomes. For example, if I am taking tennis lessons and I am learning to hit a forehand, the area in the brain involved with this activity will light up on the PET scan. The more I practice the forehand, the more developed the neurosignature becomes, and the more pronounced its visibility on the PET scan. Similarly, if I sit in a chair, close my eyes and visualize performing the activity of hitting a forehand, the same neural activity, i.e., neurosignature, lights up and is evident on the PET scan. The same is true if I dream about the activity.

From a genetic standpoint, the brain has what is called "hard-wiring." There are a number of ways in which we are hard-wired. Our innate will to live is a hard-wired response originating within our brain. So are many of our biologic functions, such as the beating of the heart, spontaneous breathing, the function of the immune system and many others. The fight-or-flight response is also a hard-wired activity. But our brain also possesses the ability to change. This ability is called *plasticity* or *neuroplasticity*. Neurosignatures are made up of both hard-wiring and the various changes that occur as a result of adaptations. Scientists recognize that we function in both "bottom up" and "top down" ways. Let me explain.

An example of "bottom up" restructuring is when you touch your hand to a hot stove and immediately pull it back because of the pain. From that point on, the experience, which created a neurosignature in your brain, prevents you from touching a hot stove again. This protects you from further injury. An example of "top down" restructuring is when you use your thoughts to change the way your brain functions. The experience Dan Jansen had in competing in the 1000 meter speed skating event during the Olympics is an example. Dan never saw himself as a long-distance speed skater and had a mental block concerning the distance and the event. His coach had him write at the top of his training schedule each day, "I love the 1000 meter event." When it came time for the Olympics, Dan Jansen not only won the 1000 meter event, but set a new Olympic record. What his coach had done was to create, through "top down" restructuring, a new neurosignature, which caused a change in his physiologic and physical performance.

Belief systems are excellent examples of "top down" or thought-induced brain restructuring. Our belief systems are very powerful in filtering the information that we receive. Although our minds react in certain ways based upon our neurosignatures, the good news is that we can rewire and change our reactions. This is a process called *cognitive restructuring*. Every time you develop a new awareness or understanding based upon some new experience or information, the neurosignatures within the brain change. Because of this, we actually change. Visualize yourself, as you experience and learn new things, changing the configuration of your neurosignatures. This cognitive restructuring has a definite impact on how you will respond to events in the future.

Once a woman confronted her husband with the analogy about the love bank. She gave him instructions about the necessity of doing nice things for her so that he would not continue to deplete his account in her love bank. What she was saying was that she desperately needed some cognitive restructuring regarding their relationship. If he would simply respond to her with acts of love and kindness, it would reconfigure her neurosignatures, which would determine her outlook and behavior toward him.

Meditating on God's Word changes us by the process of cognitive restructuring, but with the added advantage of being under the Holy Spirit's guidance and direction.

CONNECTING TO GOD THROUGH MEDITATION

Active meditation is a way we can draw closer to God and connect with Him. If you wish to have spiritual power from God

190

in your life, you need to continually ask for the Holy Spirit to fill you, literally, to permeate your entire being. I like to use the example of an electric cord. The diameter of a cord usually determines the amount of electrical current that can be carried. I ask people if they see themselves connected to God by way of that small cord that plugs into an AC/DC adapter connected to a CD player, or if they would prefer to have a larger cord, such as the one used to run several power tools simultaneously, and which carries considerably more current? I want the huge cord with the giant plug seen on construction sites that, when plugged in, conducts so much current that it has to be bolted to a wall to protect individuals from getting electrocuted!

So how do you increase the size of your cord so that you can be infused with a greater amount of God's power through the Holy Spirit? One way is through active meditation. Active meditation involves repeating a word, phrase or prayer over and over. I ask participants to meditate and invoke the relaxation response. Once they have done so, I ask them to focus on a particular phrase or prayer that they know. Some have chosen the beginning of the Lord's Prayer, *"Our Father who art in heaven."* Others have gone to the Psalms and used the beginning of the 23rd Psalm, *"The Lord is my Shepherd."* Others have turned to music and have even sung, *"Our God is an awesome God."* The choices are endless, but the word or phrase should be one that is particularly significant to you. Sometimes it is helpful to choose a phrase from a verse of Scripture that emphasizes a point previously unfamiliar to you. In this way, through meditation, the phrase becomes deeply embedded within your brain, forming its own neurosignature. It becomes a permanent part of your understanding.

After you have evoked the relaxation response, you begin to repeat your phrase over and over and over. After you have done this for several minutes, it is helpful to sit and relax. Ask God what He would like to teach you regarding the phrase. Then listen to what God has to say. I have gained tremendous insights through this type of meditation. If you have a particular problem with forgiveness, for example, you might choose a phrase that speaks about forgiveness. Many who have done this have found, after meditating, greater freedom in their ability to forgive. By choosing phrases that exalt God, meditation can also be used as an excellent form of worship. In so doing, we invite God's presence into our lives. The Scripture states, *"God inhabits the praises of His people."* Therefore, another way of connecting to God is through what I call praise or worship meditation.

I previously mentioned how, suddenly and quite unexpectedly, I became the chief executive officer and president of our medical corporation. The corporation had done very well for a number of years, but was starting to feel the pressure of all the changes occurring in the health care industry. The changes demanded that we make a number of adjustments in the way we conducted our business to ensure that we would be able to provide the medical services that our patients needed. Although I had never received any formal training in accounting, finance or human resources, I suddenly found myself in the position of responsibility for all of these functions and more. The administrative staff all looked to me for guidance and direction.

To complicate matters, despite assuming this new responsibility, I also continued to practice almost full time. To say that the next six months were stressful would be a major understatement. I often awoke during the night in a cold sweat worried about one problem or another. Many nights I slept very little. I usually got out of bed very early in the morning to begin my day. After a few weeks, I wondered if God was awakening me so I could pray and begin to turn these problems over to Him. It was at this point that I developed a very powerful form of meditation that I call Visual Prayer.

When I awoke at night consumed by fears, I would begin to visualize myself standing on one side of a small brook. On the other side of the brook was a small mountain, and at the base of the mountain was a flat grassy area. As I looked at the mountain, I saw a man dressed in a white gown slowly coming down the side of the mountain. Inherently, I knew the figure was Jesus. He walked down from the mountain and stood on the other side of the brook. He motioned for me to come across the brook. There was very little water in the brook, and it was easy for me to step across on the rocks. I knelt down reverently at His feet, and He said, "Tell me about your problems." I began to explain all of the issues with which I was confronted. Then, Jesus took out a large round wicker basket that looked like a pointed Chinese straw hat, which He held upside down. He said to me, "I want you to tell Me again about all the problems, placing each, one by one, in the basket." The Bible tells us to cast

all of your anxiety on Him, because He cares for you.

I Peter 5:7

192

I did as He instructed. I took each care and put it in the basket. As I did, after a period of time, I found that I drifted off to sleep and slept well the rest of the night. Turning my problems over to God, through visual prayer, put me in contact with the Prince of Peace. He gave me *"the peace that surpasses all human understanding,"* which allowed me to sleep well. This happened night after night, month after month, and I came to depend upon it for my strength. As I continued this nightly visual prayer, I saw a dramatic turnaround in our corporate business environment. Problems were solved. As I prayed, God sent the necessary people to our organization to help us with our problems. Eventually, God sent a replacement for me, one more qualified than I was with the CEO functions, and under his direction our corporation eventually accomplished the goals I had envisioned.

One evening, when I was teaching my class "Achieving Your Spiritual Potential," I led the group in the visual prayer meditation. Those present began to turn their problems over to God. At one point, I opened my eyes and was amazed to see more than half of the class weeping! Tears were coming down their cheeks. It was at this point I realized the tremendous power of this form of meditation.

I've mentioned the importance of being non-judgmental during meditation. It is important not to have unreal expectations, particularly when you begin to use meditation in your life. Often, people seek incredible spiritual experiences or revelations from God. I try to explain that, although at times these may occur, meditation should be seen as important to their physical, emotional, and spiritual well-being and as a way to connect to God. They should leave the rest to God. I was deeply affected by a sermon that my Senior Pastor, Gary Johnson, preached some time ago entitled "God Is Not In A Hurry." Too often, we are in a hurry to hear the voice of God. We need to pause in order to hear Him and to receive from Him His plans and His power. As we pause, we need to pray. My prescription for everyone is to take ten minutes out of each day and listen to God. Don't speak, just listen.

I have used various forms of meditation with patients in my medical practice and have seen dramatic results. As I observed personally, it has eliminated insomnia, dissipated fears and resulted in significant changes in their overall outlook. Whatever your problems, concerns or worries, these forms of meditation should be very beneficial.

SANCTIFYING THE IMAGINATION

The simplest and most basic way to meditate upon Scripture is by using our imagination. We desire to see, hear and touch the biblical narrative. In this simple way, we begin to enter the story and make it our own. We move from detached observation to active participation. Jesus taught in this manner, making constant appeals to peoples' imagination in His parables. Our imagination helps to anchor our thoughts and center our attention. Francis de Sales noted that "by means of the imagination we confine our mind within the mystery on which we meditate."

Using the imagination also brings the emotions into the equation, so that we come to God with both mind and heart. It is vitally important to understand the Scripture intellectually, but if we have not felt it emotionally, we have not fully understood it. In Christian meditation, we seek to live the experience of Scripture. With our imagination, we can apply all our senses. We smell the sea, hear the water as it laps on the shore, see the crowd and feel the hunger pains in our stomachs, as well as the hot sun upon our heads. We touch the hem of His garment. The wonderful thing about these experiences is that we quite forget about ourselves.

A major difference between Christian, Eastern or secular meditation is that Jesus confronts us and asks us to choose. We are asked to obey the Word. It is this ethical call to obedience that is the key difference. There is no loss of identity, no merging with the cosmic consciousness, no fanciful astral travel. Rather, we are called to life-transforming obedience because we have encountered the living God. Christ is truly present among us to heal, to forgive, to change and to empower us.

May God grant us the ability to speak from our hearts in the words of the Psalmist from Psalm 119:

Oh, how I love your law! It is my meditation all day long ... How sweet are your words to my taste, sweeter than honey to my mouth!
Psalms 119:97 and 103

FOCUS

TRUTH (What is the focus – the essential truth of this chapter?)
Jesus must be in the box – the very center of my life around which everything revolves.

APPLICATION (What does this truth mean to me? How is it relevant in my life?)

I need to connect to God by meditating on His Word.

ACTION (What should I do about it? How can this truth benefit my life?)

Pray: Dear Jesus, do whatever is necessary to be certain I keep You at the very center of my life.

CHAPTER 10

THE WORK OF THE HOLY SPIRIT IN YOUR LIFE

In the human species, spiritual development is the supreme law.
Alexis Carrel (*Reflection on Life*, pg. 127)

"Who is the Holy Spirit?" and "How does He work in your life?" Several years ago I was reading through the book of Ephesians, when I came to the following verse:

Now unto Him who is able to do far more abundantly beyond all that we ask or think, according to the power that works within us.

Ephesians 3:20

When I read this, I thought there was a misprint. Where it said, *"according to the power that works within us,"* I thought it should have said, "according to the power that works within God." But the more I studied and looked at some other translations of the Bible, the more I came to realize that it was, indeed, correct. God was saying that He is able to do exceedingly abundant things, according to a power that He has placed *within us*. This power is the Holy Spirit. Once I realized this, it became clear to me that the secret to achieving my spiritual potential was learning how to unleash the power of the Holy Spirit in my life.

Subsequently, my pastor, Gary Johnson, gave a series of sermons on the functions of the Holy Spirit. [1] Each of them started with the letter P. He spoke of the Holy Spirit with regard to His Person, Presence, Purpose, Pursuit, Power, Persuasion, Prompting and Prayer. As he preached, I took copious notes and even purchased the tapes of the sermon series, which I studied over and over. I went to the Scripture, reading and re-reading the verses until I was convinced that I completely understood the points he had made. From this, I learned that it is essential to understand how the Holy Spirit desires to work in our lives.

In 1997, a young man named Lyndon Rivera went with me on a medical mission trip to Guatemala. Lyndon was born and raised in Guatemala, and his family moved to the USA when he was 14 years

197

old. He had never been back to his home country. While on the trip, he surrendered his life to Jesus and became a Christian. Some time later, I sensed that he wanted to go deeper with God. I asked him about this, and he said that he wanted to but didn't know how. We began to meet. He told me that he wanted to be a better husband, a better father and a better employee at work. Over the next 3 months, I taught him about the Holy Spirit and showed him how to connect to Him.

Sometime later, I asked him how things were going in his life. He told me that his marriage had never been better, that he enjoyed being a father more than ever and that he had just received an award with a big bonus for employee of the year at work. Then I asked, "Lyndon, did I ever instruct you on how to be a better husband, father or worker?" He replied, "No, you didn't." Next, I asked, "Then how did this happen?" He knew immediately it was the result of the work of the Holy Spirit as he had yielded control of his life daily to Him. That's what this chapter is all about. I am going to tell you exactly what I told Lyndon, and you will see the same results in your life if you yield to the Holy Spirit.

The Holy Spirit's operation in your life is key to developing intimacy with God. Intimacy is drawing near to God. In James, there appears this verse:

Draw near to God and He will draw near to you.

James 4:8

There are many examples of people in the Bible who were intimate with God. The story of the prodigal son shows a father who waits in earnest for the return of his son. Finally, one day, he sees his son coming and anxiously runs to embrace him despite all that his son has done. In this story, the father represents God, our heavenly Father. This is the only example in all of Scripture where God is seen running to mankind. Another example of intimacy is described in Genesis when God is walking in the garden with Adam. It is clear from the creation account that God wants to have a close relationship with us. There are many passages in the Bible that indicate and affirm God's desire to converse with us. In Jeremiah, we read:

Call to Me and I will answer you, and I will tell you great and mighty things, which you do not know. **Jeremiah 33:3**

We also know that God wants to bear our burdens. I mentioned in the last chapter how I entrusted my burdens to God through Visual Prayer.

Some men seem to think they should only go to God with the big things. For some reason, they think they shouldn't bother Him for trivial concerns. But God wants just the opposite. He wants to hear about and be involved with all the small stuff. He is that concerned, literally, with every moment of your life.

The Lord is near to the broken hearted and saves those who are crushed (contrite) *in spirit.*   **Psalm 34:18**

The bottom line is that God wants to spend time with you. If you commit to times of solitude, you can have intimacy with Him. But it does not stop there. This intimacy can be a continual moment-by-moment experience in which you are connected to and sense God's presence. With God's presence in your life, you will have an incredible arsenal and the power to overcome and deal with all the issues of life.

WHO IS THE HOLY SPIRIT? HOW IS HE OPERATIVE IN YOUR LIFE?

In order to connect with the Holy Spirit, it is absolutely essential to know who He is and what He does. Scripture makes it clear that the Holy Spirit is God. He is all-powerful (omnipotent), all-knowing (omniscient), present everywhere (omnipresent) and immortal.

In Acts 5:3–5, we read that, after Ananias lied to the Holy Spirit, the Apostle Peter said to him, *"You have not lied to men, but to God."* Also, when Jesus gave the Great Commission in Matthew 28:19, the Holy Spirit is listed equally with God, the Father and with Jesus. These verses speak of God's omnipresence.

Where can I go from thy Spirit? Or where can I flee from your presence?   **Psalm 139:7**

There are many other examples of God's omnipotence in Scripture. Perhaps the greatest example is given in Romans 8:11, which states that Jesus was raised from the dead by the power of the Holy Spirit. In fact, the many miracles that Jesus performed were due to the power of the Holy Spirit within Him. Jesus received the Holy

Spirit when He was baptized by John the Baptist just before beginning His ministry.

You know of Jesus of Nazareth, how God anointed Him with the Holy Spirit and with power ...   **Acts 10:38**

The Scripture also speaks of God's omniscience. Paul's first letter to the Church at Corinth states:

... the Spirit searches all things, even the depths of God.
1 Corinthians 2:10–11

Finally, we know that the Holy Spirit is immortal. Hebrews 9:14 says that the blood of Christ was offered by Jesus *through the eternal Spirit.* Just like God, the Father and Jesus, the Son, the Holy Spirit always was and always will be.

EIGHT STEPS TO UNDERSTANDING AND CONNECTING WITH

THE HOLY SPIRIT

To connect with the Holy Spirit, it is vital to understand the various aspects of the Holy Spirit and how He operates in your life. Each of the eight steps described below challenges you to connect with the Holy Spirit. This chapter contains a lot of information about the Holy Spirit and how He is available to transform your life. I suggest you take each step and focus on it for one week. Then move on and add the next one. At the end of the eight weeks, I guarantee you won't believe the difference in your life.

Earlier in the chapter I mentioned my good friend, Lyndon. Here is his personal account of how he connected to the Holy Spirit.

On October 10, 1996 my wife gave birth to our first child, a daughter. As expected, our daughter, Paloma, brought many changes to our lives. The most dramatic change came through a promise that I had made to my wife Mistie, many years earlier. Mistie reminded me soon after Paloma's birth that I had promised to bring our children up in a church.

Through a series of what many would consider coincidences, we visited a church just a few miles from our home that had a ministry established in my home country of Guatemala. Through a series of

200

additional "coincidences," I met Dr. Mike Elmore, who was in charge of the mission trips to Guatemala. In short, I went to Guatemala and accepted Jesus Christ as my Lord and Savior on my first mission trip, only 4 months after Paloma's birth.

So I was going to be able to keep my promise and not be miserable, after all. I could live my life Monday through Saturday and take a few hours on Sunday for church - promise kept! This is not to say that my acceptance of Jesus into my life was not legitimate. I just thought that the extent of my relationship with Jesus and God was going to be Sunday mornings and an occasional prayer throughout the week as required by my personal needs.

Four years later, I saw my life the same as it had been prior to my trip to Guatemala in 1997. We still attended church every Sunday, and I still paid my taxes and drove the speed limit. In my heart, however, I felt the same, if not worse, than before. Surely, God intended more than this for my life and the lives of all who claim Jesus as their Lord and Savior. It seemed ridiculous that Jesus would die on the cross for the sins of mankind, and through this we would find forgiveness in God, but then we just go on living our lives like before. After all, why would we call ourselves followers of Jesus and not go through a drastic life transformation? I was the same guy as before, with the exception of attending church on Sunday mornings.

I shared my frustration with Mike over breakfast one October morning in 2000. I told Mike that I wanted to be a better husband, a better father (now of two), a better son and so on. Mike's challenge to me was that I begin to pray for the Holy Spirit to fill me and control me. I had a few problems with that advice. First, I just wanted some sort of formula that I could work on for a few days or weeks and voila! Second, I had a problem with praying to the Holy Spirit. It sounded like something for the fanatics. Besides, I remembered that I had read somewhere that God is a jealous God, and I did not want to offend Him.

I drove to work that morning puzzled, not sure of what to think of my mentor's advice. That night, however, I spoke with God and explained to Him that I wanted to do something to be closer to Him. In advance, I asked God to forgive me if I was entering into something that I shouldn't by praying to the Holy Spirit. I had read enough in the Bible to know that God is manifested in three persons: God, the Father, God, the Son and God, the Holy Spirit. God in His perfection created a way for us to be reconciled to Him through the sacrifice of His Son, Jesus Christ. But He did not stop there; God also gave us His very own Spirit to be in us so that, while we wait for the return of our Savior, we can live triumphantly in this world (John 14:16-17, 1 Corinthians 2:12).

So I began to pray to the Holy Spirit; I asked Him to permeate me, to change me and to help me recognize and accept God's will in my life. Soon after, I began to experience chaos in my life, which was manifested most dramatically in my career. Things had been going very well for 7 years, but now it was as if the proverbial rug was pulled from under my feet. I prayed over and over for God to change my circumstances, but things did not improve. Instead, they got worse.

I will never forget one dark and cold January morning sitting in my car ready to leave for work. I was dreading the idea of heading into another day of extreme pressure and uncertainty at the office. I felt sick to my stomach. Suddenly, I remembered another challenge that Mike had posed to me during that October breakfast: "Thank God for all things." I braced myself with a tight grip on the steering wheel as I began to pray, "God, thank you." I was honest with God and told Him that I didn't completely understand why I was praying this. I told Him that I was through asking for my circumstances to be changed and instead I thanked Him for allowing those circumstances in my life. I told God that He promises us that in all things He works for the good of those who love Him (Romans 8:28), and I wanted to take Him up on that promise.

I was beginning to accept God's will over my life, regardless of what it looked or felt like. Aside from accepting Jesus Christ as my Savior, this was the most important moment in my entire life. I don't think this is an overstatement or an exaggeration. Sitting there in my car that early morning, I truly **surrendered** *my life to God for the first time. My circumstances at work continued to deteriorate, but in the next few days I began to experience a peace that I had never known before, the peace that surpasses all understanding (Philippians 4:7). It was only through the work of the Holy Spirit that I was able to pray what I did that morning and trust God in the midst of turmoil.*

Mike never did tell me how to become a better husband, father or son. He did much better than that; he pointed me to the God of love and mercy. He pointed me to God's very own Spirit who is in me, the Spirit that has the power to transform lives.

202

Paloma turned 10 years old 2 weeks ago. As expected, she brought many changes to our lives. The most dramatic changes in my life, however, came through a promise that Jesus made to all of us, the promise of the Holy Spirit.

STEP 1: THE PERSON OF THE HOLY SPIRIT

Jesus stated:

I will ask the Father, and He will give you another Helper, that He may be with you forever; that is the Spirit of truth, whom the world can not receive, because it does not see Him or know Him, but you know Him because He abides with you and will be in you.

John 14:16-17

Isn't it amazing to realize that the Holy Spirit wants to come alongside you? He promises not to leave you and desires intimacy with you. Think of this as the three "Cs" of companionship, commitment and communion.

1. Companionship. The Scripture gives the picture of the Holy Spirit running alongside to give us just what we need in every situation. Jesus said that the Holy Spirit would be "just like Me," in other words, another helper, just like Him. The Holy Spirit is God. Jesus sends Him to direct and help us the same way Jesus did His disciples. Other words used to describe His function include counselor, advocate and intercessor. He can be all of these to you if you want.

The Holy Spirit is not an "it" but "He." He is a personality, full of emotion and capable of being grieved. He is not a ghost, vapor or force, but rather, fully God. The word *ghost* in the King James Version of the Bible was probably used because He could not be seen.

2. Commitment. Jesus promised we would not be alone and that the Holy Spirit would be with us "forever." The Holy Spirit is continually with us, in the same way that, after cardiac surgery, a nurse is with you in the recovery area. You sense her touch, know her hand and sense her presence. So too, you can learn to sense the presence of the Holy Spirit in your life as you draw near to Him.

3. Communion. God wants intimacy with us. Because the Holy Spirit is in us, we have the potential for intimacy with Him. We can communicate with Him at all times.

The Holy Spirit comforts us by His companionship, by His eternal commitment and by His communing (intimacy) with us. Allow yourself to be led by the Holy Spirit. Talk with Him.

Challenge: I encourage you to begin to recognize the work of the Holy Spirit in your life. Do this by practicing the following:

1. **Talk with the Holy Spirit.** Pray directly to the Holy Spirit, just as you have to your heavenly Father and Jesus. Don't exclude or ignore Him.
2. **Walk with the Holy Spirit.** Recognize He is with you every moment in each activity of your life. Speak to Him throughout the day. Listen to His voice speaking to your heart. Observe His presence working in your life.

STEP 2: THE PRESENCE OF THE HOLY SPIRIT
(His presence = the filling of the Holy Spirit)

Unfortunately, it seems we have filled our lives with everything but the Holy Spirit. We must be filled with the Holy Spirit if we are going to be "salt" and "light" to the world around us. It is only through the presence of the Holy Spirit in us that we are enabled to be different from the world. The Apostle Paul instructs us:

And do not get drunk with wine, for that is dissipation, but be filled with the Spirit. **Ephesians 5:18**

He also tells us to be renewed in the spirit of our mind:

... and that you be renewed in the spirit of your mind
Ephesians 4:23

These verses mean that, by the Spirit, we adopt a new attitude. The Holy Spirit overhauls our mind. The very spirit of our mind must be constantly renewed:

... and put on the new self, which in the likeness of God has been created in righteousness and holiness of the truth.
Ephesians 4:24

In these verses, Paul is telling us to clothe ourselves in this new nature, i.e., put on the clean fresh clothes of the new life, which resemble God. These clothes are righteousness and holiness and spring from truth, where there is no illusion. If we do this, Paul indicates that our life will look different and that we will be capable of more, once the Holy Spirit dwells in us with His power. He instructs us as follows:

"... lay aside the 'old self'... don't give yourself up to sensuality ... put on the new self ... laying aside falsehood ... speak truth ... be angry and yet do not sin ... steal no longer ... let no unwholesome word proceed from your mouth, but only such a word as is good for edification according to the need of the moment, so that it will give grace to those who hear ... let all bitterness and wrath and anger and clamor and slander be put away ... be kind to one another, tender-hearted, forgiving ... be imitators of God ... walk in love ... immorality or any impurity or greed must not even be named among you ... walk as children of Light ... trying to learn what is pleasing to the Lord."

Ephesians 4 & 5

In other words, let your light become brighter daily.

Now, don't get discouraged by this list. The good news is that you can't and are not expected to do any of these things on your own. If you yield your life daily to the Holy Spirit, He will begin to work in and through you, and you will be amazed by the changes you see. You may not even be aware of the changes, but others around you will point them out to you.

The Bible says we can't even control something as small as our own tongue:

But no one can tame the tongue; it is a restless evil and full of deadly poison. **James 3:8**

We need to learn to depend on the Holy Spirit daily to receive power from Him so that we can live the life He desires for us. Let me explain this "filling of the Holy Spirit." We know from Scripture that the filling is:

1. **For everyone** – In Greek it is a command, an order.
2. **Forever** – It is constant, continual and never ending. It is for every moment of every day.
3. **Forsaking** – As wine permeates our whole being, so we are to permit and allow the Holy Spirit to take control and permeate our entire being, so that we can be transformed into the image of Jesus Christ. He does the filling, not us, and it is a process.

We are not always able to yield to the Holy Spirit in every moment. It is a learning process, and it comes with time. Compare this process with little children who are learning to walk. They fall and get up, then fall and get up, over and over. So, in this way, we too, must yield to the Holy Spirit. In actuality, it is not us getting more of the Holy Spirit, but rather, it is the Holy Spirit getting more of us as we progressively surrender to Him.

Challenge:
1. **Ask the Holy Spirit to fill you daily.** Ask Him to permeate your very being. The word *permeate* comes from the Latin, meaning "to flow through or to pass into and affect every part." It is like a drop of black ink dropped into water. The ink permeates the entire glass.
2. **Depend on the Holy Spirit.** Yield control and surrender passively to His power and will in your life. He will permeate you with His **power** and **presence**.

   Pray: Oh, Holy Spirit, I am asking you to permeate my entire being. Enable me to live the life you want me to live. I need you in this and every moment.

STEP 3: THE PURSUIT OF THE HOLY SPIRIT

Did you know that the Holy Spirit is constantly pursuing you? He wants to help you resist and overcome temptation. Paul wrote to the church at Rome:

For those who are according to the flesh set their minds on the things of the flesh, but those who are according to the Spirit, the things of the Spirit. For the mind set on the flesh is death, but the mind set on the Spirit is life and peace, because the mind set on the flesh is hostile toward God; for it does not subject itself to the law of God, for it is not even able to do so, and those who are in the flesh cannot please God. However, you are not in the flesh but in the Spirit, if indeed the Spirit of God dwells in you. But if anyone does not have the Spirit of Christ, he does not belong to Him. And if Christ is in you, though the body is dead because of sin, yet the spirit is alive because of righteousness. But if the Spirit of Him who raised Jesus from the dead dwells in you, He who raised Christ Jesus from the dead will also give life to your mortal bodies, through His Spirit who indwells you.

Romans 8:5-11

We need to recognize that we face a daily struggle between our flesh and our spirit. There is, literally, a war going on inside us. Even the Apostle Paul acknowledged this battle in his own life. Listen to what he said:

For the good that I want, I do not do; but I practice the very evil that I do not want; But if I am doing the very thing I do not want, I am no longer the one doing it, but sin which dwells in me. I find then the principle that evil is present in me, the one who wants to do good. For I joyfully concur with the law of God in the inner man, but I see a different law in the members of my body, waging war against the law of my mind and making me a prisoner of the law of sin which is in my members. Wretched man that I am! Who will set me free from the body of this death? Thanks be to God through Jesus Christ our Lord! So then, on the one hand I myself with my mind am serving the law of God, but on the other, with my flesh the law of sin.

Romans 7:19-24

When Paul stated, *Who will set me free from the body of this death?,* he was making reference to an ancient form of Roman execution in which a corpse was tied to a condemned man. The rotting corpse infected the living, condemned man with disease, and he died a long painful death. But Paul went on to say that Jesus could set him free from this corpse of sin that was tied to him. We can win. We can endure. God says so!

Our bodies are controlled by our sinful nature. Our thoughts give birth to sin. Sin starts in the mind, then we act on it. A series of small sins can bring down a great man. This is similar to what happened to the Titanic, a great ship that sank because of the small slits made in its hull after it brushed alongside an iceberg. If we are filled with the Spirit, then we can set our minds on Him:

For those who are according to the flesh set their minds on the things of the flesh, but those who are according to the Spirit, the things of the Spirit.

Romans 8:5

Your mind is essential to win the daily battle. It all begins in the mind. Paul tells us:

207

And do not be conformed to this world, but be transformed by the renewing of your mind, that you may prove what the will of God is, that which is good and acceptable and perfect. **Romans 12:2**

Set your mind on the things above, not on the things that are on earth. **Colossians 3:2**

We must do all that we can do to *be transformed by the renewing of your mind* and to *set your mind on things above.* This requires focus and discipline. We must do our part, but God promises that we can do it and that the Holy Spirit will empower us. We must believe we have won the war against sin; then we can win the battle over temptation. We are a new creation in Jesus Christ. We have been set free from the sin that formerly bound us.

Therefore if any one is in Christ, he is a new creature; the old things passed away; behold, new things have come.
II Corinthians 5:17

Who is controlling your mind? The flesh or the Spirit? Paul wrote to the believers at Corinth:

We are destroying speculations and every lofty thing raised up against the knowledge of God, and we are taking every thought captive to the obedience of Christ. **II Corinthians 10:5**

There is power available to you from the Holy Spirit so that you can overcome temptation. You can take every thought captive. That is why the Holy Spirit comes alongside you, literally pursues you.

Challenge: Recognize that the Holy Spirit is constantly pursuing you. Ask Him to transform and renew you, to enable you to take every thought captive. Here is how to deal successfully with your thoughts and temptations:

1. Immediately - Don't let that thought linger.
2. Completely - Every thought. Deal with every thought, not just some.
3. Capture - To capture means to constrain, hold it tightly and control it. We don't let just anyone come into our home, so why would we allow thoughts to remain in our minds and dwell on them?
4. Christ - Make every thought obedient to Christ, to bend to His standard. God has given us His Word to strengthen us and protect

us from deception. His Word is described as a *sword,* which is an offensive weapon.

This week, practice taking every thought captive. Yield every thought to the Holy Spirit and ask Him to help you in taking it captive. Use your sword to defend yourself from Satan's attack.

... the sword of the Spirit, which is the word of God.

Ephesians 6:17

The psalmist realized the importance of the Word and said:

Your word I treasured in my heart, that I may not sin against You.

Psalm 119:11

STEP 4: THE PURPOSE OF THE HOLY SPIRIT

Just as the Holy Spirit transformed the disciples, He can transform you. Some of the disciples were uneducated fisherman. The Holy Spirit changed them from ORDINARY to EXTRAORDINARY. Once they became *"in Christ,"* they became new creatures.

Therefore if any man is in Christ, he is a new creature; the old things passed away; behold, new things have come.

II Corinthians 5:17

For we also once were foolish ourselves, disobedient, deceived, enslaved to various lusts and pleasures, spending our life in malice and envy, hateful, hating one another, But when the kindness of God our Savior and His love for mankind appeared, He saved us, not on the basis of deeds which we have done in righteousness, but according to His mercy, by the washing of regeneration and renewing by the Holy Spirit.

Titus 3:3-5

We were saved by the washing of regeneration and renewing by the Holy Spirit. **The purpose of the Holy Spirit is to change us.** When this happened to Peter, a radical change occurred. He was changed from an ordinary man to someone quite extraordinary. The same Peter who had denied Jesus three times, now spoke powerfully by the Holy Spirit. He had never had a speech class, yet he taught doctrine and quoted Scripture because he was *"filled with the Holy Spirit."*

If we call ourselves Christians, why have our lives never been

209

radically and completely changed? Some of us have the Holy Spirit, but we like being in charge. We have never surrendered to His inside-outside changing. Hence, we live weak lives. It is the nature of man to reject and resist change. So too, we reject what the Holy Spirit wants to do in our life - transform us into the image of Christ. Will you yield to God's control?

Before being filled with the Holy Spirit, Peter acted *COWARDLY* and was afraid. After Jesus was arrested, Scripture says that Peter:

... was following Him at a distance.   **Matthew 26:58**

Peter was afraid he would be punished the same way Jesus would be, since people were sometimes found guilty by association. But after being filled with the Holy Spirit, Peter changed to acting **COURAGEOUSLY.** Peter was also changed by the Holy Spirit from being *CONFUSED* to **CONFIDENT.** Just like Peter, if you are filled with the Holy Spirit, you will be able to speak with confidence about what God has done in your life. The Holy Spirit will give you the words to speak if you are willing in faith to speak boldly.

Peter also changed from being *COMPROMISED* to **COMMITTED.** Peter denied knowing Jesus three times. Later, he was so discouraged he decided to go back to fishing. But after being filled with the Holy Spirit, he demonstrated his commitment as he spoke:

And there is salvation in no one else; for there is no other name under heaven that has been given among men by which we must be saved.   **Acts 4:12**

Peter was emphasizing the truth. In our pluralistic society that emphasizes diversity, there is still only one way to God. We can't be compromised. When we submit to the Holy Spirit's purpose in our life, those around us will repeatedly see **courage, confidence and commitment.** Then they will know we have been with Jesus in a real way. Those who work in banks always start out as tellers who have to count cash and feel money so they can tell the difference between the real thing and counterfeit. So too, in our lives, people will see a genuine relationship with Jesus Christ. They will be able to "feel" the real thing in our lives.

Challenge:

1. **Ask the Holy Spirit to empower you each day.**

2. **Ask Him to give you commitment, courage and confidence.**

When others see and ask about the difference in you, don't be afraid to tell them what He has done in your life. He will give you the right words to speak.

STEP 5: THE POWER OF THE HOLY SPIRIT

Paul wrote this to the believers in Corinth:

And when I came to you, brethren, I did not come with superiority of speech or of wisdom, proclaiming to you the testimony of God. For I determined to know nothing among you except Jesus Christ, and Him crucified. I was with you in weakness and in fear and in much trembling, and my message and my preaching were not in persuasive words of wisdom, but in demonstration of the Spirit and of power, so that your faith would not rest on the wisdom of men, but on the power of God. **I Corinthians 2:1-5**

Do you ever feel pressure in life like Paul did? Paul was speaking to believers in Corinth, yet there were many pressures there. Many were slaves. Corinth was a center of trade, wisdom and the worship of many gods with gross immorality. Because of what he had experienced on his missionary travels, Paul wrote that he came to them in weakness, fear and trembling. It pressed heavily on him. Paul was very well educated but chose not to rely on his training. Nor did he want them to base their faith on his human argument but on the demonstration of the Spirit's power. John wrote,

... greater is He who is in you than he who is in the world.
I John 4:4

The Holy Spirit provides you with power. The Greek word for power is *dunamos*. It is the same root from which we derive our word dynamite. This word indicates a supernatural work of God enabling you to live the life He wants. Your body becomes the active temple of the Holy Spirit when you surrender to Him. Today, we have a problem of extremes. On the one hand, some Christians are like a surge protector for a computer. They deny the power of the Holy Spirit for today. They refuse to permit God's power to come into their lives. On the other hand, there are other Christians who believe they can harness the power of the Holy Spirit to "name it and claim it." We need the balance that Paul had. We need the power of the Holy Spirit to make it through the struggles of life. Paul was successful because he recognized his shortcomings and limitations. He stated that he was a sinner among sinners:

> *... among whom I am foremost of all.*   **I Timothy 1:15**

Paul knew that, apart from God, he could do nothing. He focused on the blood of Jesus and what had been done for him. This enabled him to constantly see the hand of God in his life and thank God for it despite the circumstances. Paul put aside everything, his education and his own strength, and trusted in God totally.

Challenge: Did you know that God wants to give you His power to make you capable of living as He desires? Recognize two things:

1. Are You Wanting? God has made each of us unique, but you will never reach your spiritual potential unless you are filled with the Holy Spirit. Then you can reach your potential for the glory of God. You have to ask yourself if you want God to prompt, guide and direct you. Do you want Him in charge of your life?

2. He's Waiting! He is here! He came on the day of Pentecost and never left. He's waiting for you to turn and yield to His leading, not to just harness His power for your own purposes. He wants to harness your life. Turn to Him and pray daily, "Yes, Holy Spirit. Take charge of me, for you are God. Harness my life."

STEP 6: THE PERSUASION OF THE HOLY SPIRIT

Jesus said to His disciples:

I have many more things to say to you, but you cannot bear them now. But when He, the Spirit of truth, comes, He will guide you into all truth; for He will not speak on His own initiative, but whatever He hears, He will speak; and He will disclose to you what is to come. He will glorify Me; for He will take of Mine and will disclose it to you.

All things that the Father has are Mine; therefore I said that He takes of Mine and will disclose it to you.　　　　　　　　　　**John 16:12-15**

The Holy Spirit is the "Spirit of Truth." Jesus was speaking in the Upper Room, and had something profound to say. He declared that He was going to His Father. His disciples were afraid to ask Him where He was going. Grief had filled them, and their hearts were troubled. Jesus said to them:

Where I am going, you cannot come.　　　　　　　　　　**John 13:33**

Peace I leave with you ... Do not let your heart be troubled, nor let it be fearful.　　　　　　　　　　**John 14:27**

A little while, and you will not see Me; and again a little while, and you will see Me ... because I go to the Father.　　**John 16:17**

What did He mean? Confusion was mounting. Simon Peter asked:

Lord, where are You going? ... Lord, why can I not follow You right now?"　　　　　　　　　　**John 13:36-37**

Jesus told them:

Behold, an hour is coming, and has already come, for you to be scattered.　　　　　　　　　　**John 16:32**

That hour occurred that very night. But He also reassured them:

These things I have spoken to you, that you may be kept from stumbling (not go astray).　　　　　　　　　　**John 16:1**

The disciples struggled with their faith, and so do we when we have a crisis in our life and are confused. Sometimes the crisis is financial or marital. It can be a problem with one of our children. As the confusion mounts, we are in danger of straying and falling away. Even John the Baptist's faith in Jesus was in question as a result of being in prison. John sent some of his followers to ask Jesus:

Are You the Expected One, or shall we look for someone else?　　　　　　　　　　**Matthew 11:3**

If this can happen to John the Baptist and the disciples, it can happen to us. At times, we all fall asleep spiritually and drift off the

213

path we should be on. The evil one seeks to lead us astray. But Jesus said the Holy Spirit would guide us in three ways:

1. **BY STAYING** - When the Holy Spirit came, He came right in the midst of their trouble. Jesus said,

I will never desert you, nor will I ever forsake you.

Hebrews 13:5

When you are struggling on the road of life, the Father sends the Holy Spirit to come alongside you. Compare this with the Olympic athlete in Barcelona who ran in the 400 meter race, but fell after pulling a calf muscle. His father walked down out of the stands, came alongside his son and helped him up. Together they walked across the finish line. So too, the Holy Spirit persuades you to cross the finish line. He enables you to say, like the Apostle Paul,

I have fought the good fight, I have finished the course (race)*.*

II Timothy 4:7

2. **BY STEERING** - He will give you proper guidance based upon what is right.

... He will guide you into all the truth.   **John 16:13**

The Greek word for *guide* was used to indicate that you are in a foreign land and don't know the way to go. The Holy Spirit steers you into "all truth," i.e., the right direction: light vs. darkness; purity vs. impurity; righteousness vs. evil.

If we live by the Spirit, let us also walk by the Spirit.

Galatians 5:25

The word *walk* literally means to march with the Holy Spirit. The Holy Spirit is calling the cadence in life since you are a part of God's army. He wants you to follow His lead <u>step</u> by <u>step</u>. You have a choice.

3. **BY STATING** – He will not speak on His own, only what He is told. Only the Holy Spirit knows the thoughts of God. Jesus said that the Holy Spirit would take what He had taught the disciples and make it clearer.

But the Helper, the Holy Spirit, whom the Father will send in My name, He will teach you all things, and bring to your remembrance all that I said to you. **John 14:26**

The Holy Spirit expounds upon what Jesus said. Your conscience is not a proper guide. My father always told me, "Your conscience is like an alarm clock. It goes off right where you set it." It is the Holy Spirit who will bring to your mind Jesus' teaching to steer you back into the light.

Challenge: The Holy Spirit will persuade you to go on in the truth so you can always finish well.

Pray daily: "Holy Spirit, thank You for always being with me, especially in times of trouble. Please guide me this day and show me truth in every situation I face."

STEP 7: THE PROMPTING OF THE HOLY SPIRIT

Now there were at Antioch, in the church that was there, prophets and teachers: Barnabas, and Simeon who was called Niger and Lucius of Cyrene, and Manaen who had been brought up with Herod the tetrarch, and Saul. While they were ministering to the Lord and fasting, the Holy Spirit said, 'Set apart for Me Barnabas and Saul for the work to which I have called them.' Then, when they had fasted and prayed and laid their hands on them, they sent them away.

Acts 13:1-3

We need to be able to make **SOUND** and **SATISFYING** decisions. With the prompting of the Holy Spirit, we can do so. The Holy Spirit came as a "mighty wind." We should desire this in our life. We need His moving and prompting because we have questions and need to make decisions.

The church at Antioch was being prompted by the Holy Spirit to make a decision. The people there were glad about many of the things that were happening. They were growing both numerically and spiritually. Barnabas had been hand picked and sent to Antioch from the church in Jerusalem. Then Barnabas went and got Paul. Paul and Barnabas spent one year in Antioch. They had good leaders in the church, and they were an actively serving church. They were devoted to the cross of Christ and sent gifts to the cause of Christ, despite a famine. The whole family of God at Antioch was waiting on the Holy

Spirit. The whole church was seeking the Holy Spirit.

The believers in Antioch wanted the prompting of the Holy Spirit. They were intense and their fasting and waiting indicated their depth of desire. **We also need to express to the Holy Spirit our desire for Him to lead us.**

Prayer and fasting were linked together. Fasting is going without food and replacing it with prayer. The believers in Antioch waited on the Holy Spirit's prompting. They did not run out ahead of God, but rather, waited on Him. God is on His own time schedule.

Cease striving and know that I am God. **Psalm 46:10**

This is an almost alien concept to us in the United States. "Still" means to stand or sit without moving. We need to go off and be alone with God to hear Him and encounter Him. The believers in Antioch acted and walked in what the Holy Spirit said. The church actually sent their main leaders, Paul and Barnabas, away! Think how difficult this must have been. They sent their ministers off to other churches. When we are seeking the Holy Spirit, we must have an open mind.

Challenge: Are you open to the leading of the Holy Spirit? Are you reading His Word regularly? You must know His Book to make good decisions. It is the bread of life. Are you asking for the Holy Spirit's prompting daily? Do you seek His advice in making decisions?

Pray each day: "Holy Spirit, I desperately need Your prompting today and every day to make good decisions at work, in my home, and in every aspect of my life. I yield my life to You and depend on You to do this."

STEP 8: THE PRAYERS OF THE HOLY SPIRIT

And in the same way the Spirit also helps our weakness; for we do not know how to pray as we should, but the Spirit Himself intercedes for us with groanings too deep for words; and He who searches the hearts knows what the mind of the Spirit is, because He intercedes for the saints according to the will of God. **Romans 8:26-27**

In Greek, the word for *weakness* means without strength. We have times in our life when we lack strength. When we are weary, we may not know how to pray or are often wrong in the way we pray. In times of spiritual weakness, we are unaware and unwise regarding how we should pray. But the Holy Spirit is there, praying and interceding on our behalf. Three times Paul prayed for the "thorn in his flesh" to be removed. Yet God said, "No." Even Paul, when weary, prayed incorrectly.

The Holy Spirit takes up a position on our behalf. *Intercede* in Greek means to come alongside; to rescue in time of peril; speak on behalf of. The Holy Spirit does this. He will not stop or desert us. Jesus is at the right hand of the Father interceding for us. In Hebrews, it states that Jesus "lives to intercede" for us. When we can't keep our heads up anymore, then the Holy Spirit comes alongside us and lifts up our heads.

The Holy Spirit makes our petition. The Bible says He "groans." Apparently, there are times when even human words cannot express what needs to be said. The content of what the Holy Spirit prays on our behalf is:

1. **Profound** – beyond human understanding.
2. **Perfect** – never unwise; He always prays the will of God. Its content is perfect.
3. **Powerful** – it was the power of the Holy Spirit that raised Jesus from the dead. We can see the effective unity between what Jesus and the Holy Spirit do.

Challenge: I challenge you to enter into a prayer partnership with the Holy Spirit and center your life on God. When the Holy Spirit's power is unleashed in your life, you have the opportunity to soar and reach your spiritual potential.

Pray: "Holy Spirit, thank You for interceding for me. Thank You for praying for me profoundly, perfectly and powerfully. I yield my life totally to You today. Please empower me to accomplish all You desire."

ARE YOU INVITING THE HOLY SPIRIT INTO YOUR LIFE DAILY?

We see that Jesus depended daily on the Holy Spirit throughout His ministry. How can we do less? Jesus is our example. We are to pattern our lives after Him. Have you presented your body to God daily as instructed?

Therefore, I urge you, brethren, by the mercies of God, to present your bodies as a living and holy sacrifice, acceptable to God, which is your spiritual service of worship. And do not be conformed to this world, but be transformed by the renewing of your mind, so that you may prove what the will of God is, that which is good and acceptable and perfect.   **Romans 12:1-2**

Have you really committed your life to Jesus? Are you afraid of doing so or of what He might ask you to do? Don't be! You have nothing to fear. He is the God of love. He loves you more than anyone on this earth. As your loving Father, He delights in giving you the "very desire of our hearts." Whatever you surrender to Him, He will return to you many fold.

I strongly urge you, if you have not already done so, to put all you are, all you own, on the altar of God. Give it all to Him. And when you do, a most amazing thing will most assuredly happen. The love of God will magically and mystically fill your heart, empowering you to accomplish great things for the Kingdom of God.

... because the love of God has been poured out within our hearts through the Holy Spirit who was given to us.   **Romans 5:5**

Only by surrendering to God completely can you experience the Spirit-filled and Spirit-controlled life. You cannot begin to imagine the freedom you will experience by giving everything over to God. It is, indeed, one of the great paradoxes of Christianity. It is the greatest investment you can ever make in your entire life. It is one investment that will pay big dividends. It truly is "a piece of the rock." Only in this instance, it is Jesus, the Rock of our salvation. Invest in Him completely and without reservation. It is natural to hold back and to have reservations, but go beyond them, in faith, to commit to Him. You can say as one man did, "Jesus I believe, but help me in my unbelief." Be honest with Him. He knows what is in your heart anyway. Just take the first step. He will meet you where you are. When you do, you will receive "the peace that passes all understanding."

Now the Lord is the Spirit, and where the Spirit of the Lord is, there is liberty.   **II Corinthians 3:17**

FOCUS

TRUTH (What is the focus – the essential truth of this chapter?)

The Holy Spirit is available to me. He wants to live within me and change me into all that God wants me to be.

APPLICATION (What does this truth mean to me? How is it relevant in my life?)

I must invite the Holy Spirit to dwell within me. I must do this daily to receive the power necessary to live the life God desires. I can't do it on my own.

ACTION (What should I do about it? How can this truth benefit my life?)

Pray: Holy Spirit, I ask You to permeate my entire being – spirit, soul and body. Empower me to accomplish today all that You desire.

CHAPTER 11

ANSWERING THE QUESTIONS OF LIFE FOR YOURSELF

THE UNIVERSALITY OF TRUTH

The pursuit of truth and the pursuit of God are parallel,
since God is the author of both.
Thomas Aquinas

Throughout history, there has never been a civilization that did not have faith in some form of god or supreme being. As long as man has existed, he has sensed a need to have reverence for the Creator. Our society has been victimized by much of Western culture because of the separation of faith and reason. The 17th century philosopher and mathematician, Renée Descartes, was the first to state that the body could function quite well, independently of the mind. As a result, the body was viewed as nothing more than a machine. This view has been passed down from generation to generation and, even today, permeates the science of medicine to a remarkable degree. All of our technological breakthroughs in transplantation, genetic research, and other areas have fostered this view. It is understandable that Descartes' thinking led science along a secular and materialistic path. Science promised to provide us with the answers to all of our questions; however, we see now that science has failed us. *Science has never been successful in helping us answer the real questions of what life is all about and what happens when we die. Nor has science been able to provide for or satisfy us spiritually.*

Similarly, with ever-increasing knowledge, the promise of the Enlightenment was to give us solutions to the problems of mankind. Have the problems of hunger, poverty, war or pestilence gone away? No! That's because knowledge in and of itself is not enough. It ignores the most basic problem of man. The Bible states,

The heart is more deceitful than all else and is desperately sick.
Jeremiah 17:9

Martin Luther aptly recognized this problem when he stated, "Reason is the greatest enemy that faith has; it never comes to the aid of spiritual beings, but, more frequently than not, struggles against the divine Word treating with contempt all that emanated from God."

With science promising to provide us with all of the answers we need, the church abdicated its mission of healing. Science and medicine were left to provide these answers. The result has been the development of a progressively larger spiritual vacuum.

Fortunately, in some of our newest discoveries, God, or at least the spiritual dimension, is again being considered. The "new physics" describes the world of matter and form as quantums of energy that comprise everything. Eastern mystics have always seen the universe as one indivisible whole. This new physics seems to fit that concept better than our prior thinking. What is this energy that comprises everything? Is this somehow the spiritual energy or dimension we have been missing?

William James, a 19th century philosopher, noted in his book, *The Varieties of Religious Experience,* that people of every culture have common experiences in worshipping a supreme being. [1] Similarly, Dr. Herbert Benson, in his book, *Timeless Healing,* concluded that the experience of a deity, by whatever name it is called, is universal. [2]

In my book, *Stress & Spirituality*, I explored much of the information now available to us in the medical literature. There has been an explosion of information showing the importance of faith in God in the healing process. This so-called "Faith Factor" can no longer be denied. The integration of these data into the practice of medicine has been and continues to be exciting. In my medical training, I was taught about the physical and emotional aspects of man. The spiritual aspect was completely ignored and, even if mentioned, often disdained. Now, all of that has changed. The spiritual dimension of man is acknowledged; however, medicine and science have had a difficult time defining spirituality. I defined spirituality in Chapter 2 in my consideration of the tripartite nature of man – a being made up of spirit, soul and body.

IN SEARCH OF TRUTH

Man has always sought truth. Belief systems have played an important part in this continual search, shaping and defining our interpretation of truth. All of us have been raised with internal biases that make it literally impossible for any of us to seek truth in a truly impartial way. Most of us are quite opinionated about what we believe to be true. I frequently ask people, "Why do you believe what you believe?" I often receive interesting responses such as, "I feel like it is true." You don't have to live too long on this planet to recognize that feelings are like the wind and change for all kinds of reasons. But it is often a ticket to disaster to equate what you believe with what you feel. Others say, "I was taught that in school." Think back. Was everything you were taught in school correct? Still others respond, "My parents told me that." It is a sobering moment in life when a child comes to realize that something mom or dad told him was incorrect. It is disturbing to realize that mom and dad are not the invincible, all-knowing parents that a child has thought. So, how do we deal with this dilemma?

THE PRINCIPLE OF INTELLECTUAL HONESTY

For more than 30 years, I have been actively engaged in teaching. For a number of those years, I was an Associate Clinical Professor of Biochemistry with the Department of Biochemistry at the Indiana University School of Medicine. During that time, I offered an elective course on Clinical Nutrition to biochemistry students, and gave them the opportunity to use their biochemistry when evaluating and treating patients at the bedside. I made it a point the very first day to say to the class, "You are responsible for not believing a single word I tell you." They often looked shocked and perplexed. I went on to explain that I would impart as much knowledge as I could, but I was human and made mistakes like everyone else. I explained that, even though I firmly believed everything I would teach them, occasionally I might be wrong. There could be many reasons for this. One reason is that truth in medicine keeps changing based on new discoveries. Therefore, I encouraged my students to question absolutely everything. Just because something is printed in a textbook does not mean it is right. That is why textbooks have to be rewritten every few years. The principle I was teaching them is invaluable for all of us. I call it **The Principle of Intellectual Honesty**.

The principle is applicable to all areas of life. When applied to each area, it forces us to question absolutely everything we believe. It demands that, when we find something new we believe to be correct, we must discard the old and insert the new. Although this makes perfect sense, many refuse to do it. Why would anyone want to hold on to a belief that is untrue? It is amazing how common it is. In fact, I would challenge you by saying that I believe most people are not intellectually honest, especially in certain areas of their lives such as their religious and, many times, scientific beliefs. I have seen professors defend scientific positions that they know are incorrect, because these positions represent their whole life's work and have made them famous. Rather routinely, people defend their religious beliefs without ever critically evaluating why they believe what they do. What they believe is oftentimes a combination of what their parents taught them, what they learned at church or school and the environmental effects of the community in which they were raised. The questions are: **Is there a way to know truth, and is there such a thing as absolute truth?**

No one is truly free to do whatever he wants without suffering the consequences. I sometimes challenge my medical students by asking them if they believe the statements, "There are no absolutes," and "You can do whatever you want as long as you don't hurt anyone." Some have said they do believe these statements. I then point out that if the first statement is true, then the second statement must be false. The second statement would need to be, "You can do whatever you want," because the phrase "as long as you don't hurt anyone" is an absolute that cannot exist. How often do you take for granted the things that people around you say and accept them as true?

We are all constrained by some boundaries and are accountable to authority figures. Paradoxically, the acceptance of boundaries and limits is our gateway to freedom. Freedom is defined as "exemption from arbitrary power; liberty; independence." But freedom always costs something. We have our liberty because of those who lost their lives in the Revolutionary War. We have liberty in Christ at the cost of Jesus' death.

In the United States, our understanding of what is true and, therefore, acceptable has certainly changed since the 1950s. The following table demonstrates the radical shift that has taken place in our thinking since then.

THE CRISIS FOR TRUTH IN THE USA

THEN (Pre-1960's)		NOW (1960's and Beyond)
TRANSCENDENT VALUES	*vs*	RADICAL INDIVIDUALISM (MORAL RELATIVISM)
SELF SACRIFICE	*Replaced By*	SELFISHNESS
COMMITMENT	*Replaced By*	"FREE LOVE"
BEST INTERESTS OF THE COMMUNITY	*Replaced By*	"EXTREME INTERPRETATION OF INDIVIDUAL RIGHTS
GOD IS ALIVE Underlying system of values based upon the laws of God		"GOD IS DEAD" Life has no meaning but individual meaning and pleasure
TRUTH Moral Order of the Universe Absolutism Character & Duty		TRUTH IS GONE Naturalism & Evolution There are no absolutes. Loss of Character Increased Crime

I first met Jim Bricker at Faith Community Church on the south side of Indianapolis shortly after he was saved in 1979. I will never forget all those times he sat in my Sunday School class. He was always the most attentive person and took notes all the time. Jim was a truck driver with an infectious personality and smile, who was on fire for Jesus. A teacher hopes that one day he will have a pupil who exceeds what he himself has accomplished. Jim was that student of mine. Here is his story of how God helped him in his search to answer the questions about life.

It was Jeff's 21st birthday. The big party with more than 75 guests that we planned for him was on a hot summer night in August. Jeff was a strong, burly, young man with a heart of gold and one of the most loyal friends one could ask for.

Jeff looked up to me like the big brother he never had. He only had a little sister whom he adored. Now that Jeff was turning 21 he was asking a lot of questions about life. Even as our friends were gathered in the back yard of his parent's house having the time of their lives with plenty of free booze and illegal drugs, Jeff called me aside. He wanted to have a soul searching conversation, one I was far from prepared for. I hadn't figured out the meaning of life or the purpose of my own existence. How could I possibly answer Jeff's deep questions about life? It was like the blind leading the blind.

All of the sudden and without warning, a fist fight broke out. In a moment's time, the fun and friendly party turned into an every-man-for himself rumble. In the midst of the panic, with people punching and kicking each other, I couldn't help but notice this one guy who appeared to be the instigator of the terrible nightmare. He was swinging wildly at people and appeared to be out of his mind. I grabbed him by the left arm and fell to the ground on top of him.

People were fighting madly in total rage. I jumped up, and as I looked to my right, I saw Jeff slowly take his glasses off and hand them to his mother. He came to my rescue by standing up against the bully who started this mess.

After a brief confrontation, Jeff, standing up as straight as an arrow, suddenly fell over backwards. He lay on the ground silently on his back. His parents and I rushed to his side and noticed a shining object sticking out of his chest with blood around it. It was a knife with a five-inch blade.

Jeff's body quivered. He was alive for only a few more moments before he took his last breath. My good friend had just been asking me about the meaning of life and was now dead. There was nothing we could do to bring him back. His death was a terrible tragic loss!

After Jeff's death, I begin to privately ponder those deep heart felt questions about life and why we exist. I couldn't help but wonder what happened to Jeff and where he might be now. I asked myself about life and death, about God, about heaven and hell and all of those other soul-searching questions that each and every one of us ask from time to time. I had lots of questions, but I had no answers. So began my soul searching quest for purpose and meaning in life.

I went to church and asked questions. I even read the Ten Commandments. The more I sought to know, the more I realized I did not know. I realized that for so many years I just did not know what life was really all about, and that was pretty scary!

Then it happened. As I was having a conversation with my cousin Steve, he told me that I mattered to God, and that God had a purpose and a plan for my life. He said I could be awakened to this new found reality by asking Jesus into my life to be my forgiver and friend. What a concept to know God, the one and only true and living God, the Creator of heaven and earth, as my friend in a personal way! Now that's the most incredible good news I had ever heard. Why not? I said a big loud "Yes," to the person of Jesus to be my Savior and the Lord of my life.

Everything changed from that day on. I now had discovered purpose in life beyond myself. I seemed to view life through a new set of lenses. My whole life before was all about getting, and now it was all about giving. Every girl I'd ever known was for my own satisfaction and ego, but now I understood that relationships were much more than personal satisfaction and gratification. I understood for the first time that meaningful relationships are all about trust, commitment, respect and sacrifice and that real happiness is discovered in giving, not just in receiving.

Over the next several years, I continued to grow spiritually in my relationship with Jesus and in the knowledge of His Word, the Bible. I learned to relate to women in a new way, as sisters in Christ, and not as objects of pleasure. I learned a lot about respect through several God ordained relationships which were in preparation for the one that would become my wife. 1982 was the best year of my life. I was not only married, but also ordained as a pastor.

In July 2007, my wife and I will celebrate 25 years of marriage. We have two children, and we are all actively involved at our church Vineyard Community Church. I have had the privilege of serving in the ministry as the founding and senior pastor of VCC. I also serve the Vineyard denomination at large as Regional Coordinator for starting new churches in the Great Lakes Region of the USA.

God has blessed our church in Greenwood, Indiana, with several thousand people in regular attendance. I'm grateful to God for the male role models, mentors and coaches in my life. I appreciate my friend Dr. Mike Elmore, who took me under his wing while I was in my early 20s and spoke into my life. He believed in me and added value to my life with his Godly counsel. By patiently and carefully listening

227

to me and answering my questions, he showed me the way to godliness through his example.

Today, I spend time with lots of young people. I hope to be a biblically-oriented male role model and a mentor for them like Mike and others were for me. One of our greatest needs today is for men to be real men. As the Apostle Paul wrote in 1 Corinthians 16:13,14 "Be on your guard; stand firm in the faith; be men of courage; be strong. Do everything in love." Modeling real manhood is all about being men of character, consistency, courage and compassion.

THE PARADOXES OF CHRISTIANITY

God expects men to be the spiritual leaders in their home. Many men struggle with this because they are uncertain about what they believe. Perhaps this is because there are some basic understandings of Christianity that frequently cause confusion. These are what I call the Paradoxes of Christianity. A clear understanding of these will be of significant help to you in becoming the spiritual leader in your home. Every ship needs a captain, and the captain needs to know where the ship is going at all times.

The **Paradox of Salvation**. For me, salvation is like a door. If you look above the doorpost, there is a sign that displays Scripture verses.

Come to Me all who are weary and heavy-laden, and I will give you rest. **Matthew 11:28**

... if you confess with your mouth Jesus as Lord, and believe in your heart that God raised Him from the dead, you will be saved. **Romans 10:9**

Believe in the Lord Jesus, and you will be saved. **Acts 16:31**

Once a man looks at these verses, considers them and accepts them to be true, he walks through the door of salvation. But what does he find? On the other side of the door, above the doorpost, is written,

Before the foundation of the world was made, I called you, I foreordained you, I chose you and I predestined you. **Romans 8:29**

Now, these are very sobering words. So what is it that God does, and what is it that man must do? If our salvation depends upon our accepting His offer, but our selection is predestined, then we are not free to choose. Yet, we *are* free to choose. We can only understand this up to a point. The rest we must accept by faith. It is like looking at a mountain whose top is covered by clouds. We can see both sides of the mountain, but not the peak. But if we start to climb, we can walk up the mountain into the clouds and continue to walk over the top and down the other side. The top of the mountain is there, although hidden by the clouds. We can't see it by looking, but we are able to experience it by climbing into the clouds. Salvation is like this mountain. We can see the sides, but not the top. We understand each side, but can't fully comprehend what goes on at the top. Nonetheless, even though we don't completely understand it, we can still experience it.

The **Paradox of the Trinity**. The Bible says that God is a trinity. How can there be just one God, yet we speak of God the Father, God the Son and God the Holy Spirit? The best explanation I have heard for this is that there is only one true God, yet three divine eternal manifestations of God. I mentioned previously how water can exist as a gas, a liquid or a solid depending on the temperature. This idea is similar to the three divine eternal manifestations of God. Obviously, God is God, and He is not bound by our limited understanding. He exists in a realm not bound by space, time or the limits of knowledge. We cannot even begin to comprehend this. He is truly awesome. We should be grateful that He has given us the understanding that we have of Him. Faith is essential, but it is not blind faith. The Apostle Paul, in his letter to the Church at Rome, stated that none of us is without excuse when it comes to understanding that God exists.

For the wrath of God is revealed from heaven against all ungodliness and unrighteousness of men who suppress the truth in unrighteousness, because that which is known about God is evident within them; for God made it evident to them. For since the creation of the world His invisible attributes, His eternal power and divine nature, have been clearly seen, being understood through what has been made, so that they are without excuse. **Romans 1:18-20**

These verses explain how God revealed Himself to all mankind in creation. How can anyone honestly look at the complexity and the expanse of our universe and not believe in a God who purposed it all?

Doesn't the complexity demand a designer?

The **Paradox of the Sacrament of Communion**. The Bible tells us that, when we partake of the bread and the wine in Communion, it is the body and the blood of Christ. Some churches look to the limits of man's reason and simply state that, since our senses perceive only bread and wine, Communion is merely symbolic of the body and blood of Christ. Catholicism endorses the principle of transubstantiation, which states that, despite what our senses tell us, the bread and wine are literally transformed into the body and blood of Christ. I am not convinced that either is correct. Personally, I like the way Martin Luther phrased the idea when he stated, "It is the bread and wine, in, with and under the body and blood of Christ." What does this mean? It means that Luther knew he could not fully understand it either. His statement makes no sense, but it does express as eloquently as possible, within the limits of language and our understanding, the paradox that we face in Communion.

The **Paradox of the Nature of God → Love and Judgment**. People are often confused about how God can be so loving, yet also be a righteous judge preparing to hand out punishment. It is easy for people to accept that God is a God of love. Many religions accept this and refuse to acknowledge the existence of hell. They accept heaven readily and ignore the possibility of hell. But the Bible teaches that God is not only a God of love, He is also a God who expects holiness and is prepared to judge us. This paradox achieves meaning when we realize that God sent His Son to die for us and all we have to do is accept Him. The sacrifice He made is acceptable to God our Father on our behalf for our sins, past, present and future.

When our Father looks at us, He does not see our sins, but rather sees us covered with Jesus' precious blood. Covered with this blood, we are seen as holy. Ask yourself these important questions: **If there was no such place as hell, would God have sent His Son to die such a cruel, merciless death on our behalf? What would have been the point?** When God created man, He created man with a free will. This means man can choose to either accept God or reject Him. When man turned away from God and sinned, the rejection of God by man began. It continues to this day. Is there no price to be paid for this rejection, which separated us from Him? Man was no longer holy. Only through Christ's intervention and being covered with Jesus' blood can we again be holy before our Father.

Each of these paradoxes, and many others within Christianity, confront us with the limitations of our understanding. This is when faith in God is necessary.

THE BEATITUDES

In medical school, I learned two ways to approach new information. One of my professors said, "You can learn a lot and use it a little, or you can learn a little and use it a lot." Although I was smart, I realized I was no genius. So I chose the latter. I went into biochemistry believing that if I understood the biochemical basis of medicine, it would extend to everything I would be taught. That turned out to be true, and it served me well. Later in my Christian walk, I found a parallel. If I could find out the very basis of what Jesus taught, it, too, would extend to everything in the Bible. I found another way "to learn a little and use it a lot." You can, too.

Many years ago, I was asked to teach a Sunday school class on the Sermon on the Mount. At first I thought, "This is going to be dry and boring." But I couldn't have been more wrong. I had been given a guidebook to use for the series of classes, and I sought other books to help me. I noticed that each one referenced a book written by D. Martyn Lloyd-Jones, entitled *The Sermon on the Mount*. [3] So I thought, "Forget all these other books. I'll read this one." It is, bar none, the best book I have ever read. There was something about the way he wrote that I could relate to. Then I found out that he had been a doctor of medicine in Great Britain for three years, from 1914 to 1917, and then gave up his practice of medicine for a "higher calling." He became a minister and pastored Westminster Church in London for many years, until his death in the 1980s. My son and I had the opportunity to visit the church a few years ago. It was such an honor to stand on the church steps of my spiritual mentor. Dr Lloyd-Jones opened up Jesus' foundational teaching in the Beatitudes for me. I hope my discussion of the Beatitudes will do the same for you.

We don't use the word *beatitude* much anymore. It comes from the Latin and means "happy, blessed, perfect blessedness or happiness; a blessing." The word happiness relates to "hap-en-stance" which indicates that happiness is dependent upon that which "stands around," i.e. circumstances. But, this is not what the Bible means. Quite the opposite is true. The blessedness refers to a state of joy independent

231

of your circumstances.

The Beatitudes follow a logical progression, as indicated by the following discussion. Jesus gave them in a particular order because they are interdependent; and one is a prerequisite for the next.

Before we begin this study, you must understand one very important thing. *You can't "do" any of these Beatitudes! They are "be"-atitudes not "do"-atitudes*. The danger in reading them is to think that's what God wants you to do. That is not true. It is only the work of the Holy Spirit in you that will enable you to live as the Beatitudes describe. Now you know why I focused on how you can connect to God in Chapter 9 and how to ask the Holy Spirit to change and work through you in Chapter 10. If you have done the things described there, you are ready to hear what Jesus said.

The Sermon on the Mount indicates how Christians should live (not live like this and then become Christians). Jesus knew that we would need a greater power than our own to live the life He desires; in other words, we need the life of God within us. A Christian must BE something before he DOES anything. The Sermon on the Mount is an elaboration of what it means to love God with our heart, mind and will and our neighbors as ourselves. Jesus gave His life to enable us to live out these principles.

... (Jesus) who gave (sacrificed) Himself for us, that He might redeem us from every lawless deed (rescue us from our evil ways) and purify for Himself a people for His own possession (secure Himself a clean people), zealous for good deeds (ambitious of noble deeds).

Titus 2:14

It is important for you to be intellectually honest and recognize that you are utterly helpless in and of yourself. It is only through a spiritual rebirth, by receiving the life of God within you, that you can live the way God wants you to live. The Sermon on the Mount provides you with great comfort and encouragement. If you live out this sermon in your life, you will be blessed.

Quality of life comes from God. When the world sees you empowered by the Holy Spirit, acting in love, it will be drawn and attracted to you just like people were to Jesus. **Each Beatitude is NOT a natural tendency, but a disposition produced by grace alone through the operation of the Holy Spirit within you.** Hence, you can obtain the Beatitudes IF you simply yield to Him.

BEATITUDE 1

Blessed (happy, to be envied, spiritually prosperous) are the poor in spirit (those who sense spiritual poverty; who feel their spiritual need), for theirs is the kingdom of heaven. **Matthew 5:3**

The first Beatitude forces you to be intellectually honest about yourself. It says in effect, "I need help; I can't do it alone! I need God's help for salvation, guidance, knowledge, and wisdom." When you realize what God wants, viz. perfection – holiness, you realize your spiritual poverty and your need for God. This is where Jesus started when He began His ministry, and we must start here, too.

We all need to acknowledge our weakness and ask for help. Men are often afraid to admit their needs because they fear others will reject them or see them as weak. In actuality, if we admit our faults, then others will come to respect and trust us. This helps build strong relationships. People need to be needed. Admitting our needs causes people to trust us and see us as having emotional integrity. We gain self-esteem.

If we pretend we are something we are not, then we are always playing games. People will find out who we really are. For example, in Alcoholics Anonymous, you must admit, "I'm an alcoholic." Openness and honesty are signs of self-respect. We admit we are wrong when we say, "I'm sorry." King David said, *Oh, God be merciful to me a sinner.* The prodigal son returned home to his father and admitted all he had done.

Intellectual honesty means we know why we believe what we believe, and at any moment are prepared to change what we believe if we are shown to be incorrect. It is important to recognize that no one comes to God unless he admits his spiritual poverty. The secret of living the Christian life is total dependence on God.

Here are some questions for you to think about:
1) Why is it so difficult for people to admit they cannot be good enough on their own to enter heaven?
2) How does *poor in spirit* differ from poverty?
3) What is the difference between "poor in spirit" and low self-esteem?

There is a form of pride that is healthy. It is self-esteem and self-respect as God's loved and redeemed creation, empowered by Him to do good works in the Kingdom of God on earth. Listen to what God spoke through the prophet Isaiah.

> *For thus says the high and exalted One*
> *Who lives forever, whose name is Holy,*
> *I dwell on a high and holy place,*
> *And also with the contrite (humble, crushed, broken)*
> *and lowly of spirit*
> *In order to revive the spirit of the lowly*
> *And to revive the heart of the contrite.*
>
> **Isaiah 57:15**

Be honest with God. If you have doubts about Him, go to Him in prayer and tell Him.

In summary, being *poor in spirit* means that we feel hopeless when we compare ourselves to God. He demands we be perfect, and we realize we can't be. Peter became poor in spirit after he denied Christ the third time.

The First Beatitude is the solution to the following problems:

1) Arrogance – It causes us to take the credit for success.
2) Pride – Pride prevents us from crying out for help.
3) Fear – We fear men rather than fearing God.
4) Lack of Humility – True humility enables us to say, "I'm sorry."
5) Lack of Self-Esteem – As we empty ourselves and contemplate standing before Him, we come to know who we are in Him.

Challenge: **HOW DO YOU BECOME POOR IN SPIRIT?** You must first recognize that it is not something you produce in yourself. You must look to Jesus and what He expects of you. The more you look to Him in utter submission and dependence, the more you become poor in spirit. Ask the Holy Spirit to make you poor in spirit.

BEATITUDE 2

> *Blessed are those who mourn (Happy are those who are sad), for they shall be comforted (consoled, given courage and comfort).*
>
> **Matthew 5:4**

Are you sincerely sorry (mourn) for what you have done wrong? When you do, God promises to forgive.

Webster defines mourn as "to be anxious, to remember, think of, 1. to feel or express sorrow, lament, grieve, 2. to grieve for someone who has died.

Sorrow is mental suffering caused by loss or disappointment. Scripture gives us a variety of reasons why we mourn:

1) Romans 7:18 – *"nothing good dwells in my flesh."*
2) Mark 7:21-23 – *"man's heart is evil."*
3) Romans 3:10-12 – *"none is righteous."*
4) Romans 7:24-25, 8:1 – *"Wretched man that I am! Who will set me free from the body of this death?"* (this body doomed to death, deadly lower nature, sinful nature)

Sorrow for sin is the attitude necessary for conversion, but also throughout our entire life. It takes us back to our knees seeking forgiveness when we do wrong.

Challenge: HOW DO YOU DEVELOP THIS ATTITUDE?
When you meditate on the Scriptures and pray for the Holy Spirit to reveal your sin to you, then you will mourn and be comforted.

BEATITUDE 3

Blessed are the meek (patient, gentle, humble-minded, those who claim nothing), for they shall inherit the earth (the whole earth shall belong to them). **Matthew 5:5**

Webster defines meek as "literally - pliant, gentle, 1. patient and mild, not inclined to anger or resentment, 2. submissive, easily imposed upon, 3. kind." Note: Meekness is not weakness, intolerance or laziness. I prefer to use the word "malleable" in place of "meek." We are given the analogy of the potter and the clay in Isaiah.

But now, O Lord, Thou art our Father, we are the clay, and Thou our potter; and all of us are the work of Thy hand. **Isaiah 64:8**

The person who is meek is one who has a quiet, approachable spirit, ready to listen and learn, i.e., a teachable spirit. He lacks the spirit of retaliation and leaves everything in the hands of God. He is easily bent and shaped by God's hands and becomes what God desires.

Challenge: HOW DO YOU BECOME MEEK/MALLEABLE?
You can't make yourself meek. Only the Holy Spirit can humble you

and produce within you the right view of "self." When you become a Christian, you give up all your "rights," especially the right to be offended, the right to do things your way, the right to control your life and the right to take credit for what you do. As you give up your rights, you allow Jesus to come in and wholly possess you. He then molds you and forms the clay of your life into something beautiful.

BEATITUDE 4

Blessed are those who hunger and thirst for righteousness, for they shall be satisfied.   **Matthew 5:6**

This is a desire to be free from sin because sin separates us from God. This desire is two-fold: 1) to be free from the power of sin, and 2) to be free from the desire of sin. It is a desire to manifest the fruit of the Holy Spirit described in Galatians 6:22 – "love, joy, peace, patience, kindness, goodness, faithfulness, gentleness, and self-control" in your every action. This verse shows that the world is controlled by sin and Satan. We can never determine to be righteous. The righteousness of Jesus is "imputed" to us. It occurred when we were saved. When it occurred, our Father saw us covered with Jesus' blood and, therefore, holy.

He made Him who knew no sin (had no knowledge of, had never sinned) to be sin on our behalf (God made Him one with the sinfulness of men), that we might (through union with Him) become the righteousness of God in Him (turned into the holiness of God).
                                                    II Corinthians 5:21

Not only have we become the righteousness of God, but we are also filled with righteousness as a continual, progressive process. It is the work of the Holy Spirit continually delivering us from the power of sin.

Challenge: HOW CAN YOU EXPERIENCE THIS? As the Holy Spirit lives within you, you are able to conquer things that come against you. True joy and happiness comes ONLY as you hunger and thirst for God's righteousness. It never comes as the world constantly seeks happiness, which is some kind of evanescent vapor that can never be found or grasped in a lasting fashion.

BEATITUDE 5

Blessed are the merciful (compassionate, those who show mercy) for they shall receive (obtain, be shown) mercy. **Matthew 5:7**

Mercy is a sense of pity combined with a desire to act to relieve the suffering of others. Examples of mercy are the account of the good Samaritan and God the Father sending His Son. My sister once said to me, "Justice is receiving what we deserve; mercy is not receiving what we deserve; and grace is receiving what we don't deserve."

If we compare the statement *shall receive mercy* with the Lord's Prayer (*forgive us our sins, as we ourselves also forgive everyone who is indebted to us*) and the parable of the debtors in Matthew 18:21-35 (*So shall My heavenly Father also do to you, if each of you does not forgive his brother from your heart*), it is easy to misinterpret the meaning. Does it really mean that God will only forgive us to the extent that we forgive others? If this were what it meant, then none of us would have a chance. If this were what was meant, it would negate the doctrine of grace, since our forgiveness would depend upon each of us. What is meant is that, because we know that we have been truly forgiven, we are grateful and able to forgive others.

Challenge: HOW CAN YOU BECOME MERCIFUL? After your new birth experience, you will see others differently than before. You will see them as victimized by Satan and respond like Jesus did as He looked upon those who were crucifying Him and said, "*Father, forgive them for they know not what they do.*"

BEATITUDE 6

Blessed are the pure in heart (utterly sincere), for they shall see God. **Matthew 5:8**

The *pure in heart* are those who mourn their impurity. Although doctrine and intellectual understanding are important, Jesus emphasized the condition of the heart. If you are *pure in heart*, you will have a sincere desire to know Him and will be undivided in your love and single-minded in your devotion to Him. You will seek to live to His glory in all you do. Christianity is more than decency, morality and an intellectual interest in church doctrine. It is a commitment of the whole person.

These are the ones who will *see God.* What does it mean to *see God*? It is to sense and enjoy His presence daily, to come to know Him personally, to see Him in nature and to recognize His hand in the events of history. One day we will have the opportunity to literally see Him face to face.

For now we see in a mirror dimly, but then face to face: Now I know in part, but then I shall know fully just as I also have been fully known. **I Corinthians 13:12**

Challenge: HOW CAN YOU BE PURE IN HEART? Only God can make you pure in heart. He promises, as James stated:

Draw near to God and He will draw near to you.

James 4:8

Pray that the Holy Spirit will make you pure in heart.

BEATITUDE 7

Blessed are the peacemakers, for they shall be called sons of God. **Matthew 5:9**

A peacemaker seeks to make peace, and does all he can to produce and maintain peace. He is the opposite of quarrelsome. He is always ready to humble himself and do anything to promote the glory of God. It is quite obvious that this requires a change of your heart that only God can bring about.

Jesus came as the Prince of Peace. He gave Himself so we could be at peace with God and with one another. Paul stated:

Have this attitude (mind) in yourselves which was also in Christ Jesus. **Philippians 2:5**

When Jesus came, He obviously was not thinking of Himself.

Challenge: HOW CAN YOU BECOME A PEACEMAKER? This is totally the work of the Holy Spirit in you. It usually happens slowly and progressively as you yield yourself daily to Him.

Blessed are those who have been persecuted (endured persecution) for the sake of righteousness (for being and doing right) for theirs is the kingdom of heaven.   **Matthew 5:10**

Why will you be persecuted? You will be persecuted for the same reason that Jesus was persecuted. Jesus was persecuted not because He was a good man, but because there was something about Him that condemned those around Him. He exposed false righteousness. If you are righteous, you may condemn even if you say nothing, just because of what you are. Those who feel condemned will hate you and find fault with you. Your new nature loves God and wants to become like Him. The light you become exposes darkness around you. As a result, you should not expect to be praised by everyone around you because the Bible says that the *"natural mind is enmity against God."*

In Romans 8:7, the Apostle Paul said that, although we live in this world, we are citizens of another kingdom.

For our citizenship is in heaven.   **Philippians 3:20**

Currently, your citizenship in heaven is essentially spiritual, but the kingdom of God exists in any realm where Jesus is reigning. Does He reign in your heart? Does He reign in your marriage? Does He reign in your work? Do you exhibit that essential difference? If you do, you will be persecuted.

Challenge: ARE YOU BEING PERSECUTED FOR DOING WHAT IS RIGHT?

THE QUESTIONS OF LIFE & ANSWERS IN THE BEATITUDES

You may have recognized that, with each of the challenges for the eight Beatitudes, there is nothing you can really do to achieve them. The only thing you can do is relax and yield to God every moment of every day. Remember, no one loves you more than He does. So I encourage you to just relax in His presence at every moment, and allow Him to have His way with you. I promise that if you will do this, God will do incredible things in your life. And as a result of the changes within you, you will have a profound impact on those around you.

Recognize that you have the ability to write your own history. As you yield to God, He promises to lead you into all truth by His Holy Spirit.

There is a time when we must firmly choose the course which we will follow or the endless drift of events will make the decision for us.

Herbert V. Prochnow, Banking Executive and Toastmaster

FOCUS

TRUTH (What is the focus – the essential truth of this chapter?)

It is critical that you not only know what you believe, but why you believe what you believe.

APPLICATION (What does this truth mean to me? How is it relevant in my life?)

I must start where Jesus started – at the Beatitudes. I must first realize that I can't lead my life alone. I need His power to enable me to accomplish all that I need to do in life.

ACTION (What should I do about it? How can this truth benefit my life?)

Pray: Oh Holy Spirit, I yield every aspect of my life to You. Please help me to live the Beatitudes. Unless you change and empower me, it is hopeless. I can never be what You want me to be. But with Your power, I can be all You want me to be.

CHAPTER 12

THE PROBLEM OF SUFFERING
"WHY?!!!"

There are some things you learn best in calm,
and some in storm.
Willa Cather, Writer

Why would I include a chapter on suffering in a book designed to help men understand women and strengthen their marriages? The answer is simple. In every family there will be suffering. The Bible says that the sun shines and the rain falls on the just and unjust alike. Because of the curse on the earth that resulted from man's sin, we are all subject to suffering in various forms. When suffering and trials come, our wives and children may question why God would allow it. We need to be able to intelligently and appropriately respond to this question.

I regularly encounter patients who ask the question, "Why? Why would God allow this to happen to me?" Some assume that God hates them or is punishing them. Usually nothing could be further from the truth. I have studied suffering many times, and recently, I was asked to speak at a church on this topic. I put together a handout that was well received and prompted a lot of questions. I spoke on two subjects: 1. Types of suffering, and 2. Possible reasons why God would permit suffering in our lives.

TYPES OF SUFFERING

1) **SELF-INFLICTED** → Some suffering is self-inflicted. We bring suffering on ourselves by sin, ignorance, carelessness or stupidity. If I smoke heavily for 30 years and develop lung cancer or severe emphysema, who do I have to blame for the problem but myself? If I drink too much, drive my car and end up in an accident that leaves me paralyzed, whose fault is that? If I am promiscuous sexually and get AIDS, do I blame God?

241

Sometimes we suffer as the result of ignorance. We are aware of many dangers in various work environments that we were not aware of previously. For example, the dangers of asbestos are now well understood. It can cause a form of chronic obstructive lung disease called *asbestosis* and produce a form of cancer called mesothelioma.

If we are careless, it stands to reason we may get ourselves into trouble. We can't blame anyone but ourselves for the problems we suffer as a result of careless actions.

Lastly, sometimes we just do stupid things! Have you ever pulled onto an interstate and then realized, "Oh, my goodness! I never even looked! If a semi had been barreling down that lane and was unable to move over, I would have been killed!" Well, some people have died that way. We all do things at times without thinking. Some of those things are stupid, and some of those things can cause suffering.

2) **CHOSEN** → Some suffering comes as the result of a conscious choice. The Bible instructs us to *Take up your cross daily* ... When we choose to take a stand for what we believe, it is not always popular. The eighth Beatitude says, "Blessed are those who are persecuted for doing right." Most of the men who signed the Declaration of Independence lost their lives for what they believed. So too, we may have to pay a price for declaring and standing up for what we believe.

When we go to those who are suffering and extend our compassion, sometimes we pay a price. Every year I lead mission trips to Central and South America. Those who go give up a week of their vacation, pay approximately $1,200, step outside their comfort zone into the third world and intend to serve others for that week. Most do not speak the language of the country they are going to. Some get sick during the trip. However, the suffering they incur is usually more than offset by what they receive from those they choose to serve. I have always said, "It is impossible to outgive God. When you give up a week to serve those in need, God will richly bless you for it." Many who have gone and suffered in one way or another have still told us that it was the best week of their entire life.

3) **RANDOM** → Suffering is the collective result of sin - man's rebellion that led to the curse on the earth. As a result of this curse, terrible tragedies occur. When tragedies occur, the normal human response is, "It's not fair!" But think about it. We rebelled against

242

God. We walked away from Him, and now we blame Him for the consequences. I suspect that when we blame God, He, too, says, "It isn't fair." He is correct.

Some people are fatalists. They believe in fate and say, "What good is it to pray to God when I am just a victim of fate?" They seem to think that what is going to happen is going to happen and there's not much they can do about it. I have never been able to understand this "whatever will be, will be" logic.

Some people speak of good and bad luck, a variant of fatalism. They see life like a card game in which you sometimes have good luck and sometimes bad luck.

When your mind entertains some of the thoughts I have mentioned here, I encourage you to think about the following:

a) The Bible states,

The sun shines and the rain falls on the just and unjust alike.
Matthew 5:45

b) God is far bigger than our limited minds can conceive. Remember the question God put to Job:

Who is this that darkens my counsel with words without knowledge? **Job 38:2**

c) God is far greater than the evil in the universe and will one day triumph over it.

d) God is sovereign but won't do anything contrary to His nature. In a world of natural law and human freedom, He is able to accomplish His perfect will and yet remain true to His character and the principles He has built into the universe.

e) God watches over His people personally and individually.

REASONS FOR SUFFERING

There are two ways of meeting difficulties: You alter the difficulties, or you alter yourself to meet them.

Phyllis Bottome, Writer

While some TV evangelists preach that God *always* wants to make you happy, I am here to tell you that will not always be the case. In fact, do you realize God promises us suffering, trials and difficult

243

times? The Apostle John recorded Jesus' words:

> *In the world you have tribulation, but take courage, I have overcome the world.* **John 16:33**

People confuse the joy of the Lord, which can always be with us, and happiness, which is a feeling. It is joy that sustains us through difficult times when we are unhappy. So, let's look at some reasons why God allows suffering.

1)   PUNISHMENT OR DISCIPLINE – We sometimes punish ourselves by our own disobedience, ignorance and stupidity. At times we are deliberately disobedient.

> *Then when lust has conceived, it gives birth to sin, and when sin is accomplished, it brings forth death.* **James 1:15**

God's moral laws were given for our good. When we suffer because of the evil we do, Jesus also suffers. He is in relationship with us. God promises to discipline us because He is concerned about us. In the same way, we discipline our children because we love them.

> *For whom the Lord loves He chastens.* **Hebrews 12:6**

At other times, we suffer the consequences of just doing dumb things! At the time of Christ, the Jews believed that suffering was always a punishment for sin. We must resist the temptation to be like those Jews and Job's comforters and jump to the conclusion that when someone is suffering it is punishment for wrongdoing.

2)   PREPARATION FOR MINISTRY – A good example is when Joseph was sold into slavery by his brothers. The act ultimately led to the saving of the nation of Israel from famine. Too often we focus on "being blessed" rather than "blessing others." We are to "stand in the gap" and "intercede" for others. What happens *to* us affects what happens *in* us and that affects what happens *through* us. We live to comfort others and to be channels of God's love, not reservoirs.

> *God ... who comforts us in all our affliction so that we will be able to comfort those who are in any affliction with the comfort with which we ourselves are comforted by God.*
>
> **II Corinthians 1:3-4**

3) REVELATION OF TRUTH – There may be some things we need to honestly face up to. Calamity is often the voice of God shouting to us to turn around and come back. C. S. Lewis said, "Pain is God's megaphone to a lost world." Sometimes we lose our way through life. When God permits or allows us to suffer, we need to reflect and realize that there may be some area of our life that we still need to change. Suffering both makes us and reveals what we are made of (our character). Are we willing to change, to grow? Without character we are nothing.

... tribulation brings about perseverance ... proven character ... hope.   **Romans 5:3-4**

We always learn the most during the difficult times in our life.

4) DEMONSTRATE TO US THE SINCERITY OF OUR RELATIONSHIP TO GOD, DRAW US TO HIM AND REVEAL OUR DEEP NEED FOR HIM – How would you be if you were left with nothing but God? That would be a true test of faith. For example, all Job had left was his faith in God. He was not sure where God was or what God was doing. He did not know (could not know) the conflict behind the scenes. But, we do know! Job did us a wonderful service – he proved Satan a liar. So today, when you suffer, you can know God is working out His perfect purposes in your life. As you walk with Him and learn to depend on Him, you become more comfortable with Him and your relationship grows.

We also have a way of drifting away. Like sheep, we stray and end up in trouble. We need difficult situations in our life. Paul needed the *"thorn in his flesh."* When God did not remove it, he accepted it, and God told Paul *"for power is perfected in weakness."* God's people have access to Him. Job cried out for *"an arbitrator"* (Job 9:33). We have such a person in Jesus Christ.

For there is one God, and one mediator also between God and man, the man Christ Jesus.   **I Timothy 2:5**

Jesus, as the God-man, brings God and man together. He is a merciful and faithful High Priest on behalf of heaven. Because of Jesus Christ, God's throne is a throne of grace (not of judgment) for His people. We go to Him for our healing. We find the true meaning of suffering only in God. Apart from God, there are no answers to the

245

difficult problems and questions of life.

5)   DEFINE OUR FAITH – Satan says to us, "Do what is right and you will escape pain and receive blessings." But is that why we obey God? Or do we obey God because we love Him, regardless of how much pain He may permit in our lives? A person with "commercial faith" has two options: 1) Bargain with God to get Him to change the circumstances, or 2) Blame God for breaking the contract and reject Him. Job's friends chose the first option and his wife chose the second. Satan loves both options, but Job rejected both. Instead, he blessed God and maintained his integrity. Peter said we suffer trials so that our faith can be proved genuine:

> *In this you greatly rejoice, even though now for a little while, if necessary, you have been distressed by various trials, so that the proof of your faith, being more precious than gold which is perishable, even though tested by fire, may be found to result in praise and glory and honor at the revelation of Jesus Christ.*   **I Peter 1:6-7**

6)   STRENGTHEN OUR FAITH, BUILD OUR CHARACTER AND MAKE US TOUGH – At times of confusion when we don't understand what is going on, there must be faith. We trust God because we know He is the kind of Person Who can be trusted, even though we may not always understand what He is doing. God's ways are often hidden from us.

> *... the testing of your faith produces endurance. And let endurance have its perfect result, so that you may be perfect and complete, lacking in nothing.*   **James 1:2-4**

The Hebrew word for *hope* means "to wait with confidence." Have you ever prayed for more faith? God may have answered that prayer by permitting suffering in your life. God does not solve our problems by substitution. For example, He does not necessarily choose deliverance from sickness. But He transforms us by victory in the situation. The Holy Spirit dwells in us, and He reproduces the character of God in our lives (Galatians 5:22-23 and Matthew 5:3-11). Suffering will either tear us down or build us up. We are free to choose how we will respond. God uses the tool of suffering in our lives (the raw material) to produce character.

> *... tribulation brings about perseverance, and perseverance,*

proven character, and proven character, hope.   **Romans 5:3-4**

I spoke in Chapter 5 about the innate differences between men and women. Trials help men develop the right side of the brain. When we have gone through several trials, we become more sensitive and relational.

7) **PROTECT US FROM EVIL** – Sometimes suffering detains us from what we might do and prevents us from going in a particular direction. Although this often frustrates us, God uses it to protect us without our ever knowing, or knowing only in retrospect.

The righteous man perishes, and no one takes it to heart (cares or heeds it); and devout men are taken away, while no one understands. For the righteous man is taken away from evil.   **Isaiah 57:1**

Death can be used by God to protect us from future evil. We are not given a guarantee as to how long our life will be.

Precious in the sight of the Lord is the death of His godly ones.
Psalm 116:15

A number of years ago, the daughter of one of our best friends was killed in a small plane crash. My wife and I immediately rushed over to their home to be with her parents. It was a very difficult and emotional time for everyone. What do you say when a young life is suddenly erased? All you can do is be with those who are suffering, and share the suffering with them. That night I had a very vivid dream. In my dream, one of my daughters was returning to college. She was driving along the highway as a semi truck approached her. Just before the truck passed, the driver bent down to pick up something that had fallen on the floor. As he did so, his truck suddenly veered into the opposite lane, striking my daughter's car head-on and killing her instantly.

Then God spoke to me and said, "I can turn back the time and cause the truck to go straight so that you daughter will not be killed, and she will live out her life normally with all that is in store for her. Or I can leave it the way it is, and she will be with Me in eternity from now on. You decide." At first, I naturally wanted my daughter back. But the more I thought about it, I realized that, from the moment she died, she would forever be with Him in perfect peace, with no pain or suffering. How could I deny her that just for my own sake? Who knows what suffering might lie ahead for her that the accident saved her from? In the end, I told God to keep her, and I would see her later when I died. Although this was only a dream, it was so real and settled in my mind what my response to such a question from God would be.

8) DEVELOP OUR COMPASSION AND EMBRACE THE WORLD'S PAIN – Suffering increases our awareness, sympathy, and empathy. It makes us merciful. The word compassion means "to suffer with." When we know what it means to suffer, it is easier to help others who are suffering.

We can choose to either ignore the suffering in the world or take the pain into ourselves. It is natural to want to flee when we encounter pain. It will be too big, too much for us, so we must turn it over to Jesus. That's when we begin to understand God's heart and passion for the world. He will use us to intercede for those suffering. We are told to *take up our cross daily* (Luke 9:23). This simply means going where He wants you every moment of every day and doing what He shows you to do. Suffering is revealed to us daily. We live in a world of hurting people. God gives us many opportunities to comfort them.

Truly I say to you, to the extent that you did it to one of these brothers of Mine, even the least of them, you did it to Me.

Matthew 25:40

Do we dare accept it? Do we dare involve ourselves? As we yield our lives to God daily and let Him control our lives, He causes His love and compassion to rise in us. <u>The needs of others become our need to help them</u>. What we do for them, we do for Him. We are united with Him in suffering.

9) ALLOW US TO WITNESS – When we suffer, people watch to see our response. They want to know if our relationship with God is real and if He will sustain us in tough times. This is "Lifestyle Evangelism." How we act and respond to life's trials should be different compared to the rest of the world. The world's response to suffering includes comparing, complaining, rudeness and restlessness rather than joy, kindness and peace. Suffering can be your master or your servant. You can be a victim or victor. It's up to you to choose whether suffering will master you or you will master it.

10) HELP US UNDERSTAND GOD'S GLORY AND BETTER KNOW CHRIST – Jesus' suffering was the most glorious display of God's love. To understand the Kingdom of God, we must properly understand suffering.

Kingdom of the World	Kingdom of God
People associate money, power, abundance of possessions, fame, success, and beauty with glory. Examples are King Solomon and his Temple, Einstein's intelligence, "Old Glory" (our country's flag, which symbolizes political success and power). People expected Jesus' ministry to be about political power, vast riches, territorial expansion and military conquests. They turned away when this did not happen.	Jesus' ministry was misunderstood. Isaiah 9:7 foretold how He would reign on David's throne. But when Jesus arrived, His ministry diverged sharply from their expectations. His ministry was about humility, simplicity, submission, love and finally, suffering.

Even Jesus' disciples did not understand. James and John wanted to sit on Jesus' right and left hand *"in your glory"* (Mark 10:37). They wanted worldly glory. Jesus said, *You don't know what you are asking. Can you drink the cup I drink ...?* Suffering was not part of the glorious kingdom they had in mind. But Jesus' suffering would bring glory to the Father in a most unexpected way.

When Jesus spoke of His impending suffering, Peter said, *Never Lord ... This shall never happen to you!* (Matthew 16:22). Jesus reprimanded him. Later, Peter cut off the ear of the High Priest's servant, and again Jesus explained, *Shall I not drink the cup the Father has given to me?* (John 18:11). Peter demanded that Jesus distance Himself from suffering and death. It was the same seductive suggestion of Satan in the wilderness. Peter wanted the Kingdom to come without suffering. But Jesus was a willing sacrifice for our sins. This is God's great glory – a love so deep for each person that He endured all the mockery, torture, pain, suffering and death.

We prefer the Jesus of huge revivals, crusades, big churches,

Who healed the blind, versus the Jesus Who was rejected. Jesus offered the cup to each disciple in the Upper Room (Matthew 26:27-28). Not only did they drink of salvation, but of His suffering. The cup of salvation, suffering and glory are the same cup. Paul said,

I want to know Christ and fellowship in His suffering.

Philippians 3:10

Also, I Peter 2:21 states:

For you have been called for this purpose, since Christ also suffered for you leaving you an example for you to follow in His steps.

Like the pain and suffering of childbirth, our suffering can be endured and even embraced if it brings the desired result. We are called to share not only His glory but also His suffering.

... if indeed we suffer with Him so that we may also be glorified with Him.

Romans 8:17

Jesus was in a relationship with the pain of the world, so must we. Jesus was all about relationships. His intimacy with those in pain is our model. God suffered for us through Jesus giving us life. Imagine how you suffer when your child is in pain. Therefore, I must suffer for others to bring them His life and hope. His love within us will propel us and compel us to show His compassion to hurting people. He uses us to touch the world with His love. Rick Warren, author of *The Purpose Driven Life*, stated: "We learn things about God in suffering we can't learn any other way." [1]

What would it be like to depend completely on God? Sometimes suffering can take us there (without family, friends, money or our own strength to depend upon). We are united with Him in His death, resurrection and suffering.

11) FOR THE GLORY OF GOD – God can use suffering to refute Satan's charge that we obey only to escape trials and enjoy blessings. There is often something bigger than ourselves involved in the trials we are called to endure. We were made to glorify God in all we do; that is our purpose in life. We glorify God with our faith and our praise in times of trial.

When Jesus' disciples saw a man born blind they asked,

Rabbi, who sinned, this man or his parents, that he would be born blind?

Jesus responded,

It was neither that this man sinned, nor his parents; but it was so that the works (power) of God might be displayed in him.
John 9:1-3

Sometimes we suffer for doing what is right.

But if when you do what is right and suffer for it you patiently endure it, this finds favor with God. **I Peter 2:20**

The eighth Beatitude states:

Blessed are those who have been persecuted for the sake of righteousness, for theirs is the kingdom of heaven. Blessed are you when people insult you and persecute you, and falsely say all kinds of evil against you because of Me. Rejoice and be glad, for your reward in heaven is great; for in the same way they persecuted the prophets who were before you. **Matthew 5:10-12**

The last time people criticized you for doing the right thing rather than the wrong thing (like paying the taxes you owed versus cheating), did you rejoice? You should have, because your behavior was pleasing to God.

12) EXPERIENCE THE BENEFITS OF HELPING OTHERS – If we reject suffering, we also lose the benefits. If we could only see suffering as God does and accept it, it would free us to help. Jesus said:

For whoever wishes to save his life will lose it, but whoever loses his life for My sake, he is the one who will save it.
Luke 9:24

The question is, "Will we make ourselves available to help?" It was Jesus' incredible love and compassion that drew the crowds. If we open our hearts, He will put His love within us, and we will no longer be able to ignore the needs of those around us. Their needs will become our need to help.

My observation is that people who pursue happiness and self-gratification usually end up miserable, but those who pursue worthy causes and help others find happiness, satisfaction and fulfillment.

People react in different ways to suffering. One of the more common ways is to blame God. I have always wondered, "Why is it that God always gets the blame for suffering?" Dr. Benjamin Carson, former neurosurgeon at Johns Hopkins, observed that, sometimes, after a miracle has occurred, other doctors concluded that "it was a spontaneous remission." Ben would look them squarely in the eye and say, "You guys wouldn't know a miracle if it bit you in the rear-end!" On the other hand, if a miracle doesn't occur, people blame God for the disease and the suffering. People are inconsistent. If a miracle occurs, they say "spontaneous remission," and if it doesn't and the patient dies, they say, "God took him."

Why is it that we never hear people blame Satan for the problems in life? All we ever hear is, "The Devil made me do it!" I believe that Satan is wreaking havoc in today's world, producing all kinds of suffering to take out as many people spiritually as possible. One of the primary ways he does this is by deceiving us. He somehow convinces us that he doesn't exist, or if he does exist, he is not operating in our lives. The result is that we blame God for everything.

Doug Harty is a dentist who has participated in over forty international mission trips. I first met Doug when he was once hospitalized. We became fast friends and have gone on several mission trips together. Doug knows what it means to suffer. Listen to his experiences.

"Doug, this is Liz from Transplant. It's time. How soon can you be here?" These are the words I heard from the phone at 5 AM one morning. Eight years earlier while shaving, I had noticed I was very jaundiced. As a dentist, I recognized that the jaundice was a symptom of a liver problem. Less than a week later, my gall bladder was removed. Forty-five minutes into the surgery, the doctor came out to tell my wife that I had a slowly progressive liver disease that would eventually require a liver transplant for me to survive. We had two children, ages 4 and 2, a home and a new dental practice. The news was not exactly on the agenda of how we saw our life together. These two words, "It's time," have stuck with me all of these years.

We had been Christians since we were married. Following Christ, and being faithful to Him does not protect one from the problems of life, but it does teach one how to deal with those problems. The years passed and our children grew. My liver disease progressed, requiring me to stay in the hospital more frequently. The bills kept coming in, and I worried what kind of father, husband and provider I was. My wife considered life alone as a single parent. We found ourselves stressed with more than a little anxiety. But we were blessed with a church, family, friends and doctors that cared for us and loved us and kept us steady. We found ourselves moving closer to God.

One night when I was particularly sick, my wife and I were lying in bed awake, talking, crying and worrying. We could not do this any more and then we realized we didn't have to. This was not our job. We have a Lord who promises us, "Come to me, all you who are weary and burdened, and I will give you rest. Take my yoke upon you and learn from me, for I am gentle and humble in heart, and you will find rest for your souls. For my yoke is easy and my burden is light" (Matthew 11:28-30). "It's time" - we gave it over to Him, and our life changed drastically. The truth of how these sorts of things make a relationship grow closer or divide it is true. As we focused more on God, we focused on each other a lot more and our marriage grew. When you love God the way He intends, you cannot help but love people around you the way He intends.

We also began praying diligently for my donor. We knew that when the time came, someone would have to die for me to live. We prayed for the family of my donor. We knew that during the most tragic moment in their lives, someone would have to ask them if they would be willing to allow others to live through harvesting of their loved one's organs.

As the sun was rising, we drove to the hospital for my transplant. I thought, "This may be the last time I see a sunrise this side of heaven." Looking at my wife's beautiful face as the dark orange sun grew brighter and rose higher made me realize how blessed I had been. One agrees to "for better, for worse, in sickness and in health," but does anyone really believe at the time one says it that it will ever occur? She had fulfilled every letter of that vow. She loved me as deeply, as hard and as well as she possibly could. Before I was taken into surgery, we had time alone in the "pre-op" area. These were the most frustrating few moments of my life. How do you begin to tell your wife how much you love her in a short period of time? Will she ever understand how I felt when I rolled over in the middle of the night just to see the outline of her figure under the sheets? Is there a painting or photograph that will make her understand? Is there a *texture or a fabric that she could touch to give her a hint of what I felt when I touched her? Would she ever be able to understand what happens to my heart when I kiss her? The answer was "no" and "yes" at the same time. She had the same frustrations. That is what "I love you" means. Every emotion, smile, tear and memory of our life was in those words. That was all we could utter to each other in those few minutes. But it was enough.*

My donor's liver continues to work great, and the change in my life has been remarkable. If I had to live my life over and go through it all again, I would. I am a better man, a better husband, a better father, a better boss and a better Christian for having had this experience. I have a better understanding of what Jesus did for me by dying on the cross. Someone had to die for me so I could continue to live on earth. Jesus had to die for my sins so I could live eternally in heaven with Him.

Recently, God blessed me again. I am recovering from successful cancer surgery. Once again, we gave it over to God and focused on His will. As a result, we found ourselves loving each other more than we ever thought possible.

THE POWER OF SACRIFICE

I once asked my pastor, "How come we never hear any sermons about sacrifice?" In all the years I had attended church, in several different denominations, I could only remember one or two such sermons. Shortly thereafter, Tom Morris, one of the associate ministers, preached a sermon entitled "Strengthened By Sacrifice." [2] I would like to share with you some of the insights of his message.

Both celebrities and heroes sacrifice. The difference is that celebrities sacrifice for themselves to achieve their personal goals, and heroes sacrifice for others. The Church is about building people up. After Jesus ascended into heaven, the early Church was characterized by giving and sharing. The members gave to one another as each had need. They recognized that they were simply stewards of all that God had given to them. The ownership of their things belonged to God. He had simply entrusted them with the responsibility of looking after them. If we say that Jesus is Lord of our life, we must each decide regarding this issue of ownership. This is important because, if God asks us to part with our "stuff," we won't have a problem. When we give, we are only giving what God has given to us.

Once as I was driving home, I was just about to pull into the driveway, when I suddenly saw in my mind our home completely burnt to the ground. It was a deep impression that God gave me. In that moment God asked, "How do you feel?" At first I was devastated. All I could think about was all that had been lost. All the clothes, picture albums of our family, computers, etc. were gone. Everything had been lost. Then a deep peace swept over me. It was almost like I had been liberated from the stuff of my life. It didn't matter. It was just stuff. God used that event to help me. I have never struggled with the stuff of life since.

The Church today has been corrupted by three aspects that characterize our self-centered culture.

1.   Individualism – Ask yourself, "Are people ruder today or more polite?" Rudeness is a symptom of individualism. The overall attitude expressed by individualism is, "Others don't matter," "It's my way or the highway" and "I did it my way." The Book of Proverbs states,

He who separates himself seeks his own desire, he quarrels against all sound wisdom. A fool does not delight in understanding, but only in revealing his own mind.   **Proverbs 18:1-2**

He thinks only of himself.

2.   Secularism – The attitude of the secularist is that God doesn't matter. Although polls in the USA have shown that 90% of people believe God exists, their attitude is, "God, you stay on your side of the fence, and I will stay on mine."

They say to God, 'Depart from us! We do not even desire the knowledge of Your ways.'   **Job 21:14**

Many people attend church on Sunday, but during the week, God is irrelevant and has nothing to do with the way they live their lives.

A wicked man in his pride thinks that God doesn't matter. In all his thoughts there's no room for God. (GNB)

Psalm 10:4

255

Have we become so busy, so full of ourselves, that there's no room for God? Look at the titles of some of the best-selling books in the past decade: *Re-creating Yourself, When All You've Wanted Is Not Enough, Looking Out For Number One, How To Be Your Own Best Friend, Pulling Your Own Strings, Total Self Confidence, Trusting Yourself, How To Keep Control Of Your Life After Fifty.* The overall attitude is, "I don't need God. I don't need other people. I certainly don't need anybody to cramp my style. All I need is me."

3. Narcissism – This is the philosophy that says, "All that matters is me." It's exemplified by the T-shirt that says, "It's all about me!" We are so self-absorbed. All I am interested in is *my* goals, *my* dreams, *my* desires, *my* self-fulfillment, *my* happiness, *my* career, etc. Everything in my life is evaluated by the question, "What's in it for me?"

For he flatters and deceives himself in his own eyes, that his iniquity (sin) will not be found out and be hated. (AMP)

Psalm 36:2

As a result of this self-centeredness, the Church has been weakened. People come to church asking, "What kind of programs do you have for me and my children?" "Do I like the music?" "How can you help me?" Think about it; if everyone came to church with this attitude, who would do the serving? Who would look out for the others and care for them?

Not only has the Church been weakened by such ideology, but so have marriages. A mother or father leaves the family to go "find" herself or himself. There was a study done on America's search for self-fulfillment in which hundreds of people were interviewed in several cities. The conclusion: "Among married people interviewed, those most devoted to their own self fulfillment were those having the most trouble in their marriage." That should not surprise us. It's no accident that during the "Me" decade, the divorce rate has soared.

Finally, self-centeredness has resulted in generalized frustration and despair. If you are at the center of your world, it's not too long before your world becomes meaningless. Proverbs 28:25 states, *"Selfishness only causes trouble."* If you make yourself the center of the universe, eventually that universe will crumble because you can't control everything around you. You need a higher power, a greater authority, a focus and a moral compass to give your life meaning and significance.

FOCUS

The happy and efficient people in this world are those who accept trouble as a normal detail of human life and resolve to capitalize on it when it comes along. H. Bertram Lewis

TRUTH (What is the focus – the essential truth of this chapter?)

Times of suffering WILL occur in my life. But I know that God will not allow anything to happen to me that He can't use for my good.

APPLICATION (What does this truth mean to me? How is it relevant in my life?)

I need to do the opposite of what I feel and thank God for times of suffering, because I know He will keep His promise and work them for my good.

ACTION (What should I do about it? How can this truth benefit my life?)

Pray: Dear Jesus, I thank you for the difficult times in my life and look forward to all the good You will bring out of them.

CHAPTER 13

GETTING ON THE ANCIENT PATH
WHAT DOES GOD WANT?

There is a path that God intends for men. I have called it the Ancient Path. It is not new. It is dependable and has proven reliable over time. If you choose to take this path, it will be your best shot at success in life and your marriage.

God wants nothing more from you than He has given - a 100% commitment. Do not be intimidated by this. In the Sermon on the Mount, Jesus stated,

Blessed are those who hunger and thirst for righteousness, for they shall be satisfied.   **Matthew 5:6**

It is clear from God's comments to the Church at Laodicea in Revelation that He is disgusted by lukewarm Christians. He is no different than we are in this regard. Think for a moment about the significant relationships in your life. Are you satisfied with half-hearted commitments?

If you fear a full commitment to God, let me point out this important spiritual principle: It is impossible to out give God. No one loves you more than God. No one has done more for you than He has. No one extends to you promises that even begin to compare to those that God gives to you. Sometimes our imperfect earthly fathers prevent us from seeing our heavenly Father in the proper light. But you can be assured that your heavenly Father is pure and holy and has only your best interests at heart. God is not in any way capricious. He loves you and wants to bless you. Like a loving earthly father wants to give his children everything, so too, does your heavenly Father. I love this Scripture verse from Psalms:

Delight yourself in the Lord; and He will give you the desires of your heart.   **Psalm 37:4**

I previously quoted this passage from II Chronicles:

The eyes of the Lord move to and fro throughout the earth that

He may strongly support those whose heart is completely His.
II Chronicles 16:9

God longs to have a relationship with you. He longs to strongly support you. All He asks from you is that you come and yield to Him. Although I thought I had run my life successfully for the first 26 years, it was not until I completely submitted to Him that I found out what real living was all about. It was only in surrendering everything that I then received so much more of God's bounty.

The First Epistle of Peter states:

But you are a chosen race, a royal priesthood, a holy nation, a people for God's own possession, so that you may proclaim the excellencies of Him who has called you out of darkness into His marvelous light.
I Peter 2:9

It is worthy to note that, as you yield and submit to Him, you become part of God's family, His chosen race. You become royalty, a part of a holy nation, a people whom God possesses. As you achieve your spiritual potential, you will find through the Holy Spirit that you will proclaim the excellencies of God, who called you out of the kingdom of darkness into the kingdom of light.

ACHIEVING BALANCE IN LIFE

The Ancient Path will help you achieve proper balance in life. Let me begin by sharing a few important facts to help increase your faith.

1.) God loves you beyond measure!
We are told in John's Gospel:

For God so loved the world, that He gave His only begotten Son, that whoever believes in Him shall not perish, but have eternal life. For God did not send the Son into the world to judge the world, but that the world might be saved through Him.
John 3:16-17

I am amazed by Christianity. There is no other religion on earth, in which a loving God sends His only Son to suffer and die, to restore us in our relationship with Him. God is passionate about having a relationship with you. God's sacrificial giving for mankind sets

Christianity on a pedestal far above any other religion.

The Apostle Paul wrote to the Church at Rome:

For I am convinced that neither death, nor life, nor angels nor principalities, nor things present, nor things to come, nor powers, nor height, nor depth, nor any other created thing, will be able to separate us from the love of God, which is in Christ Jesus our Lord.
Romans 8:38-39

You can take great comfort in knowing that there is literally nothing in the universe that can separate you from the love of God.

2.) God expects you to believe in Him.

The author of the Book of Hebrews wrote:

Now faith is the assurance of things hoped for, the conviction of things not seen ... And without faith it is impossible to please Him, for he who comes to God must believe that He is and that He is a rewarder of those who seek Him. **Hebrews 11:1 & 6**

It is faith which gives you the eyes to see how God can use adverse circumstances for your good.

3.) God expects you to pray to change circumstances.

Matthew records:

Ask, and it will be given you; seek, and you will find; knock, and it will be opened to you. **Matthew 7:7**

The verse gives you a picture of how you should pray. It is not just a matter of *asking*, but going to God and *seeking* the answer and literally *knocking*. Notice the tenacity and persistence with which you are instructed to pray. But note, this tenacity is not your attempt to manipulate God. Remember, God's focus is on His kingdom. Are our prayers directed at changing our circumstances or His kingdom here on earth?

The Gospel of Mark says:

Truly I say to you, whoever says to this mountain, "Be taken up and cast into the sea," and does not doubt in his heart, but believes that what he says is going to happen, it shall be granted him. Therefore I say to you, all things for which you pray and ask, believe that you have received them, and they shall be granted you. **Mark 11:23-24**

Jesus instructed us to come to God like a little child. Remember how little children come. They ask for all kinds of things. Many requests are foolish and would be detrimental if answered. But this is how we are encouraged to come to God. Our function is to ask. It is God's function to answer. As we grow in Him, our petitions become more mature, although our attitude should remain childlike.

The Book of James states:

Is anyone among you suffering? Then he must pray. Is anyone cheerful? He is to sing praises. Is anyone among you sick? Then he must call for the elders of the church and let them pray over him, anointing him with oil in the name of the Lord; and the prayer offered in faith will restore the one who is sick, and the Lord will raise him up, and if he has committed sins, they will be forgiven him. Therefore, confess your sins to one another, and pray for one another so that you may be healed. The effective prayer of a righteous man can accomplish much. **James 5:13-16**

A logical question is, "If God wants us to pray in faith, why isn't everyone healed when we pray?" Only God knows the intricacies of each life. You can be sure that He is at work in your life for the ultimate best. Remember, sometimes that means that when you pray and request something from God, His answer may be "Yes," "No," or "I have a better idea." We do not know all that He knows. However, you can be certain that He always hears and always answers. He knows what is best for you. He knows your needs better than you do and promises that all your needs will be met. That doesn't necessarily mean you receive all that you want. You need to have a clear understanding of the difference between your needs and your wants.

4.) While on earth, suffering will be inevitable.
I Peter states,

But to the degree that you share the sufferings of Christ, keep on rejoicing, so that also at the revelation of His glory, you may rejoice with exultation. **I Peter 4:13**

And also in James:

Consider it all joy, my brethren, when you encounter various trials, knowing that the testing of your faith produces endurance. **James 1:2-3**

I will not belabor the point after my comments in the last chapter. But, it is essential that our response to suffering be dramatically different from those who do not know Jesus.

5.) God has a perfect plan for your life.

We have seen this verse in Romans:

And we know that God causes all things to work together for good to those who love God, to those who are called according to His purpose. For those whom He foreknew, He also predestined to become conformed to the image of His Son, so that He might be the first born among many brethren. **Romans 8:28-29**

God promises to work all things for your good. However, it does involve a condition. He has predestined you to become conformed to the image of His Son Jesus. I must admit that, on some days, I do not always want to be conformed to that image. His answer to this promise involves me doing my part to yield to Him (indicating my wish to become conformed to the image of His Son). Once you understand that, as a committed believer in Christ, nothing bad can happen to you unless allowed and permitted by God. You are assured that God can make good out of what appears to be a terrible situation. As a result, you go beyond just enduring and praise God, not only in the midst of the circumstance, but literally *for the circumstance*. The circumstance merely represents an opportunity for God to work in your life, perfecting you. Remember the metaphor used in the Old Testament. God, our Father is the master potter and we are the clay. If you will yield to Him, the clay of your life being malleable and of the perfect consistency, then your heavenly Father can fashion your life into something beautiful.

6.) God expects you to live in joy and peace.

The Apostle Paul stated:

But in all these things we overwhelmingly conquer through Him who loved us. **Romans 8:37**

It is through the power of the Holy Spirit working in us that we achieve our spiritual potential, and we "overwhelmingly conquer" through Christ.

In Philippians, we read,

Rejoice in the Lord always; again I will say rejoice! Let your gentle spirit be known to all men. The Lord is near. Be anxious for nothing, but in everything by prayer and supplication with thanksgiving let your requests be made known to God. And the peace of God, which surpasses all comprehension, will guard your hearts and your minds in Christ Jesus. **Philippians 4:4-7**

There is a difference between peace and joy. Webster defines joy as: "1. a very glad feeling; happiness; great pleasure; delight." Peace is defined as: "1. freedom from war or civil strife, 2. freedom from disagreement or quarrels; harmony; concord, 3. an undisturbed state of mind; absence of mental conflict; serenity."

It takes faith for you to live as God desires. You must put your whole trust in Him. I am reminded of the story of a burning house. A little boy named Bobby was trapped in an upstairs bedroom. He was able to open the window. When his father saw him, he yelled, "Bobby, jump and I will catch you!" But Bobby was afraid. Because of the smoke billowing out the window, he could not see his father. "I can't see you, Daddy!" he cried back. "Bobby, don't worry; I can see you. Just jump. I will catch you." Fortunately, Bobby put his entire trust in his father's words and jumped to safety into his father's arms. Sometimes because of all the "smoke" in your life, you can't see, sense or feel God's presence, but He is always there watching you. At those times, you need to jump into your Father's arms. He will catch you.

As a Christian seeking to achieve your total spiritual potential, you can be assured of the facts described above. Focusing on them will give you understanding. They will help you create the balance you need. They will permit you to overcome and endure, allowing you to go on and become all that God intends.

VICTORIOUS LIVING

A number of years ago, I went through a period when I was down right depressed. It was accompanied by discouragement and confusion regarding my life and its direction. The period lasted for some time, and I became progressively more miserable. I suppose I was waiting for my circumstances to change for the better and for God to intervene and rescue me. Neither happened!

I even began to doubt my relationship with God. In retrospect, I now realize that God permitted this, and it turned out to be one of the most valuable times in my life. In the midst of my depression, I had to figure a way out of the mess. Over the next several months, God instructed me on the Ancient Path. I will describe the process I went through.

I went back to the Bible and re-examined all I had been taught and all that I believed. It forced me to crystallize exactly my faith.

I began by defining for myself two very important points. First, I knew that *GOD LOVED ME*. Second, I believed that *GOD HAD A PERFECT PLAN FOR MY LIFE*. These facts became my anchor and starting point. It was God's Word and the Holy Spirit working in my life that made these truths real to me. No matter what, I knew I could depend on these truths.

If you don't believe these, then you are in the stage I call *nonunderstanding*. In this phase, you are always asking, "**Why** did this happen to me?" "**How** could God do this?" The trials you face cause stress, confusion, unhappiness and doubts. Your prayers always *focus on the circumstances* at hand, and you ask God to change them. When we are new Christians, or what I call baby Christians, God often answers our prayers by changing the circumstances. However, as we mature in our relationship with our Father, He benevolently says, "No," to these requests. This confuses us, until we begin to realize that He has something to teach us. The Bible says, "God's ways are not our ways." Man, is that ever the truth!

Compare this to a little child learning to walk. If his parents help him with each step, he will never learn to walk. We learn to walk by repeatedly trying and failing. Finally, we get it. So too, are the lessons of life that God wants you to learn to grow up to be a mature individual, able to stand on your own two feet and walk with confidence in the midst of the storms of life. Entering the stage of *understanding* brings great freedom. It is exciting to know that God is at work in your life. It is during this stage that you come to realize that *GOD LOVES YOU* and *GOD HAS A PERFECT PLAN FOR YOUR LIFE*. Remember, the Bible says that God, your Father is the potter and you are the clay. He desires to make something beautiful out of your life. However, for this to happen, you must realize that He uses the trials in life for your own good. Sometimes my children were frustrated by trials. I always told them, "God loves you even more

265

than your mother and I love you. He promises *to make good out of every situation.*"

And we know that God causes all things to work together for good to those who love God, to those who are called according to His purpose.   **Romans 8:28**

After reminding them of this verse, I told them, "You will never find a better deal than this anywhere in the universe." In essence, you really have only two options. You can complain about your circumstances and rebel against what God wants to do, or you can submit to His loving plan and recognize that the trials He permits He uses to change you so that you can become all He desires. I call this latter stage *acceptance*. Acceptance comprehends that circumstances are allowed for your good to produce strength, endurance, patience and a variety of other qualities that God knows you need to develop.

Consider it all joy, my brethren, when you encounter various trials, knowing that the testing of your faith produces endurance. And let endurance have its perfect result, that you may be perfect and complete, lacking in nothing.   **James 1:2–4**

Our way is to develop a rigorous self-improvement program that only leads to frustration. Why? Because only God can change you. Therefore, you have to commit to Him and trust that He will transform you. This transformation actually makes you able to *"prove what the will of God is."*

Therefore, I urge you, brethren, by the mercies of God, to present your bodies as a living and holy sacrifice, acceptable to God which is your spiritual service of worship. And do not be conformed to this world, but be transformed by the renewing of your mind, that you may prove what the will of God is, that which is good and acceptable and perfect.   **Romans 12:1-2**

To achieve your spiritual potential, you must make this commitment. Once you have made it, you must believe that God has taken over. Then, eagerly accept with thanksgiving and praise *all* the circumstances God uses to bring about His transformation in your life. Sounds a little crazy, doesn't it? "Praising God for the bad things going on in your life? Are you nuts?" Keep reading – it should make sense shortly.

You will notice that, with acceptance, comes a decided difference in how you pray. You are no longer focused on the circumstances, because they are simply part of God's wonderful, purposeful plan for your life. Your focus has changed. Instead of focusing on the circumstances, you are now *focusing on Jesus*. You delight in Him.

Delight yourself in the Lord; and He will give you the desires of your heart. **Psalm 37:4**

If you have an attitude of thanksgiving despite your situation, you will experience true joy in life. You are less anxious. You continually cast all your cares upon Him because you know He cares for you. The trials of life don't seem to adversely affect you as before. You are walking and living your life by faith - faith that God does indeed love you and is working out His purpose in your life.

Faith is an interesting quality. It is often difficult to define. We understand it better when we experience it. I remember several years ago touring Biosphere 2, just north of Tucson, Arizona. It was a self-contained glass and steel enclosure in which eight Biospherans lived. They planted and grew their own food and raised animals. The project was designed to give us the information needed to, one day, develop a fully functional and independent space station on the moon or another planet. One problem that occurred inside Biosphere 2 was that, as the trees grew larger, they suddenly broke halfway up the trunk. The explanation was that, although all the other conditions necessary for proper growth were present in Biosphere 2, there was no wind. Wind was needed to not only strengthen the trees as they grew, but to also make them resilient. Without wind, the trees were brittle and weak and broke from their own weight.

So too, in our lives we need the winds of adversity to make us strong and resilient. If we have no trials in life, we will never need faith. There really would never be an opportunity to trust God. We are called by God to walk by faith. Faith is a deliberate determination to trust and rely on God's Word in spite of the circumstances and what our senses tell us. Faith enables us to live in a new dimension. We must be broken of our habits of trusting only our senses, emotions and intellect.

Notice Paul's attitude in writing to the Church at Rome:

... we also exult in our tribulations, knowing that tribulation

brings about perseverance; and perseverance, proven character; and proven character, hope; and hope does not disappoint, because the love of God has been poured out within our hearts through the Holy Spirit who was given to us. **Romans 5:3–5**

God is love, and His power working in you and through you is love. His message to the world is love, and we are His messengers. God wants us to be "full and complete." God is continually changing you for the better. The problems or habits you previously could not solve, you are now overcoming as the Master Potter shapes your life. You are living life in a new dimension. You are beginning to experience eternal life right now here on earth. This is what Jesus meant when He said:

I came that they might have life, and have it abundantly. **John 10:10**

Acceptance allows you to experience real joy and peace in the midst of difficult situations. This leads you to the stage of *praise*. Many Christians make it to the stage of acceptance, but never progress any further. Praise is what I call the "pole vault" stage. Why do I call it this? Because in my personal experience and in counseling others, I've seen that it is the progression from acceptance to praise that requires the greatest leap of faith. This leap of faith only occurs once you have completely internalized the following facts:

1. God loves me beyond measure.
2. God has a perfect plan for my life that gives purpose in all that I do.
3. As a result of man's sin, I will experience trials and suffering.
4. God promises to use every unpleasant circumstance in my life for my good. He can make good out of each tragedy.
5. Because the above facts are true, I can **deliberately praise God**, not just in the midst of, but actually **for my trials**.

When you begin to deliberately praise God for the bad things occurring in your life, the people around you will think you are definitely crazy. It will not make sense to them. It only makes sense when you understand the facts above and combine them with faith. These make up the pole that you need to cross the chasm between acceptance and praise. If you achieve this, you will notice some incredible changes. First, you will begin to see things through God's eyes. Second, being able to praise God for bad situations provides an avenue for tremendous release from the burden of these situations. You will sometimes find yourself overwhelmed with His peace "that surpasses all understanding."

Lastly, being willing to deliberately praise God for your trials somehow magically *releases the power of God.* In effect, praise says to God, "Father, I don't like the current problem I am facing, but I know that somehow You will use it for my good, so I thank You for it." It sounds so simple to do, but initially it can be very hard. With practice it gets easier and more natural. With time and by faith, it actually begins to make sense.

PRIORITIES AND FOCUS

God's command is that you seek His kingdom first and that you love God with all your heart, soul, mind and strength. The key to life is focus. When you are driving, you can't stay in your lane without proper focus. So too, focus is essential to stay on the Ancient Path. Here's a simple example of the importance of focus.

I always had trouble filling empty ice cube trays with water and putting them back in the refrigerator without spilling some of the water. It frustrated me to no end. One day I thought to myself, "I know I can do this if I just focus and concentrate." After I filled one of the empty trays, I looked at it and refused to look away. My focus was on nothing else. To my amazement, I didn't spill a drop. I thought, "This must be an accident. I always spill some water." So I did it again and again, never spilling a drop. For those of you who have never spilled a drop of water filling ice cube trays, I suppose you can't relate. My problem has always been that I get in a hurry, and I'm always thinking about what I am going to be doing next and not focusing on what I am doing now. An ice cube tray helped me apply the principle of focus to other areas of my life, specifically in regard to my priorities and staying on the Ancient Path.

Since Jesus is truly "the way, the truth and the life," you can do no better than to let Him be your focus. Your priorities give you focus. What are your priorities in life? Are they what you really want them to be? Or have other less important things forced their way into your life? What is your passion? What are your choices in life?

Priorities are what you make them. Your choice, or lack of choice, will determine how you spend your time.

I spoke about priorities in Chapter 9. If you did not complete the exercise on priorities in that chapter, I encourage you to do the following. First, list all the things you do in a typical week. Then, add the things you do less frequently. Second, put them in the order of how they have taken precedence in your life. These are your current priorities. Look at the list. Are they in the order that you want them to be? Third, rearrange them to what you want them to be. Lastly, develop a strategy to actually rearrange your priorities to what you want them to be in your day-to-day life. If you are unsure as to what the exact order of your priorities should be, seek the counsel of God, your spouse and your best friend. Don't forget, relationships are the key to life.

I have referred to Dr. Richard A. Swenson's book, *Margin, Restoring Emotional, Physical, Financial, and Time Reserves to Overloaded Lives*. In this book, he describes a "new morbidity" which he defines as marginless living - an insidious disease that is widespread and virulent. He is referring to the frenzied pace at which we live our lives. The velocity of our lives results in our relationships being starved to death. "We don't have time to listen, let alone love. Our children lay wounded on the ground, run over by our high-speed good intentions." He contends that our success and progress have been defined by money, technology and education. The problem is that none of these speaks to our transcendent values and needs.

He recommends that we stop and redirect our lives. We must make progress subservient to what is most important to us, especially our relationships. After all, it is relationships that God focuses on, and He certainly defines progress quite differently than our current society. Swenson defines *margin* as "room to breathe," and he gives examples of how Jesus created margin in everything He did. I was challenged by this book to find ways of deliberately creating margin in my own life, and using the breathing room to facilitate the development of my relationships.

GOD CAN USE YOU TO MAKE A DIFFERENCE

The population of the earth recently exceeded 6 billion. Sometimes, we feel small and easily overwhelmed. Have you ever felt that you are too small to make a difference? The good news is you aren't. In Acts 1:8, Jesus said that we would be His witnesses *"even to the remotest part of the earth."* That doesn't mean you have to travel to the ends of the earth. You can be His witness wherever you are. The amazing thing is that our sovereign God uses imperfect people to accomplish His purposes. God has chosen to do His work through us. In the Bible, God repeatedly used people who were "small" and "insignificant" to accomplish great things. God searches for the humble, not the proud. In essence, if you see yourself as too small, then you're perfect! We must be small enough to be used. Remember the first Beatitude; we must be "poor in spirit." Remember also that His strength is made perfect in your weakness.

There are many ways that God can use you to make a difference. Let's look at some of them.

1. **Availability** – Isaiah said, "Here am I Lord, send me." So wherever you go, adopt the attitude of being available to God to be used. Jesus used a small boy who had five loaves of bread and two fish to feed 5,000 people. The point is that it isn't what you have, it's what you are willing to give. Will you give what you have to Jesus?

2. **Experience** – Jesus called four fishermen and said, "Follow Me and I will make you fishers of men." He was saying that He would use their past experiences for His purposes. Whatever your past experiences, whether good or bad, God wants to use them.

3. **Prayer** – Prayer is God's tool to change the world. Among other things, we are told to pray for those in authority. Prayer can change the way our rulers run the country. Are you willing to be used by God to pray?

4. **Pain** – God comforts us in our pain. Likewise, we can comfort others, especially those with problems similar to those we have experienced. Pray to God and say, "Lord, you can use even my pain." Remember, people are watching us to see if the gospel of hope still works for us in the midst of our pain.

5. **Faith** – Are you willing to step out of the boat in faith as Peter did, trusting that Jesus will hold you up? Are you willing to let God use your life to reach people with His love?

Many Christians seem confused and frustrated by the concept of evangelism or witnessing. The heart of being a Christian is sharing the Good News of what God has done in your life and what He can do for others. This begins with "lifestyle" evangelism. If you are traveling along the Ancient Path, people will see the joy in your life, the unique way you respond to difficulties and the concern you have for those around you. They will be drawn to you. How hard is it to tell them why you are the way you are and what God has done for you? Remember, we must earn the right to be heard.

In Matthew 28, Jesus gave the Great Commission telling us to go *"make disciples."* The lost are valuable to God. Jesus ate with sinners and told them stories about how much God loved them. Who wouldn't want to hear about how much someone loves them?

I want to ask you three questions:

1. What kind of witness are you for Jesus?
2. Do you realize that God brings people in your life for you to be a witness to?
3. Do you know that God will give you power through the Holy Spirit to be an effective witness?

What Kind of Witness Are You for Jesus?

Jesus said, *If I be lifted up, I will draw all men unto Me.* Is our behavior such that people are being drawn to Jesus, or are we driving them away? Our behavior is determined not only by what we know, but by how we use that knowledge. There is a difference between wisdom and knowledge. Webster defines them as follows:

Knowledge – "have a clear perception or understanding of."

Wisdom – "having or showing good judgment, prudent, discreet. Following the soundest course of action based on knowledge, experience, understanding."

As I meditated on the difference between knowledge and wisdom, I realized that you can be smart and have knowledge, but still be dumb! You can know a lot but have little wisdom. Wisdom guides you in the use of what you know.

I see this in my office when patients come in with a lot of information they have downloaded from the Internet. They come with a significant amount of knowledge (information) about their symptoms and medical condition. Sometimes, by the time I see them, they are convinced they actually have several different diseases. Even though they have all this knowledge, they lack the wisdom to put it all together.

God Brings People into Your Life for You to Witness to

Recently, one of my fourth-year medical students, who was about to graduate, said to me, "May I ask you a question I can't ask anyone else?" He was questioning all he had been taught about religion. He was afraid he would offend and upset his family and friends if he called into question their beliefs. After he outlined for me his many concerns, I gave him a book entitled *How You Can Be Sure That You Will Spend Eternity With God,* by Erwin W. Lutzer. Each morning, I sent him to the library to read for one hour; then he would return and we would discuss what he had read. After reading the first chapter, he commented, "I am not sure where he is going. He's already dismissed every way I've ever heard of how to get into heaven." Each day, I simply asked the Holy Spirit to fill him with wisdom and knowledge. The changes that occurred in him over the following month were remarkable.

Jesus said that He is the *"way, the **truth** and the life."* You must come to a place in your life where you decide who you will believe. When the Apostle Paul wrote to the Church at Corinth, he stated:

For Christ did not send me to baptize, but to preach the gospel, not in cleverness of speech, so that the cross of Christ would not be made void. **I Corinthians 1:17**

And my message and my preaching were not in persuasive words of wisdom, but in demonstration of the Spirit and of power, so that your faith would not rest on the wisdom of men, but on the power of God. **I Corinthians 2:4**

You don't have to be concerned with the words you use when telling others about Jesus. You only need to tell what He has done in your life. God will give you the right words. They may not seem eloquent, but if they are sincere, they will be effective.

God Will Give You Power Through His Holy Spirit to Be an Effective Witness

Has God done things in your life? Has He changed you? Your testimony about what He has done in your life is your witness. Just as His power changed your life, your witness gives hope to others of how God can change their lives, too.

If you are a Christian, it is probably because someone, such as your mom, dad or a friend, invited you to become one. Jesus has compassion for people. If you are truly compassionate and love people, you will reach out to them with the best that God has to offer. They may not accept or believe what you tell them, but they can't deny the testimony of what God has done in your life. I suggest you begin by praying and asking the Holy Spirit to give you the opportunity to speak to one lost friend.

YOUR T-SHIRT

If I were to give you a plain white T-shirt with nothing on it, and I asked you to write or draw on it your logo for life, what would it be? How would you synthesize what your life is all about in a picture or a few words?

I was challenged to do this a number of years ago. For months, I worked on my logo. At first it was very detailed. I drew a raging river with banks that were quite steep. To cross the river without a bridge would be very dangerous. Next, I drew a walking bridge over the river with the initials of the not-for-profit foundation that my wife and I had established written on it. The water of the raging river symbolized life with its many difficulties. So many of the people I come into contact with have trouble getting across the river of life. The purpose of our foundation is to help them. In my mind, I saw my wife and I taking the hands of people and walking them across the bridge one at a time.

For example, our mission trips to South and Central America have been designed to help the poor. Our teams have included doctors and dentists to help those who have little or no access to health care. Construction teams have built homes, churches, medical-dental clinics and buildings for in-country mission organizations. We have distributed food, clothing and toys to the needy. The big surprise to both my wife and I has been that the people who have gone with us have been the most blessed. By their sacrificial giving, they received abundantly more then they gave. Of course, this is exactly what God promises. So often, those who have traveled with us have been going through some crisis. We have been amazed to see how team members have ministered to them. New friendships that can last a lifetime have been formed.

But the more I looked at my logo, though it made sense to me, I realized it was too detailed and required a lot of explanation to help others understand our mission. So I started thinking about the essence of the logo. I asked myself, "What are we really all about?" I wanted a logo so simple that it immediately conveyed a message to everyone who saw it. It finally dawned on me. I sketched two outstretched hands. They simply represented the hands of love that we want to be to all we meet.

When I get up every morning, I think of the outstretched hands and pray, "Oh, Lord, I want to help as many people today in as many ways as I possibly can." That's it. That is the essence of my life. It's that simple.

So, let me challenge you. What is the essence of your life? What are you all about? In what ways do you want your life to count for something? How do you want to make a difference? What would your logo look like?

FOCUS

TRUTH (What is the focus – the essential truth of this chapter?)

God wants me to get on the Ancient Path because He loves me and wants to bless my marriage and my life.

APPLICATION (What does this truth mean to me? How is it relevant in my life?)

If I treat my wife the way that God intends, I give my marriage the best chance of success and allow God to work in our lives.

ACTION (What should I do about it? How can this truth benefit my life?)

Pray: Dear God, please help me to get on and stay on the Ancient Path. I surrender every aspect of my life completely to You, and give you total control of my life. Empower me to become the man, husband and father you destine me to be.

CONCLUSION

Many men have chosen to travel the Ancient Path. I want to encourage you. No matter how old you are or what direction your life has taken, you can decide to get on the Ancient Path. I can assure you, God is ready to meet you right where you are.

The Ancient Path will help you clearly see the phases of your life. It will allow you to make success and significance congruent, and show you how to live every moment of everyday in the present.

The Ancient Path will empower your marriage, making it better than you ever dreamed possible. You will be able to become the father you always wanted to be.

Most important of all, the Ancient Path will connect you to God in a deeply personal and powerful way, such that you will accomplish *far more abundantly beyond all that we ask or think according to the power that works within us.* (Ephesians 3:20)

Tim Rogers is a pharmaceutical representative who was kind enough to review the manuscript for this book. He had this to say:

Life and relationships don't have to be a hardship, although it does take work to make for joyful times. I believe that what God wants most is for a man to be, first and foremost, wholly committed to Him.

As I pored over these pages, I often thought about my twenty years of marriage, the ups and downs, and how helpful this book would have been at many different stages in my life. As I see other men around me, all at different stages in life, I realize how this book can create great discussions and build strong relationships that can have lasting impact.

This book, "The Ancient Path," is a great resource for either personal or small group study. Each section explores what men desire to know more about. It is an inspiring book that you can read many times through life's journeys.

In the end, it is each man's decision to allow the Holy Spirit to reveal some new truth that will help teach, inspire or require action in his life that will help him get on "The Ancient Path."

The decision is yours. Will you set this book aside, or allow God to use it as a manual to enable you to become the man God desires, and the husband and father your family so desperately needs?

I will be praying for the Holy Spirit to guide, direct and empower each of you.

BIBLIOGRAPHY

Introduction
1. Elmore, M. F. *Stress & Spirituality, Conquering the Stress of Life & Achieving Your Spiritual Potential.* Indianapolis, IN: MCK, Inc., 2002.

PART I

RECOGNIZING HOW LIFE WORKS

Chapter 1 – Finding Significance and Purpose In Life
1. Buford, B. *Halftime.* Grand Rapids, MI: Zondervan Publishing House, 1994.
2. Buford, B. *Game Plan.* Grand Rapids, MI: Zondervan Publishing House, 1997.
3. Buford, B. *Stuck In Halftime.* Grand Rapids, MI: Zondervan Publishing House, 2001.

Chapter 2 – Made in His Image
1. Eadie, B. J., Taylor, C. A., Morse, M. *Embraced by the Light.* Placerville, CA: Onjinjinkta Distribution, 1992.
2. Rawlings, M. S. *Beyond Death's Door.* Nashville, TN: Thomas Nelson Publishers, 1978.
3. Rawlings, M. S. *To Hell & Back: life after death – startling new evidence.* Nashville, TN: Thomas Nelson Publishers, 1993.
4. Gallup Poll, "Religion in America: 1990." Princeton Religious Research Center 1990.
5. MacArthur Foundation. *USA Today*, February 16, 1999.
6. Reed, W. S. *Surgery of the Soul: Healing the Whole Person – Spirit, Mind, and Body.* Tampa, FL: Christian Medical Foundation, Inc., 1969.
7. Elmore, M. F. *Understanding Your Digestive System.* Indianapolis, IN. MCK, LLC, 1991.
8. Elmore, M. F., Johnson, G. *A Christian Physician Looks at Stress & Healing.* Indianapolis, IN: MCK, Inc., 1996.
9. Crick, F., Orgel, L. "Directed Panspermia." *Icarus,*

1973: 341-346.

10. Blackmore, S. *Dying To Live: Near Death Experiences.*
    Buffalo, NY: Prometheus Books, 1993.
11. Benson, H. *Timeless Healing, The Power Of Biology &*
    Belief. New York: Simon & Schuster, 1996.
12. Conference: "Creativity & Madness – Psychologic
    Studies Of Art & Artists." La Fonda Hotel, Santa Fe,
    NM, February 19 – 22, 1998.

Chapter 3 - Real Christianity
1. Miller, D. *Searching For God Knows What.* Nashville,
   TN. Thomas Nelson, Inc., 2004.
2. Miller, D. *Blue Like Jazz.* Nashville, TN: Thomas
   Nelson, Inc., 2003.
3. Senge, P. M. *The Fifth Discipline, The Art & Practice of*
   The Learning Organization. New York, NY. Doubleday,
   1990.

Chapter 4 – The Importance of Relationships
1. Lamott, A. *Plan B Further Thoughts On Faith.* New
   York, NY. Riverhead Books, 2005.
2. Peck, M. S. *The Road Less Traveled, A New Psychology*
   of Love, Traditional Values & Spiritual Growth. New
   York, NY. Touchstone, 1978.
3. Keller, P. *A Shepherd Looks At Psalm 23.* Grand Rapids,
   MI. Zondervan Publishing House, 1970.

PART II

UNDERSTANDING WOMEN

Chapter 5 – Men & Women: Why Did God Make Us So
Different?
1. Eldredge, J. *Wild at Heart, Discovering The Secret of A*
   Man's Soul. Nashville, TN: Thomas Nelson, Inc., 2001.

Chapter 6 – Becoming the Husband and Father God Wants
You to Be
1. Hagee, J. *What Every Man Wants In A Woman, 10*

Essentials for Growing Deeper in Love. Lake Mary, FL. Charisma House, A Strang Company, 2005.

2. Dubner, S. J. & Levitt, S. D. *Freakonomics: A Rogue Economist Explores the Hidden Side of Everything.* New York, NY. HarperCollins Publishers, Inc., 2005.

3. Waite, L. J. & Gallagher, M. *The Case for Marriage: Why Married People Are Happier, Healthier, and Better Off Financially.* New York, NY. Broadway Books, 2000.

4. Thomas, K. B. "General Practice Consultations: Is There Any Point in Being Positive?" *British Medical Journal of Clinical Research,* 1987; 294:1200-1202.

Chapter 7 – The Abdication of Leadership

1. Warren, R. *The Purpose Driven Life, What On Earth Am I Here For?* Grand Rapids, MI. Zondervan Publishing House, 2002.

2. Harley, W. *His Needs Her Needs, Building An Affair-proof Marriage.* Grand Rapids, MI. Fleming H. Revell, 1986.

3. Alessandra, T. & O'Connor, M. J. *The Platinum Rule, Discover the Four Basic Business Personalities and How They Can Lead to Success.* New York, NY. Warner Books, Inc., 1996.

Chapter 8 – The Purpose of Work

1. Swenson, R. *Margin, Restoring Emotional, Physical, Financial, and Time Reserves To Overloaded Lives.* Colorado Springs, CO. NavPress, 1992.

2. Hughes, R. K. *Disciplines of a Godly Man.* Wheaton, IL. Crossway Books, 1991.

PART III

ESTABLISHING YOUR SPIRITUAL FOUNDATION

Chapter 9 – Connecting to God

1. Bargh, J. "Brain May Tag All Perceptions With A Value." *New York Times,* August 8, 1995, pg. C1 Quoted by D. Goleman.

Chapter 10 – The Work of the Holy Spirit in Your Life

1. Johnson, G. "Sermon Series on the Holy Spirit." Available through the tape ministry at Indian Creek Christian Church, Indianapolis, IN.

Chapter 11 – Answering the Questions of Life For Yourself

1. James, W. *The Varieties of Religious Experience.* London, New York & Bombay. Longman's, Green and Co., 1905.
2. Benson, H. *Timeless Healing, The Power Of Biology & Belief.* New York: Simon & Schuster, 1996.
3. Lloyd-Jones, D. M. *Studies In The Sermon On The Mount.* Grand Rapids, MI. Wm. B. Eerdmans Publishing Company, 1959-1960.

Chapter 12 - The Problem of Suffering – "Why?"

1. Warren, R. *The Purpose Driven Life, What On Earth Am I Here For?* Grand Rapids, MI. Zondervan Publishing House, 2002.
2. Morris, T. Sermon, "Strengthened By Sacrifice." Available through the tape ministry at Indian Creek Christian Church, Indianapolis, IN.

Chapter 13 – Getting on the Ancient Path

1. Swenson, R. *Margin, Restoring Emotional, Physical, Financial, and Time Reserves To Overloaded Lives.* Colorado Springs, CO. NavPress, 1992.
2. Lutzer, E. W. *How You Can Be Sure That You Will Spend Eternity With God.* Chicago, IL. Moody Press, 1996.

MCK Mission Foundation &
People Helping People Network

When is the last time you donated a week of your vacation time, paid $1000 or more of your hard earned money, went to a foreign country where you don't speak the language and spent your time serving the needs of others not expecting anything in return? Most Americans never have! However, those who have gone on one of our mission trips will tell you that it is an experience of a lifetime. Without exception they tell me that they feel like they received much more than they ever gave. I always tell them, "You can't out give God! It is impossible."

To everyone who considers going with us, I give the same warning, "This may be the most dangerous thing you ever do!" I am sure at first they think I am speaking about some sort of physical danger in a third world country. But, that is not what I mean at all. Once you have gone on a mission trip, it changes you forever. So, beware! If you go, you will not return the same person, and it will affect how you see every aspect of your life.

In 1989 I was invited by Dr. Julio Fuentes, a surgeon from San Marcos, Guatemala, to come and work with him to train him in the techniques of endoscopy (the passage of a flexible instrument into the intestinal tract for the diagnosis of intestinal problems) and to do digestive clinics for the people. San Marcos is a town of 60,000 which serves some 300,000 indigent Mayan Indians in the surrounding villages. In 1990, accompanied by two others, I went to Guatemala for the first time. Each year since then, I have returned with groups to do medical/dental evangelistic clinics. As a result of the many physicians, dentists and allied health professionals that have accompanied me, strong relationships have been developed with the residents of San Marcos. I have also led trips to Costa Rica, Nicaragua, El Salvador, Peru and Colombia.

In the Spring of 2003, Jeff Cardwell, Founder and President of The People Helping People Network, and I joined forces for the first time on a trip to Guatemala. Two homes were constructed working with Habitat For Humanity, a medical clinic was held in the village of Santa Teresa with the help of Dr. Julio Fuentes and food was distributed with the World Food Program. As a result of this trip, the scope of our future trips grew by networking with other organizations with similar interests and goals. This led to larger teams, sometimes with our teams filling an entire airplane.

I have received the direction from God that He wants to send 3000 people a year on short-term mission trips. This vision will be a huge undertaking and will be accomplished only with God's leading, guiding, strength and power. The partnership of The MCK Mission Foundation and The People Helping People Network is a major step forward in accomplishing our goal. MCK is an acronym for "Making Christ Known" emphasizing our commitment to Christ's Great Commission which is an integral part of each of our mission trips.

If you would like to know more about our mission work or would like to go with us on one of our trips, please go to www.mckcorporation. com and click on "Missions." We would love to have you join us!

Michael F. Elmore, MD

ORDER FORM
The Ancient Path
Rediscovering Manhood
By
Michael F. Elmore, MD

Book Title	Unit Price	Total
The Ancient Path *Rediscovering Manhood*	$14.95 For orders of 5-9 books deduct 10% & for orders of 10 or more deduct 15%.	
Subtotal Price: Quantity x Unit Price =		
Sales Tax Indiana Residents add 6%		
Shipping & Handling	$2.75 for 1 book $4.00 for 2 books $5.50 for 3 books $7.00 for 4 books $8.50 for 5 books $10.00 for 6 books $11.50 for 7 books $13.00 for 8 books $14.50 for 9 books $16.00 for 10 books Add $0.50 for each additional book.	
Grand Total:		

Name: _____

Street Address: _____

City, State & Zip Code: _____

Make Check Payable To: MCK, LLC
                                       8051 S. Emerson Ave., Suite 200
                                       Indianapolis, IN   46237